been there, done that

been there, done that

FAMILY WISDOM FOR MODERN TIMES

AL ROKER & DEBORAH ROBERTS

with Laura Morton

 NEW AMERICAN LIBRARY

NEW AMERICAN LIBRARY
Published by New American Library,
an imprint of Penguin Random House LLC
375 Hudson Street, New York, New York 10014

This book is an original publication of New American Library.

First Printing, January 2016

For more information about Penguin Random House, visit penguin.com.

LIBRARY OF CONGRESS CATALOGING-IN-PUBLICATION DATA:

Names: Roker, Al. | Morton, Laura | Roberts, Deborah
Title: Been there, done that: family wisdom for modern times/Al Roker,
Deborah Roberts with Laura Morton.
Description: New York : New American Library, [2016]
Identifiers: LCCN 2015031342 | ISBN 9780451466365 (hardback)
Subjects: LCSH: Roker, Al—Anecdotes. | Roberts, Deborah—Anecdotes. |
Parenting—Anecdotes. | Family life—Anecdotes. | African American
television journalists—United States—Anecdotes. | BISAC: FAMILY &
RELATIONSHIPS/Parenting/Fatherhood. | FAMILY & RELATIONSHIPS/
Parenting/Motherhood. | FAMILY & RELATIONSHIPS/Parenting/General.
Classification: LCC PN4874.R555 A3 2016 | DDC 070.4/30922—dc23 LC record
available at https://protect-us.mimecast.com/s/JqkJBxFxZwArSn

Printed in the United States of America
10 9 8 7 6 5 4 3 2 1

Designed by Tiffany Estreicher

Penguin
Random
House

To the memory of my parents, Al and Isabel Roker:
thank you for teaching me that parenting is a fluid thing and
that marriage is a marathon as opposed to a sprint.

And to our children, Courtney, Leila and Nick:
you bless us every day even as you challenge us to be better
parents today than we were yesterday.

—A.R.

If you are fortunate enough, you will look back on your life
and recall a secure and happy childhood. I feel very fortunate to have
had one, thanks to the firm and loving hands of Ben and Ruth Roberts.
I owe everything to your selfless example of love and devotion.

My deepest desire is that my children will look back and feel
the same way. I love you, Nick, Leila and Courtney, and pray that
my mistakes will make you stronger and wiser people.

—D.R.

Contents

been there, done that

Introduction

By most measures, we are just your average American family. Yes, we may be in the public eye, but we share a lot of the same struggles, challenges and dilemmas other families face every single day, especially when it comes to raising our children.

We're not perfect.

Far from it.

We're not even *striving* for perfection . . . Well, maybe Deborah is. (Al, I admit it!) But still, we know we're fallible, and that's what keeps life interesting. What fun would perfection be anyway?

Although Al has written a number of books, collaborating was a new challenge. As we kept sharing our ideas, our goals and our memories—some funny . . . some of them serious—we realized that what we most wanted to write about were the values and lessons we hope to convey to our children. Passing on our values is one of the most important responsibilities of parenthood, and sometimes the lessons we've learned the hard way can spare our kids an ounce or two of struggle. Many of these lessons came from our own parents, while others came from friends, colleagues or people we've been privileged to meet all around the world. All have gifted us, in words or by example, with tremendous insight and wisdom. Some of those lessons were small and easily absorbed; others were deeply painful, but valuable and necessary. These are the things we want to teach our children and, we agreed, to share. We hope these stories will help inspire, entertain and connect with you in the process.

We are truly excited to take this project on together because outside of our family, which we're extremely proud of, we haven't had the chance to collaborate on many other projects. Someone once said to us, "The couple who works together stays together!" Ever wonder if the person who said that actually worked with their partner? We're here to tell you, if you can survive writing a book that's personal, revealing, open, honest and full of intimate details about your life, then you can survive anything! (We did it! In fact, the experience brought us closer.)

We come from very different backgrounds, which has given us a broad perspective on all the things we have faced as individuals, as a couple, as parents, as journalists and, most of all, as a family.

One thing we do have in common is being raised in a large family, with Deborah being the seventh of nine children and Al being the oldest of six. When we think back to our childhoods, the happiest and most vivid memories that bring us the greatest joy are those family moments that shaped us into the people we've become today. Deborah's life was shaped by her small hometown in Georgia and Al's by his close-knit neighborhood in Queens, New York. Deborah's conservative Southern values and Al's urban savvy have combined to make a well-balanced, albeit sometimes feisty and spirited, home environment, one that never gets boring or old! (Well, not unless it's the argument about who's driving.)

Despite our differences, we've both carried our childhood lessons into our roles as partners and parents, and we think we've been mostly successful in creating a balance that has helped blend our family into one filled with unity, love and togetherness. Above all, we share an understanding that family trumps everything. You may bicker, disagree, drift and come back together again, but at the end of the day, when the chips are down, family is who you can count on and who truly matters most in your life.

Other than the Bible, there's truly no life handbook for modern times. If your pets start lining up two by two, check your homeowners' insurance for flood coverage! Otherwise—nope, there is no user's manual to confirm we are doing this thing called "life" right. Believe us, we've searched high and low for one. It doesn't exist. So instead we hope, we pray, we discuss our choices with friends and loved ones, we look for signs, we ask professionals, we probe, we research and still we hold our breath that we are making the right decisions every day.

That's life.

And life is what this book is all about. Experiences—funny, smart, sad, real, challenging, hard-to-talk-about, got-to-do-it-anyway *experiences* and what we learn from each of them.

We haven't seen it all . . . *yet* . . . but Lord knows we've seen a lot. You might say we've really *been there, done that.*

Every day we strive to take the wisdom that our parents passed on to us and integrate their knowledge and experience with what we've learned in our own lives. As a result, we've been able to share their legacy with our children, instilling their values and ours, as we face the daily challenges of being mom and dad, husband and wife, and chief cooks and bottle washers.

So as a way to pay homage to our families, our heritage, our history and our children's future, we wanted to share some of our favorite nuggets of wisdom we've gathered along the way. We're not preachin'; we're not teachin'. We're just sharing what's worked for us. Maybe it'll work for you. If nothing else, we'll share a few laughs and a couple of tears and try to make life a little better. We hope you enjoy reading them as much as we enjoyed sharing them.

—Al and Deborah

1

Never Give Up on Your Dreams

DEBORAH

Growing Up in the Segregated South

When I was growing up in Perry, Georgia, in the late 1960s, our black-and-white television was always set to CBS. Channel 13 was the only station we could get with our flimsy rooftop antenna, so soaps like *Search for Tomorrow* and *Dark Shadows* were a part of the Roberts family's daily routine. So was Walter Cronkite on the *CBS Evening News*.

Who would have guessed then that network news reporting would be my destiny some twenty years later? As a young black girl in the still-segregated Deep South, I could only daydream of someday living in a big city such as New York, reporting on important news stories like Walter Cronkite and his correspondents.

I remember being riveted by Lem Tucker, one of the few black national reporters at the time. His bravery while reporting in the thick of the brutal civil rights struggle stirred something inside my small chest. It seemed like the only black men and women you could see on TV at the time were the ones being brutalized in the fight for equal rights. I still recall seeing blacks sprayed by water hoses or being attacked by police dogs in Mississippi—just a few hundred miles away from my little town. Although I was young, I inherently understood there was something terribly wrong with what I was seeing almost daily.

As my brother Ben and my younger sisters, Belinda and Bonita, and I ran into the house, thirsty and hot from a day of play in the broiling Georgia heat, my parents were often watching the news and would shush us. So we'd stand silently around our pedestal television set, witnessing a changing world. Usually no one said a word. But one day my mother said in a soft voice, "People are getting tired." She and Daddy exchanged a look of concern unlike any I had seen from them before. Then they quickly changed the subject so they wouldn't scare their bewildered children. But we all felt the tension, especially when we went shopping downtown. I felt the glares and the uneasiness of the white customers, and it didn't escape me that they always got preferential treatment from the store clerks. I couldn't explain or express how it made me feel, but I knew I didn't like it.

Today, as we make our lives in the diversity of New York City, my husband finds it hard to believe that I can vividly recall a time when the line between black and white was so clearly marked. To me it isn't "history," but my own lived experience. It seems like just yesterday that when I was sick my mom walked me around to the back door of Dr. Hendrick's office to sit on the wooden benches in the colored waiting room. My school, the Houston County Training School, was segregated until I was in the fourth grade—*fifteen* years after the *Brown v. Board of Education* ruling by the Supreme Court. Our books were used and tattered and our classrooms in need of fresh paint. I had no idea what it was like to sit beside a white child in school, let alone to play together on a playground. We saw white people in the grocery store or at the post office and that was it. I desperately wanted to take dance lessons, but the local dance school only accepted white girls. Somehow, though, my mother managed to shield me from the sting of segregation, turning my attention away from what I couldn't have and toward what was possible by placing my focus on school, the local black chapter of the Girl Scouts or our church choir—all pursuits to catapult me forward toward my dreams and the belief that I could achieve anything.

In our little neighborhood of Old Field, with its roads made of red Georgia clay, parents didn't talk much to their kids about the indignity of segregation or the pain of the Jim Crow laws. Like so many other black adults, who mostly worked factory jobs and struggled to get by, my parents learned to keep on keeping on, quietly praying for a better day. Mom and Dad both worked in a textile factory and then, for a time, Daddy worked in a cement factory while Mom cleaned houses. They seethed silently and yet somehow managed to see the light shining through the cracks of that dark system. Both held on to the dream that their children would someday have a better life than they had. My parents taught us to be mindful and careful while also being ready to stand up for ourselves, but like others in the community, they were reluctant to push back against an oppressive system they'd known all their lives. But as we watched Martin Luther King Jr.'s march on Selma, Alabama, on the evening news, I remember Mama and Daddy cheering, calling him a hero. My parents didn't speak often about resistance, but I saw in their eyes that they were ready for change and, most of all, *opportunity*.

Life was challenging for us—for all black people back then. It took many years of hard work in factories, but Daddy was finally able to scrape together enough money to start his own business, a carpet-installation service, with my cousins Sonny and Little Buddy. Daddy wasn't a very good businessman. He never got the hang of using an appointment book. He wrote down appointments on little slips of paper that would somehow go missing and then he'd get angry phone calls from customers who expected him to be at their home . . . *yesterday*. But Daddy built a great reputation and was well respected, installing carpet in homes, both black and white, all over the region. Even though the company never did get well organized, they did great work and clients raved about my dad's work ethic and installation skills. Somehow, like any small-business owner, he managed to make it all work, getting up early day in and day out, eking out a living, putting food on the table for his family and keeping a roof over our heads.

My mom was very traditional in her role as a wife and mother, and sometimes it makes me angry that she never had a chance to realize her full potential. Like many of her friends, she never finished high school. She had to quit and get a job to help out her family. On some level I think she felt intimidated and insecure, as if she didn't know much about the world—but she did. While she may not have had a great deal of formal education, my mom had what I think of as street smarts. She inherently understood things about life and the real world that can't be taught in a classroom. She took great pride in her civic responsibilities, especially when it came to voting, and she wasn't afraid to join a local civil rights march. At the time, I didn't know what the march was all about, but I understood that my parents wanted to help make a change in Georgia, to give their family greater opportunities than they'd had. In their quiet way, Mom and Daddy were breaking down barriers. I watched with pride and did my best to understand the significance of their resilience and contribution. And, looking back, I now realize that these two people, who were denied higher education, taught me the most wonderful and powerful lessons that would sustain me to this day—lessons that I take with me everywhere I go. Whether I am interviewing the first lady or a young mother suffering with AIDS in Lesotho, on assignment in Bangladesh or navigating office politics, I draw on the example set by a strong mother who, despite her insecurities, had a strong belief in a woman's power and sheer determination.

My mom was something of a quiet feminist. I still remember the day in 1969 when she emerged from her bedroom wearing pants. While this may not sound notable today, in the 1960s, Southern women were expected to be *ladies*. And ladies wore dresses. Mom never left the house in anything but a colorful shift or a fitted A-line dress, *always* with panty hose. But Mom had a strong sense of herself and decided she wanted to wear what stylish women in the magazines and on TV were wearing. So she made herself a pair of straight-leg red pants and rocked them. Daddy came home and said, "What are you *doing*?" Mom answered that she was making dinner and it would be ready shortly. Wow. I was impressed. Mom, usually so passive and quiet, was now shaking up the status quo. My dad wasn't crazy about the look. Even so, Mom believed a woman should set her own agenda.

While she never had the luxury to dream of a career of her own, Mom always wanted more for her children. Homework and reading were serious business in my household. Mom demanded that we stay busy, if not doing homework, then joining the library reading program or at the least playing outdoors until sundown. She believed that "idleness was the devil's workshop." Mom cracked the whip, encouraging her children, especially her daughters, to find a dream and go for it. (This must be where I get it from!)

My mom clearly wanted her girls to have the opportunities in life she never got herself. As teenagers we were expected to hold a job and make some money. I worked at McDonald's for two years and took great pride in my polyester suit and matching baseball cap. Never having had a career of her own, Mom cautioned us girls that we should never rely on a man to take care of us. We needed to be self-sufficient and make our own money, she would say. She didn't want our success to be determined by who we married. She wanted it to be about achieving for ourselves.

My older sister Bennie was the first black cheerleader at Perry High School. Pretty and charismatic, she exuded confidence and excitement in nearly everything she did. She loved fashion, and even as a high schooler, she strutted around in the latest bell-bottoms and crop tops, which she sewed herself. I fondly remember how she'd regale us at dinner with stories about her adventures, like a mock trial her social studies class had presented. Bennie was so inspiring to me. Watching her, I felt that life was full of hope and opportunities. By high school, I was following in her footsteps. I excelled in academics, made the cheerleading squad, joined the Beta Club and the Civics Club and was voted a football sweetheart. I was beginning to dream of big things.

Despite the many negative images and stereotypes I grew up seeing in the media, thanks to the love and support of my family and a healthy dose of self-confidence I developed along the way, I believed I could do more, be more and become anything I wanted to be. So when it came time for college, I wanted to step away from the pack. Bennie had ventured to Miami, Florida, for fashion college, but my sister Annette had graduated from Fort Valley State, a small, historically black college just fifteen miles from home, and Tina, four years older than me, had gone to Valdosta State, a small school just south of Perry. Many of my close friends were applying to local colleges too. Believe me, just making it to college was a huge achievement, and these women were all my role models. But I wanted to make a serious break away from home. I was accepted to the University of Georgia—the "Princeton of the South"—some two hundred miles northwest of Perry. With its renowned journalism school, strong academic program and nationally known Georgia Bulldogs football team, it was a gigantic step for me and turned out to be the perfect choice. It was the place where I would discover my true passion and find the courage to take flight. With my mom's encouraging words never far from my thoughts, it was where I learned how to stand on my own two feet.

My memories of segregation are often top of mind when I am invited to speak at a women's conference or to a group of aspiring journalists, because in many ways they truly shaped so much of who I became. I usually begin my talks with a line that sums up my life.

"I am an unlikely success story."

Throughout my career, I've had the opportunity to travel all over the country and around the world, and I've discovered that no matter where we live or what our economic station in life, most of us have the same goals: to lead happy, confident lives and to reach our full potential without bias and barriers.

Though we grew up with few advantages, my family life set me on a course of confidence and determination. That burning desire for opportunity, instilled by my parents, is probably the most common subject women want to talk about everywhere I go. Whether I'm on assignment in Africa or speaking to a YWCA group in Ohio, women are thirsty for examples of how they can overcome obstacles or grab that brass ring. When I was a junior in college I interned at a small station, WMAZ-TV in Macon, Georgia. Being new to the business, I made multiple mistakes while I was there! For example, while helping a reporter shoot video for her story, I accidently pressed the stop button when I thought I was rolling tape and never recorded her interview. Naturally, she was furious. I thought I'd be let go immediately, but I wasn't. I was reassigned, given simple typing assignments—not where I wanted to be.

After I had a few tearful conversations with my mom, she wisely counseled me that life is about learning to take the hard knocks. She'd endured her share in the segregated South, and I'd have to learn to take mine if I wanted to make it in the real world. She said, "When you get knocked down, get up and push back," and that it would make me stronger. As usual, Mom was right. I worked harder, earned another internship, and landed my first job in TV just a month after graduation.

Of course, now that I'm a mother myself, the notion of resilience is especially important to me. It is my never-ending mission to make sure my children have the opportunities to realize their goals in life and to help them change the world if they so choose. But opportunities alone are not enough. I also want to instill in our children the confidence and determination to reach out and *grab* those opportunities when they come along—or to create them through sheer will if necessary!

AL
_____

My Most Memorable Presidential Inauguration

In my thirty-seven years at NBC and the *Today* show, I have covered many historical events, from the eruption of the Iceland volcano to Superstorm Sandy. I have proudly attended six presidential inaugurations, but nothing could have prepared me for the day I witnessed a moment in American history I never believed I would live to see: the swearing in of the first black man as President of the United States.

When I drove to my location for the parade, I passed the Lincoln Memorial as I had done so many times in my life, and at first glance I couldn't figure out what I was looking at. I could see the National Mall all right, but the size of the crowd took me by surprise; it didn't look like any inauguration I'd attended in the past. I felt stunned that so many had gathered. But of course they were all there, as they had come years before to hear Martin Luther King Jr., to witness a seminal moment in history. I thought about my mom and how much she would have *loved* to see what I was seeing. After Obama's first debate against Hillary Clinton, I vividly recall her saying with a conviction I'd rarely heard before, "That man is going to be president." And she was right. Sadly, Mom didn't live to see the fruition of her dream, but I was there in her place and in her honor.

After the swearing in, I took up my place along Pennsylvania Avenue, ready to broadcast the parade as I had done so many times before, beaming with great pride and joy to be both a black man and a proud American.

Traditionally, the president and first lady get out of their car and walk the last quarter mile or so along the parade route. I am usually perched directly across from the White House, reporting for the *Today* show. I was so excited at the sight of our new president and his wife as they made their way toward my position. I felt like a starstruck kid as they got closer.

"Mr. President!" I yelled as loudly as I could over the crowd.

I saw Mrs. Obama point me out to our new president.

I knew this was my chance to connect, so I asked him the only question I could think of:

"How does it feel?"

"It feels GREAT!" he responded, as he kept walking without losing his stride.

So I like to tell people that technically I got the very first interview with the new president.

And I suppose I did.

It was certainly a moment I've never forgotten.

For a brief time that day, our country was united in hope, with the promise of a new beginning.

"Yes We Can" had become a message and a belief that gave Americans a newfound confidence and optimism when we needed it.

As I watched the president make his way to the White House that cold January afternoon, I looked around at everybody who had come to witness this event and to suspend the division of parties to give our new president his due respect. It had been a long time since that had happened. He had told us that we were not red states and blue states, but *united* states, and so it seemed at that moment.

I remember watching the election returns with Nicky and Leila the night President Obama was first elected. Deborah was covering the returns for ABC in Harlem as I tried my very best to explain the importance of this win, especially to Leila, who was old enough to understand the electoral process. It was almost surreal. In fact, as we sat watching the returns, there were even a few moments when I privately wondered, "Is this really happening?" I couldn't shake the feeling that someone was going to pull the rug out from under my feet at the last moment. Surely someone would find a loophole—a hanging chad, so to speak.

But they didn't.

One by one, each network called the race.

Barack Obama would become the forty-fourth president of the United States.

Oddly, I wasn't emotional at first.

I didn't cry that night, or the next day during our extended *Today* show broadcast. I can't say the full impact of the election hit me until the inaugural ceremony. When I saw more than a *million* people show up to support our country's first black president, I was truly gobsmacked.

The realization sank in that, despite all the imperfections of our nation, we indeed live in a country where you can be whoever and whatever you dream of.

YES WE CAN.

It doesn't mean you will achieve everything you set out to accomplish, but the potential is there, and if ever my children have doubts about that, I will remind them of watching President Obama being sworn in.

In many ways, Obama followed a traditional path to success. He attended an Ivy League college and an Ivy League law school. He was a senator whose renown spread through a bestselling book and a remarkable speech at the Democratic National Convention. But in so many other ways his path was unusual, beginning with the fact that he was half African American—and not just African American but *African* American! He grew up not in Texas or Illinois or another battleground state, but in Hawaii and abroad. He did not look like most people's picture of a U.S. president.

As a typical baby boomer, I was raised to believe that success depended on a traditional path, for example, going to college immediately after graduating high school—certainly that's what I thought my older daughter, Courtney, ought to do after she graduated. I had watched her struggle in school for years, yet despite her challenges I pleaded with her to do the right—the *expected*—thing. Instead, she kept on pushing for what she believed in, taking responsibility for her life and achieving her dream of becoming a chef.

To me, she not only personifies resilience but the courage it takes to insist on what is important to her and do what she wants to do. That independence and fierce determination couldn't make me any prouder as a parent. To watch her grow and become her own person has inspired me in ways she may never know.

We all have our own path to walk in life.

We all have the ability to become difference makers.

Not everyone is destined to make history, and that's okay. As long as you strive to make history in your *own* life, you are a difference maker. I tell my kids that each morning brings a clean slate; every day they have the opportunity to make choices, to start all over, so they must choose wisely; those decisions will determine the outcome of their day.

Four years after President Obama was first elected, I found myself on the parade route once again. Unfortunately, there were many people who didn't like the outcome of the election, and people who were filled with doubt and fear about the future of our country. Hurricane Sandy had pummeled the East Coast two months earlier, and many cities were still dealing with the aftermath. The mood just wasn't as joyous as the first time around. I had a slight feeling of melancholy as I watched the inaugural speeches, especially because it happened to be Dr. Martin Luther King Jr.'s birthday. Although I knew there would be four more years of a black president, the feeling of overwhelming unity and good-will was no longer there.

But even with all that, it was still a beautiful and exciting celebration of democracy. As I took my usual position on the parade route, my colleague Brian Williams tossed the shot to me and said, "Al Roker, the pressure is on. Can you get the president to acknowledge you again? Since you got the first interview with him after his first swearing in, let's see if you can do it one more time!"

Never one to back down from a challenge, the moment I spotted President and Mrs. Obama, I began shouting, "Mr. President!" as loudly as I could.

Once again, Mrs. Obama pointed me out to the president.

"Al, the weather's great!" he called to me.

"There you have it!" Brian Williams said.

But that wasn't the end.

"Wait a minute. Vice President Biden has gotten out of his car. Al Roker with a double down. Can you get the vice president?" Brian Williams had challenged me again!

"Mr. Vice President. Come over! Come on over!" I beckoned to him vigorously, but he said he couldn't.

"The Secret Service will kill me if I do." Yet he ran over and shook my hand anyway.

"I'm done!" I said as I dropped my mike and walked away.

My producers thought I was being funny, but the truth is that I was suddenly overcome with emotion.

I was a black kid from Queens. I had just been acknowledged by the first black president of the United States and the vice president had come over to shake my hand. All I could think about was what my parents would have said if they had lived to see this day. It was an overwhelming and special highlight of my career—one I will never forget. My only regret was not having my family next to me to share the moment of triumph and celebration—not just mine, but the collective achievement of our country. Of we, the people.

DEBORAH

Women of Influence

For as long as I can remember, I've always been in search of people and moments of inspiration that make me a stronger woman, mother and wife. They're all around us—if you simply take the time to look and listen. Many people find tremendous hope and inspiration in self-help books, but I've discovered there are valuable lessons in everyday experiences and encounters. My greatest life-changing lessons often take place on the job or during some other public event. I remember the death-row inmate I once interviewed. He was sincerely remorseful for the crime he committed and was living a remarkably philosophical life behind bars, grateful for each moment. Then there was the landscape worker I met who had vowed to devote her life to being an earthly angel, raising money to fund lifesaving and anonymous loans to people on the verge of disaster. At these moments, I walk away from the cameras humbled and changed, determined to live my life just a little better and with greater purpose.

Eight years ago I had the great pleasure to sit down with Michelle Obama just before the election that would send her family to the White House and change history. I had met her at a luncheon for *Ebony* magazine and was captivated by her warmth and lack of pretense. She was cordial and relaxed, casually blending into the sea of women, but her charisma was unmistakable. I was immediately intrigued by this brown-skinned woman who was making headlines in the black community for her competence and authenticity as she gradually stirred interest nationwide. I made my way toward her through the crowd, reached out my hand and introduced myself. I asked if we could possibly schedule a TV interview sometime to tell her story. With a gracious smile, she replied that she liked my work and asked me to give my contact info to Katie Lelyveld McCormick, her cheerful assistant.

I immediately felt a connection with Mrs. Obama. We both had made our way from humble roots. She came from the South Side of Chicago and I was from small-town Georgia. Though I grew up in a large family and she had only a brother, we were both guided by examples of hardworking, strong parents who struggled to provide for their families. Like me, Mrs. Obama knew what it was like to live in a home where money was tight. Yet Michelle Obama had excelled, graduating from Princeton and finding success in corporate America, and now with her husband making a legitimate move to change the course of political history, she was poised to make history too.

After months of negotiating logistics with Katie, I finally found myself sitting in a high-rise hotel room in downtown Chicago with a producer and a camera crew, awaiting Mrs. Obama's arrival. It was an exciting moment in my career. She walked into the room at the appointed time all smiles, projecting warmth and a supercool vibe at the same time. Though I had interviewed my share of celebrities, as she reached for my hand to say hello, I was hit by a slight case of nerves—a rarity for me. But Michelle Obama radiates power and confidence unlike anyone I have ever met.

I was momentarily awestruck.

I took a couple of quiet breaths and then we both sat down.

We made small talk about the weather and our children as we put on our mikes. I had been promised fifteen minutes with her, but she coolly whispered to me that she would give me all the time we needed, immediately putting me at ease. It's usually my job to keep the interviewee calm, not the other way around. I sure was grateful though.

I keep a picture from that day in my office as a reminder of that special day. Mrs. Obama is beaming in a white blouse and black jacket, and I'm in a classic news reporter's red blazer, holding my notepad—with an equally broad grin.

Not many people at that point—including African Americans—truly believed that a black candidate, even one with Barack Obama's sterling credentials, had a real shot at the presidency. But Michelle Obama knew in her heart that her husband would win the election.

When I asked her if minorities should support her husband and finally elect a black president, she quickly answered with a surprising "No." She said that people should support her husband if they believe in his ideals and ability to change the country.

We spoke for half an hour about her passionate hopes and dreams for the country and why she believed her husband was the answer. She was unruffled when I threw her some hardballs, pressing her about the Clintons, who many felt were dismissive of her husband's chances during the rough-and-tumble of the campaign.

"It's all politics," she said.

Some people in the media had dubbed Michelle Obama "the Closer," hinting at her ability to help close the deal between the voters and her husband. And after interviewing her that day, I understood why. Articulate, captivating and well versed on the issues, she was what we call in TV a "sound-bite machine." She had confidence and was all kinds of savvy. This was a woman who believed. She believed in possibility and she believed in her husband.

After the interview, with our mikes off, we compared notes about our hectic lives and motherhood. We have children around the same ages and agreed that we were in for big challenges as they entered adolescence. Yet another connection I felt to this amazing and inspiring woman, who wasn't just an icon but a real woman—like when I complimented the beautiful patent leather boots she was wearing and she told me where to get them! I found them on sale and still refer to them as my Michelle Obama boots.

As a reporter, I was pleased with the interview; as a woman, I was blown away by Michelle Obama. This was someone who had learned to push past barriers and to claim success despite the odds. Like me, and so many other minority women in the country, she knew what it was like to be the lone black woman in an office meeting. Yet she wasn't the least bit discouraged or intimidated. No doubt she had dealt with her share of struggles and disappointments, but here she was, hopeful and brimming with enthusiasm.

I left that meeting feeling hopeful for the future, more determined than ever to shine brighter in my own life and believing that anything is possible.

Another powerful interview that changed my perspective came a few years later. I was scheduled to interview the chart-topping singer Jennifer Hudson about her new album. Like a lot of people, I had been a huge admirer of Jennifer's golden vocal cords ever since she appeared on *American Idol*. The woman could belt out a ballad that would shake you to your toes! So I was excited to meet her. It was also the first time Jennifer would be doing an interview since the tragic shooting deaths of her mom and nephew. My producer and I were cautioned by Jennifer's PR folks that she was interested in talking only about music and her well-documented weight loss. In other words, don't grill her about her personal heartbreak.

A few days later we sat down with Jennifer at six p.m. in a studio space in Midtown Manhattan. I brought my daughter, Leila, along since she is a big fan. We both popped our heads into the makeup room to say hello and break the ice. We were surprised by Jennifer's bubbly personality as her makeup artist powdered her brow.

"How nice to meet you, Leila," Jennifer said with a huge smile.

She asked how old she was and promised to be ready in just a couple of minutes. Leila beamed, and I was touched by the kindness of such a huge star.

As promised, Jennifer, radiant in a beautiful orange dress and sky-high heels, soon slid into her chair and we began talking. We discussed her love of music and the birth of her two biggest blessings: her career break on *American Idol* and her then-eighteenth-month-old-son, David. She absolutely lit up describing her baby boy and all that he was learning.

I then asked her about her new svelte figure, which she was thrilled about and happy to discuss. The interview was going very well, with lots of fun and energy. But I knew that viewers wanted to know how Jennifer was coping with her pain. So I swallowed hard and decided to gently veer into that forbidden territory. I asked where she was finding joy, given her obvious pain.

To my amazement, Jennifer didn't flinch and began to talk about how her religious faith had gotten her through. I waited for one of her PR reps to jump in, but no one did. Though tears rimmed her eyes, Jennifer was actually at ease, talking about her deep love and admiration for her mother and how her relationship with God brought Jennifer great comfort. Her strength and unshakable faith during such a devastating time touched all of us in the room.

While Jennifer Hudson's talent had taken her far beyond her South Side Chicago roots, she still possessed a steely inner strength. After suffering such a devastating loss, one I couldn't imagine suffering through, here she was finding inspiration in her music, her work and her child. Jennifer spoke of rebuilding her life and finding her joy again. I was stunned and deeply touched by the strength I was witnessing. If she could move beyond the most unimaginable loss, then surely any of us can get past our daily struggles.

We ended the interview talking about the lullabies she sings to her baby boy. Jennifer even sang the little song she had made up for him. When she finished, we all applauded. After all, it's not every day you get a private concert from Jennifer Hudson.

After the cameras were turned off, Jennifer amazed me once again by pulling Leila aside for a private conversation. When I told her that Leila takes voice lessons, she asked Leila to sing a bit—then kindly offered to turn her head away so that my shy daughter wouldn't feel self-conscious singing for such a superstar. Leila took a deep breath and sang a few stanzas from "Listen," a song Beyoncé sang in *Dreamgirls*, the movie for which Jennifer won an Oscar. Her voice was strong, and Jennifer applauded for her! She then took the time to encourage Leila to believe in herself and to keep singing.

I'd always liked what I saw of Jennifer Hudson from afar, but now I admired her even more. She is an amazingly generous woman who made time for a starry-eyed girl. Above all, she was managing to find the beauty in life again, even after suffering through unspeakable pain. I went home that evening feeling strengthened and inspired in my own life and prayed that Leila felt the same. And before I went to bed, I called my mom, just to hear her voice and cherish her a little bit more.

2

Kindness Is Like a Boomerang— It Always Comes Back

AL

The Art of Saying Nothing

Sometimes I think I see life as a sitcom with four cameras out there and a laugh track. I find myself fighting my urge to make snappy remarks. Just as a stand-up comic getting heckled wants to come back with some biting line, I can't just let things go. Sometimes my daughter will even egg me on because (I think) she appreciates my one-liners from time to time. Leila has my mother's "tee-hee" sense of humor and that pot-stirring, mischievous demeanor, which I absolutely adore. You might say she was born with a wooden spoon in her hand to stir that pot! Like mine, her humor tends to fall toward self-effacing and self-deprecating— believing that it is a sin to be prideful. It works for us and usually gets a laugh.

My love for the zinger started when I was a boy. I loved to draw cartoon and comics, where I could have my characters say anything. I could ascribe my thoughts to other people and get away with it because it wasn't actually me lobbing those one-liners.

One of my favorite TV shows was *Winchell-Mahoney Time*. Paul Winchell was the preeminent ventriloquist of the day. His wooden "partners," Jerry Mahoney and Knucklehead Smith, were superstars of the ventriloquism world. I bought Winchell's book *Ventriloquism for Fun and Profit* and devoured every word. I had a Jerry Mahoney dummy I renamed Steven Stickyfingers, because the dummy's fingers were molded together.

My act became pretty good. Steven and I took second place in the 1964 New York City parks department talent contest. We lost to a group of four girls lip-synching the Beatles song "I Want to Hold Your Hand" while dressed in turtlenecks, tights and mop-top wigs. There weren't a lot of black kids doing ventriloquist acts in the early 1960s, so I was kind of an anomaly. I was in seventh heaven the first time I saw Willie Tyler and Lester in 1972, when they made their first appearance on *Rowan & Martin's Laugh-In*. Doing ventriloquism gave me the perfect outlet to say things as a kid I would never have gotten away with if that dummy weren't in my hand. Unfortunately, my career didn't last long because my brother broke my dummy.

Ever since, though, when it comes to going for that perfect one-liner, the obvious punch line, the "I just can't help myself" comeback, I sometimes feel like that guy you see in cartoons who has the devil on one shoulder and the angel on the other battling it out. I know if I say what I'm thinking, especially if it's directed toward my wife, she is not going to be happy with me. I actually have a dialogue with myself that sounds something like this:

"Yes, say it. It is going to be really funny."

"No! You know you should keep your mouth shut."

"Go ahead. You should definitely say it."

"No! Don't say it."

"Maybe she doesn't know that I don't know I shouldn't say it."

"Say it, damn it!"

. . . And then I do.

I just can't help myself.

It's like a pitch coming across home plate that you just have to swing at. You can't not swing unless you've been tied up, and even then, you lunge at it because you have to.

Was it worth it?

Not usually.

But in the moment, it felt so good.

It's like a drug that feels fantastic and great until the thrill wears off and the reality of my actions sets in.

And when I don't say something, I feel a great need to point it out like a loyal dog who drops a dead animal at your feet with pride and a pitiful look that says, "Love me! I brought this for YOU!" He stands there wagging his tail, looking for praise, thinking he's done something marvelous. Yeah, that doesn't pay off much either.

There is a definite art to saying nothing. I haven't exactly mastered that skill yet. Every time I think about saying something, I analyze the risk versus reward—which is what all of life really comes down to.

What are the risks of saying this?

What is going to happen if I do?

Am I going to be able to have sex tonight?

Will the evening remain pleasant?

Will we be able to go out with our friends without recrimination or reproach?

For that one moment of "YES!" is it worth it?

Sometimes less is more, especially when it comes to speaking. It reminds me of a story I once heard about a preacher, a politician and an engineer who were each led to a guillotine to meet their fate.

The preacher was first to be executed. When he was asked if he wanted to face up or down when he met his fate, he said he wanted to face upward, so he could be looking toward the heavens when he met his Maker. The preacher's head was placed upon the guillotine, where he remained still and calm, awaiting his imminent death. As the blade was released, it miraculously stopped just inches above his throat. Believing this was divine intervention, the executioners set the preacher free.

Next, the politician was placed upon the guillotine, and he too was asked if he wanted to face up or down. After witnessing the great miracle of the preacher, the politician chose to face upward, hoping he would be spared as well. Once again, the blade stopped just inches above the politician's throat. He too was released.

Finally, the engineer was placed upon the guillotine. Noting that the two men before him faced up, he chose the same position. As he laid his neck upon the guillotine and looked up, he said, "Oh, wait. I see what's wrong!"

You see, there are some things that are better left unsaid.

It would be an unusual circumstance where keeping quiet would get you into trouble, but you can bank on saying the wrong thing always putting you in the dog house. I ought to know.

Woof.

As parents, we all know that our children model what they hear us say. Sometimes, discretion being the better part of valor, we should practice restraint. Whether it's an off-the-cuff comment about my weight or a quip I thought was funny, every word I utter has the potential to shape and mold how my kids think and feel—especially when it comes to their self-image. Something we see as witty and harmless may not be received the way you intend it and may do more damage than good, whether it's a sarcastic quip or a quick knee-jerk e-mail response, all because you wanted that gratification of knowing you got off a good line. I suffer from this need often—though I know it isn't always in my best interest.

There's great power in the words we speak. They have the power to build us up or tear us down. As a celebrity, the bigger the platform I stand on, the more powerful those words become and the more responsibility I have. Sadly, there are those who use their platform to spread a message of hate, bigotry or negativity in the world. While I find that an upsetting and unfortunate by-product of fame, there are also times where an entirely innocent off-the-cuff comment can be perceived as hurtful too. That's why we all need to watch what we say. The old saw "Sticks and stones may break my bones but words will never hurt me" is simply not true. In fact, they can hurt us more than physical abuse.

When I was a kid growing up in the projects, my neighborhood was predominantly Jewish. Although no one ever used the "N word," I was often called "Blackie" by the local kids. I've never forgotten how that made me feel! It seems these kids were happy they could bully and ostracize me—perhaps it was because they came from a people who had been so recently treated so vilely. In my young mind, though, it made no sense.

Many years later, my daughter Courtney came home from school. She was around six or seven years old. She asked me a question I wasn't prepared to answer.

"Daddy, what's a nigger?"

I was quiet for a moment. My baby girl, my precious daughter, had been exposed to something I naively thought I would never have to explain to her—certainly not at this age.

I took a deep breath and said, "Well, it's a hurtful word that people use to describe black people—us. Why would you ask that, sweetie?"

"A boy in my class called me that today."

I explained to Courtney that he shouldn't have done that and I would be calling his parents, because no one should use words like that to describe others.

I promptly got out the class phone list and called the boy's parents. When the boy's mother answered, I explained the situation.

There was silence.

Not the kind of silence that conveyed embarrassment or shame.

The kind of silence that conveyed something else—something that made me mad.

"I understand. I'm sorry. Our son will apologize to your daughter, and I will make sure this doesn't happen again," she said.

"Well, he would have heard that word somewhere," I said.

"Yes. He would have."

"I trust you will take care of this . . ." That's about all of the kindness I could muster before hanging up the phone.

Although this incident happened many years ago, and I'd love to believe as a society we have come a long way, there are still times I know the words we use can hurt. I'm so glad saying something such as "He's so gay" is no longer acceptable. I recognize there's a point of becoming too politically correct, but there is absolutely nothing wrong with taking a beat and thinking about whether what you're about to say might hurt or embarrass someone. Once it is out and the bell is rung, you can't unring it. You can apologize for ringing the bell, but the sound still lingers.

The stakes are high for all of us. You don't want to be the sadistic clown who hurts others for the sake of scoring points. Whenever someone gets hurt, whether it's you or someone else, there's a casualty. And where's the payoff in that? When you think about it, isn't it so much better to build others up with the words we speak, to offer them hope, encouragement and comfort through compliments and kindness? Doing this not only helps give them courage and faith to face life's challenges but helps us live a more positive and productive life too.

DEBORAH

The Time of Day Belongs to Everyone

Like most of us, so much of my identity as a woman and a parent is not only guided by what I was given as a child, but also by what I wish I had gotten. As closely bonded to my mother as I was over the years, she was not an overtly affectionate woman. Mom wasn't exactly the type to sit on the edge of her bed and talk to me about my day or my problems. After all, she had nine kids who needed her attention and she had only so many hours in a day. As a working mom with just two kids, boy, do I get it!

Mom has always had a gentle, loving nature but has never been a truly demonstrative person. Her mother died when she was just a baby, and she was raised by a stern, no-nonsense grandmother. I remember Mom telling us how she quit school before the eighth grade to help out her family, going to work in a crate factory and sometimes as a housekeeper to help make ends meet. She married for the first time at age seventeen and gave birth to a son, my big brother Jackie, an air force retiree and stoic father of three girls. That marriage didn't last long. Several years later, Mom met and married my father, Ben Roberts Sr., and they had eight children together!

My parents had what most folks would think of as a traditional marriage. Though my parents struggled financially, they somehow managed to always make a comfortable home for us kids. Even when money was tight, we all thought that we were well-off. That image was mostly due to Mom. Like many Southern black women, cooking was a way for my mom to express herself and her love. She could fry up a mean plate of chicken, and Sunday dinners were legendary. All of my relatives begged for more of her chicken and dressing whenever there was a family gathering. Although I knew she got overwhelmed at times, my most enduring memory of her is that of a loving, strong and determined steel magnolia: tough on the outside but tender on the inside.

Mom had high standards for her children, which were built on principles of the church. Honesty, forgiveness and faith were paramount. We went to church every Sunday and kept God close to our hearts. Mom often hummed gospel hymns while doing chores around the house. I always knew when she was deep in thought or busy doing her work because I could hear her humming away.

Proper manners and kindness were very important to her. She was raised to always speak to an adult with a "sir" or a "ma'am," and of course that was only if an adult approached you first. She expected nothing less from her own children.

Given her tough childhood, I was always amazed by my mom's good nature and positive spirit. While she wasn't big on saying "I love you," she had her own special way of showing people that she cared. Whether it was a routine daily greeting of friends, acquaintances or strangers with her syrupy Southern "How ya doin'?" or a small gesture she found to let each of her kids know just how much she loved and cared for us, like making Jell-O for dessert as a special treat, Mom always took the time to make a kind gesture. I once asked Mom why she was so friendly to everyone, even people we didn't know.

She replied with a strange saying I've never forgotten. "The time of day belongs to everyone."

It was a simple but confusing phrase to me.

You see, while Mom wasn't mushy with her love or much of a hugger, she found a lot of ways to show each of her children how she felt about them. She sewed all of our clothes, making sure my sisters and I always had colorful, beautiful dresses for Easter and school. Now and again there was even a special package from Sears, Roebuck & Company with a cute blouse. And I'll never forget the day she surprised me with a beautiful powder blue pantsuit I'd longed for. I spotted it in the window of Vanity Fair—a local dress shop that was kind of pricey. I dreamed of wearing the suit to a school event. I knew it was out of our price range. So one afternoon when I returned from school and found it lying neatly on my bed, I cried tears of excitement. My mom splurged for me—no doubt denying herself something.

Even though we were on a pretty tight budget growing up, she always found a way to stretch a dollar. The aroma of her fried chicken and collard greens on Friday and baked hen and dressing on Sunday come back to me as if she were standing in my kitchen cooking it today.

And then there were the little personal things she did that were small tokens of her affection yet meant so much. Mom knew I loved to read the *TV Guide*, but money was tight, so I rarely got to buy it. Every now and then, though, I'd find a copy on the kitchen counter amid the weekly groceries just for me. Somewhere between the meat and produce, she found a way to squeeze an extra fifty cents out of the bottom line to buy me that magazine because she knew it would make me so happy. And anytime I came home from college for a weekend, she had my favorite homemade peach cobbler cooling in the kitchen. That was her way of saying, "Welcome home, honey. Let me wrap my arms around you and tell you I love you!"

With Mom now closing in on ninety years of life, I sometimes look back on her inability to be warm and fuzzy and secretly wish she would have thrown her arms around me more or said "I love you" before I did. Maybe that's the older, wistful me talking, but I think it would have stuck in my heart to actually hear her say those three words a little more often. Even so, I cherished her tender, loving kindnesses because I understood them to mean the same thing.

Eventually, I began to understand my mother's mantra that "the time of day belongs to everyone." After years of walking into grocery stores and the post office and meeting friends and strangers along the way, I finally understood her homespun expression: She meant everyone deserves a kind word. Everyone deserves a little time every day.

Several years ago, I was on assignment interviewing a man and his wife who were facing a tragic situation. After the interview, I went into their bathroom to wash my hands and noticed a sign they had hanging up on the wall that was headlined "Rules of Life."

There were a number of great phrases written on the plaque about finding peace and being positive, but the one that stuck with me that day was, "Always give people more than they expect." That resonated with me because it reminded me so much of my mother. She is the first person who taught me to think above and beyond when you are doing something with or for someone else.

Just recently I was in a cab making small talk with the driver, who told me that his wife was ill and that he was having a tough day. I was busy on my e-mails and hadn't intended to be distracted but soon realized that this guy just needed a small lift—someone who respected the "time of his day." So I gave him my attention, and when we arrived at my destination, I wished him well and offered a bigger tip than I typically would give.

Giving people more than they expect can become an everyday habit, one that fills your emotional bucket by giving to others in ways they never see coming. It can be something as simple as dropping someone off in front of their house instead of at the corner because it's cold outside or complimenting their smile just to leave them feeling a little happier.

Last winter was an especially harsh one for many parts of the country. We had more snow and bitterly cold days than I can ever remember in all of the years I've lived in New York City. On a particularly miserable day in December, in the thick of the Christmas season, I was rushing home after work and was lucky to find a cab right away. It was one of those blessed New York moments when a cab stops on the corner where you're standing. I made a dash for it at the same time another woman had spotted it. I didn't see her, nor do I believe she saw me. I jumped in on one side as she made her move on the other. She had a dispirited look on her face when she realized I wasn't about to let the coveted cab go.

Now, ordinarily, the New Yorker in me would have said, "Sorry, lady!" But something inside told me to ask where she was headed. She looked exasperated, as if she had been standing in the cold, wet snow for quite some time. I told her I was headed to Eighty-second and Second Avenue. She said she was going to Seventy-fifth and First.

"Maybe you two can share!" the cabdriver suggested.

"Sure," I said. "I don't mind at all! Hop on in."

The woman jumped in and noticed I had Pepper, our family dog, with me. She rolled her eyes, resentful of her presence and of mine, clearly asking herself why she was getting into this cab with either of us. She just looked disdainful of everything.

I could have taken an attitude back with her.

But I didn't.

Instead, I used our short ride together to try to turn her day around.

"How are you doing today?" I asked.

"Don't even ask!" she said.

"Where are we headed to first, ladies?" the driver chimed in.

"I'd be happy to drop you at Seventy-fifth and Third—it's right on the way," I politely offered.

"Ugh. I can't walk that far. I've been on my feet all day. I am exhausted."

Before she could go any further, I realized this woman needed a break much more than I did. "You know what? You can drop me at Seventy-fourth and Second and I'll walk the rest of the way so you can take this lovely woman right to her front door."

She didn't know what to say.

But I knew that in that moment she needed more than she was expecting.

With that simple gesture, she began to crack that tough facade and warmed up to me. She told me she was seventy-eight years old and was still working in the jewelry district five days a week. Her office was near Rockefeller Center, near the Christmas tree, so the traffic and the hordes of people every day had become overwhelming.

I told her I understood how hard this time of year can be and reminded her that this too shall pass. The holidays are tough for a lot of people, but they come and go and things will get better. By the time we got to my stop, she had forgotten all about her terrible day. She started to dig in her purse to pay for the cab, but before she could find her wallet, I handed her more than enough to cover the ride.

"Here, take this."

"I don't have any change," she said.

"Go home and have a hot cup of tea, put your feet up and relax," I said, offering her a smile and a wink before I got out of the cab.

"God bless you!" she called out.

I turned to her before closing the door and said, "Next time you'll give me the ride, okay?" And with that I offered her a quick wave and then Pepper and I were on our way. I had a little extra pep in my step as

I walked home that afternoon. I felt good being able to do something kind for a stranger, and I felt more gratitude about life.

Gratitude makes people happier and it allows us to accomplish more through the art of doing small things every day. Today I sometimes find myself wondering if I am living the life my mother would have wanted for me and whether or not I've lost a little of my Southern warmth after years of living in New York City. I'd like to think I have not, but to be safe I sometimes go out of my way to make sure I hold on to my upbringing in a city known for its hustle and bustle and hardened attitude toward passersby. I'm so often racing around, traveling and meeting deadlines, especially with the high demands of my job, that I feel like I don't have the time to talk to this person or that friend, when in fact I'm simply not making the time! Sometimes you just need to slow down, take a beat and remember to think about everyone you encounter— because my mom was absolutely right. The time of day belongs to everyone. If I practice this daily, I can be the best example for my kids. It's my deepest hope that they will remember my kind words or small gestures—that they will leave the same kind of imprint on them that my mother's did on me. My roots are truly a part of me, and I thank my mom for planting them so deeply. And as *her* daughter, my responsibility—my *obligation*—is to pass those timeless seeds of wisdom on to my own children with the hope that they too feel the strength and security that I did to bloom where they are planted.

So when I'm out with my children I'm especially mindful of small moments of kindness. When I see a mom struggling with her stroller as she navigates the entrance to the grocery store, I am quick to grab the door. When we're out walking Pepper and someone passes by, it's a natural thing for me to say good morning! It doesn't matter whether the person returns the greeting or not. One day Leila said to me, "It makes you look small-town or naive when you strike up conversations with strangers on the street." Maybe it does, but I'm hoping she also sees the joy of connecting with your neighbors, even in the big city and our crazy busy world. I want Leila and Nicky to learn that we can all spread a little happiness in just a few words or with a momentary kind gesture.

Like my mom always said, the time of day belongs to *everyone*.

AL

WWAD . . . What Would Al Do?

My father was always demonstrative and his emotions were never far beneath the surface. You always knew how he felt about you. You never had to guess at it. Dad was also the kind of guy who gave people the benefit of the doubt. He had a way of always seeing things from the other person's perspective. Like Tevye from *Fiddler on the Roof*, "on the other hand" seemed to be one of his favorite sayings. That attitude gave him a great ability to see both sides and accept people for who they are.

There were many times throughout his career when he got knocked down or overlooked, but he never got bitter. He just did his job and worked his way back. In his case, he always came back stronger than before because that is who he was and what made him the rock to so many people who admired him.

The word "friend" was a big deal to my dad. It meant everything to him; it meant being loyal, trusted, someone who makes a difference in others' lives. My dad had a lot of acquaintances—I suppose because he was a local bus driver and an outwardly friendly guy. People felt they knew him, but he could probably count his true friends on two hands.

Friend or acquaintance, he treated everyone with tremendous warmth and caring. At my dad's funeral, one of his coworkers told a story I'd never heard. My father had been promoted from driver to dispatcher. His job was to oversee the other drivers and their routes. One morning he noticed the smell of booze on the breath of this friend. My dad was aware he had a drinking problem but had never caught him inebriated on the job.

"Al pulled me aside," he told the crowd, "put me up against the wall and told me I was to make one run, call to say that the bus had broken down, and wait for a tow truck. He said, 'If I ever see you drunk at work again, I am going to turn you in myself.'"

My dad knew it would take the better part of the day for the tow truck to show up, and by that time, his friend would be sober enough to check out of work and drive himself home without putting anyone in danger.

"I never came in drunk again—and never touched another drop of alcohol on the days I worked. Al Roker saved my life," he said.

I learned a lot about my dad just before and after he died.

When I was growing up, dads had their work life and their home life, and the two rarely crossed paths. I don't know about your house, but my kids know all about my job. My job is discussed at the dinner table as much as homework is. It's not because of the type of work I do. I think most families are like this today. I always knew my dad drove a bus, became a dispatcher and eventually worked his way into a management position, but I didn't really understand what he did at work or the relationships he forged in the process. At his wake, someone stood up and said there was a group of black managers at the New York City Transit Authority who wouldn't be there if not for the work of Al Roker. He mentored people, brought them along and dressed them down when they needed it.

My dad was a humble man who taught me humility. He didn't teach it by lecturing or saying, "Son, this is what you do." He led by example. He lived his example, which made it easy for me to absorb growing up in our home. Of course, he set the bar for me as a dad, which I strive to reach each and every day. Whenever I am faced with a dilemma about parenting or a challenge at work, I often ask myself WWAD—What Would Al Do?

Given a moment to think about my dad and how he would respond, I usually come up with the right answer.

There isn't a single day that goes by since he passed when I don't think about him, wondering what he would do or say. I think about how proud he would be of Leila and Nicky and how glad to see how great his beloved Courtney has turned out. My dad wasn't the kind of man who worried about much—my weight was about it—but I think about him and I smile because I know deep in my heart that he has to be looking down on our family with a great sense of joy and pride.

3

The Power of an Apology

DEBORAH AND AL

It's Not About You—It's About Me

In our home, education is deeply important. Both Leila and Nicky know that school is their biggest priority. Although both of us came from limited means, our parents made sure we were given the best education possible. Al attended a Jesuit military school, on scholarship. Deborah was among the first in her family to go to a desegregated school, which meant she was given the same education as the white kids in her small Georgia town. Her parents, while cautious about the turmoil of integration, knew this meant she and her siblings would have a greater opportunity to expand beyond the limitations placed on black children in the Jim Crow South. Deborah embraced this opportunity with open arms.

As a result of her passion for education, Deborah has always held our kids, especially Leila, to a high standard of excellence when it comes to her education. Living where we do, our choices are vast. There are many specialized public schools in New York City as well as some of the finest and most prestigious private schools in the country. With our blessings of career and financial success and our location on Manhattan's Upper East Side, choosing to send our kids to private schools was an easy decision. Nearly all of our friends have children in rigorous private schools. Even though we'd all complain about the pressure and the workload, in our circle it was generally understood that our children would be better off for it in the end. With an elite private school on their résumés, the world would be their oyster.

After finishing her toddler years at a well-regarded nursery school, Leila was destined for a top-tier elementary school. She performed well on the placement tests and dazzled most who met her with a strong vocabulary, keen intellect and an easy social manner. And, of course, she was a child of color in a part of town not known for great diversity. In short, she was perfect private-school material. At age five, Leila was accepted by several of the best schools in the city. We were proud and excited. This was especially meaningful to Deborah, given her humble roots in the segregated South. We chose a well-known coed school just eleven blocks from our home, where Leila seemed to fit right in. But as she entered middle school, something changed. The academic pressure heightened tremendously and the social landscape also shifted. Good friends from earlier days paired off with other friends, and girls were showing signs of adolescence, growing thinner or plumper and in some cases shedding their childhood innocence and kindness. Though we had read about the social struggles of middle school (and of course gone through it ourselves), it was hard to watch Leila suffer. Some of her friends were becoming narcissistic or mean, and body image was a growing preoccupation, which was difficult for Leila, who wasn't as thin as many of her classmates. It was uncomfortable for her to be growing up in a culture that equated body size with beauty.

Leila was growing less happy at school. Like any parent at any school in any city, there were things about Leila's school that we didn't absolutely love, but overall we felt she was getting an enviable education and experience. Leila, however, began to complain. Some days there were even tears. Was it simply the curse of middle school or was it *this* school? we wondered. We both saw her struggling, not just in her studies but also with her classmates, many of whom were cut from the same predominantly white, super-thin Upper East Side cloth. We could sense Leila, who was not super-thin, was feeling self-conscious about herself and, despite her obvious intellect, she had started to think she wasn't quite as smart as everyone else. This is a tough combination for any teenage girl. Through conversations with other parents, we realized that Leila's feelings were completely age appropriate and similar to others in her class; their children were also struggling academically and had tutors to help them keep up with their schoolwork. We tried praising Leila and reminding her of her intellectual gifts. But she wasn't buying it. If she got a B on a test, she felt like a failure. The more we tried to chime in and help in any way we could, the more judged she felt by us. That usually escalated into some type of fight, which, of course, was the opposite of the reaction we were aiming for. Neither of us made for a great tutor because, as positive as we tried to be, she often felt there was judgment in our voices. We eventually followed the lead of the other parents and found a wonderful tutor, but even so, Leila continued to feel insecure and like she didn't fit in.

She had lots of great friends, and many days she came home laughing with fun stories about her day, but other days were loaded with self-doubt and sadness. That's not how the seventh grade should be! It should be fun, exciting and, yes, challenging. Deborah recalled her middle school years with great happiness. We worried Leila was missing out on that adolescent joy!

Leila began talking about transferring, at least for high school. Al took her to a private-school fair, and Leila soon set her sights on a boarding school in Massachusetts, an idea we weren't high on from the start. Initially, we saw her interest as more of a test than a real option. If we voiced any concern over her leaving home, we feared it might strengthen her desire to go.

However, the more we talked to families with kids happily thriving at boarding school, the more interesting the idea became, especially this particular school. Its values and principles seemed to be aligned with ours, especially its spiritual perspective, which was important to us as a church-going family. But just as we were coming around, Leila began to back off the idea! Al's reaction was, "Whew!" We dodged a bullet on that one!

Even so, the issue of changing schools still hadn't been resolved.

Deborah soon gravitated toward another private school with a sterling reputation located just outside the city. While fiercely competitive, it felt a bit calmer and it had a thriving arts program. However, there was one thing we didn't count on. Leila was becoming more and more passionate about theater. She had enrolled in a weekend theater program and loved it. The previous summer, she'd asked to go away to Stagedoor Manor, a fantastic performing arts camp located in the Catskill Mountains. The first time we saw Leila onstage, she revealed a strong and lovely singing voice, and we were blown away by her stage presence and evident joy. It was clear to us she had found herself, discovering a deep passion that left her confident and glowing. Even so, neither of us had anticipated that given the caliber of academic choices we'd placed in front of Leila, she'd come up with a wild card—the LaGuardia High School of Performing Arts, the so-called *Fame* school portrayed in the popular movie.

Leila first presented the idea of applying to LaGuardia to Al, who was fine with it. But when she broached the concept with Deborah, Deborah's response was . . . less enthusiastic.

"Absolutely not!" she said.

"But, Mom!" Leila cried.

For Deborah, it wasn't even a consideration. There were so many other great schools for Leila to consider. We had given her the choice of every top institution in and around Manhattan and she wanted to go to song-and-dance school? While a bit surprised, Al was a little more open to the idea.

"You're not really serious, are you?" Deborah asked once or twice. "What about academics?"

The more she fought Leila, the more Leila pushed back.

Eventually we realized that if we didn't listen to her now, we would surely pay a price for it later. Al made the argument that when he was in high school, his dream was to attend the New York School for Graphic Art & Design because of his interest in comic-book art and animation. His parents didn't want him to spend his high school years drawing cartoons; they wanted him to get a fine education at a Jesuit high school and go on to college, so they insisted he attend Xavier. While it turned out terrifically, and he wouldn't change a thing, he has often wondered what would have happened had he pursued his passion for animation and cartooning. He's never forgotten how his parents' decision made him feel. The more he thought about that, the more he knew we needed to give Leila this opportunity.

Deborah went to a small public school. She was a good student and a cheerleader and had a happy, active school life and wanted Leila to experience this kind of joy. But she also regretted that she hadn't had competitive school choices and hadn't been encouraged to apply to Ivy League colleges. Leila was studying world history and geometry in elementary school and reading classics like Steinbeck and Hemingway, works we never discovered until high school. She was getting a superior education, no doubt.

We kept hoping Leila would back down, give in and pick one of the other fine schools we'd lined up, but she didn't. She pouted and pontificated to anyone and everyone about how she desperately wanted to go to LaGuardia and how her mom was standing in the way.

And, of course, once we started investigating, we discovered that it is actually an elite public school. There is likely no other performing arts school in the country of its caliber. Unlike most public schools, students are accepted based both on auditions in dance, drama, music and art *and* on their academic achievement and attendance records. Some famous and varied alumni from the school include Jennifer Aniston, Diahann Carroll, Al Pacino, Ben Vereen, Lola Falana and Isaac Mizrahi, just to name a few.

After giving it a lot of thought, we allowed Leila to go through the application process at LaGuardia on the condition that she also consider the other private school that we both felt strongly about. Our thinking was simple. The application process at LaGuardia was pretty rigorous. In fact, in some ways, it was more competitive than the private schools we'd been looking at. Plus, we'd heard there were twenty-seven hundred kids vying for the seventy open spots in the drama program. The odds would be daunting for any kid.

Leila never shared with us exactly what she chose to do for her audition. Perhaps that was her way of keeping the experience as her own. What we do know is that she worked very hard to prepare two pieces—a dramatic piece and a lighthearted comedic number. She was ready and excited when the big day came. Al was out of town, so Deborah drove Leila to her audition. This was poignant for both of them. Up until that point, Leila felt like her mother hadn't been completely supportive. The drive that Saturday morning was a bonding experience for them.

Deborah will never forget the look on Leila's face when she finished with her audition that day. She came out of the school beaming and ran straight into her mom's arms. It was a proud and triumphant hug. This moment truly belonged to her. It was something she'd done on her own, and at that moment, we came together. I was so thrilled for her.

Once she auditioned, we came around to the notion that LaGuardia was a real possibility, because we suspected that Leila had killed it! Plus, we wanted to support her and we knew LaGuardia meant the world to her.

Meanwhile, lots of people began chiming in on whether or not this was a good path for Leila. Some felt it wasn't looking toward Leila's future while others thought it was great. Some thought leaving her prestigious private school would lessen her chances of going to an Ivy

League college, while others pointed out that an Ivy League college might not be what Leila wants anyway. One old friend whose son had graduated from a top private school sneered, "Oh no . . . This can't happen. No, no."

Deborah's own feelings of doubt were being fueled by the negative judgments. What would it say about us and about Leila to have her step away from the private-school world? All parents want to give their kids what they never had, and Deborah is no exception.

Al accepted Leila's path. He understood that she wasn't happy where she was and that switching to a similar school was unlikely to solve the problem. He was convinced that LaGuardia was the right choice—and that she would be accepted. He kept reminding Deborah that she ought to prepare herself for that possibility, because "it's going to happen. Isn't it more important for our child to be someplace where she feels fulfilled and successful, where she stands out a little more and is seen as terrific?"

His logic was so . . . logical. So balanced.

Meanwhile we headed south to Puerto Rico to thaw out during spring break and await the decision. We were lying by the pool when Al returned from a phone call. He sidled up to Leila, looking grim.

Leila sat upright. "What?" she asked with concern.

He broke into a grin. "You're in at LaGuardia!" he declared proudly.

"Really? Really?" she asked through a broad grin, and then squealed with delight so loudly that fellow sunbathers looked at her with concern.

She was so excited and we were very happy for her. We loved seeing that joyful look on her face. She had gone after something she wanted and got it. We couldn't have been prouder.

As we took in the good news, a solemn look fell over Deborah's face. She was happy. And at the same time, she was also sad, because she knew Leila was going to pick LaGuardia.

"Why don't we think about this for a few days, you know, let it sink in?" she said.

We could tell that Leila's joy was turning as well. She certainly didn't want to let either of us down, but she hadn't come this far to make her decision based on what was best for her mom. She had to make it based on what was best for her.

Later that night, Leila came to us and explained that she had given it a lot of thought, and the private school was too much like the school she had chosen to leave. Maybe it was a little gentler, but if she was going to change schools, she wanted to make a serious change. Otherwise, she would just stay where she was. "Let's face it. LaGuardia is totally different."

Deborah let out an audible sigh. She was trying her best to disguise her feelings, but there was no hiding how she really felt.

When we got back to New York, Deborah tried one last time to convince Leila that the private school was a better choice. We invited Leila's tutor to help us sort out the pros and cons; we thought it might be helpful to have a more impartial person in the discussion. We sat around the dining room table talking about the choices: staying at her current school, transferring to the other elite private school, or LaGuardia.

Everybody gave their opinions, but Deborah was really advocating for the private school and not hearing what others in the room were saying. She was almost lawyerly in her defense, and her argument boiled down to ABL: Anyplace But LaGuardia.

Al could feel Leila shutting down as Deborah went on and on, and he knew what was coming as we thanked the tutor and closed the front door after her. Leila, visibly upset, walked upstairs without a word.

Deborah followed her to her room, where Leila was brushing her teeth and tearing up. Then she unloaded. "You just dominated the meeting that was supposed to be about me figuring out what school *I* should go to. You know, it's not about you. At the end of the day, it's about me and what I want and what school I want to go to, and this is what I want. *It's not about you, Mom!*"

And she was right.

That's when Deborah thought about something Maria Shriver had said during a conference for women. "LIVE YOUR LIFE. Not one that someone has mapped out for you or that you envy. We can all find some measure of happiness when we feel comfortable to live our own lives and be who we are supposed to be." What an important lesson for us to remember and pass on to our children.

If choosing LaGuardia made Leila a happier and more confident kid who felt like she could soar through high school instead of struggle, then forget what everyone else thought! If it meant we had a daughter who is fulfilled and happy, then this was the right choice. In fact, there wasn't a better choice.

Leila was old enough, wise enough and tuned in enough to know what she wanted. We had to trust in her.

Deborah had been so caught up in placing her expectations on Leila that she'd forgotten to give her the leeway to have expectations for herself.

Deborah apologized to Leila.

Our daughter had truly figured out her path. And Deborah was ready to trust her.

As parents, we have to allow our children the room to learn and grow by making decisions about their lives that impact the direction in which they will go. Of course, we don't want to allow them to veer too far off their path, and if we've done a good job, hopefully, they won't fall as far as we think they will.

Leila knew what was right for her long before we did. Our job was to support her in her decision, even if it didn't meet the standard we had set for her a long time ago. Life is funny that way; the truth is circumstantial. It has a way of changing on us day by day, hour by hour. A few years ago, our daughter had no interest in performing arts. And now she attends a high school for performing arts.

We didn't want to take sides on this matter, but it was pretty clear we had. At the end of the day, Leila just wanted to be heard—by both of us. She felt like one of us wasn't listening to her—and she was right.

Being a parent comes with a lot of rights and privileges, but it isn't a one-way ticket to getting your way all of the time. Merely paying attention isn't enough. We've learned that one of the hardest parts of being good parents is seeing your children for who they are. It isn't about us—it's about them. If your child feels secure, safe and happy, you've done more things right than wrong. Like it or not, our children are going to be who they are, not who we want them to be. Although they come from our bodies, they are not an extension of us, but their own individual people.

AL

The Importance of Listening to Our Kids

When I was in the seventh grade, I brought home my report card and it said that I had flunked math. Math was not my strongest subject. The fact is, I have always struggled in math. So an F wasn't out of the realm of possibilities, especially when coupled with the usual comment, "If only Albert would apply himself." But I hadn't failed. I was one hundred percent sure. And I told my folks that.

But my father wasn't buying it. Who are you going to believe—a desperate seventh grader or The Man? Well, in this case, the "man" was actually a woman. To be specific, a *nun*.

"How did Sister Catherine make a mistake, Albert?" my father said sternly. "Tonight at the parent-teacher meeting I am going to find out if you're lying to me."

"I am not lying, Dad." I did my best to convince him, but it was no use.

I had no history of lying and yet my father still doubted my word. I couldn't believe that my dad didn't trust me!

My father went to school that night and met with Sister Catherine.

As he later told me, just as he launched into my flunking, she stopped him and said, "Mr. Roker, there must be some mistake. Albert didn't flunk."

"But it's on his report card."

Sister Catherine looked in her grade book and noted an 83 next to my name, which did not match the 63 she had written down on the report card. She had made an error. I know it's hard to believe that a nun could make such a mistake, but this was the 1960s. There were no computers, no digital entering of grades and comments. Everything was done—wait for it—*by hand*!

Hold on; it gets better—*in pen.*

Prepare for your mind to be blown even more—*a fountain pen*!

I'll wait while you pull out your phone to Google "fountain pen."

Shall we continue?

When my dad came home that night, he sat down next to me and said, "You know what, son? I made a mistake. I'm sorry I didn't believe you."

Up until that very moment, I didn't know that adults apologized to kids. I never forgot that moment. All I could think was, "Wow. My dad just apologized . . . to *me*!"

While I always trusted my dad, this moment deepened our bond. He was my protector and a wonderful mentor. He taught me that it's okay to admit when you're wrong, even if you're the adult. I have carried that lesson into my role as a dad to this very day. More so, he taught me to remember to show my kids that what they say matters.

Everyone wants to be heard and acknowledged. I don't care who you are or where you're at in life. On the last day of her show, Oprah said the one thing all of her guests shared in common was their need to be acknowledged. When you think about it, isn't that what we all want?

If you're like me, there's nothing more frustrating or patronizing than when someone says, "I hear what you are saying," while scrolling through text messages or typing out an e-mail. (If you're a parent, you know exactly what I'm talking about!) It's important that the other person knows you're really listening and you have taken in what he's shared with you. If you're not focused, you can't possibly be paying attention. You have to look *and* listen.

Being present in the moment is hard for a lot of people—now more than ever. There is a lot of "noise" in the world these days. Distractions are all around us. Giving people the attention they deserve and the time to be both heard and acknowledged opens the door to better communication in any relationship, whether it's with your spouse, your children, your friends or your colleagues at work. Taking the time to take in what they say, weigh it, respond to it and then honor it has an invaluable compound effect—especially when it comes to our children, because how else will we ever truly know them?

Parents have to do what we think is right in terms of enforcing rules and instilling manners but also be willing to let our children find their way. Life is about experiences, the good and the challenging. It's our job to be there to wipe away the tears and bandage the scraped knees. The truth is, in the real world, we can't prevent them from happening.

You cannot fit a square peg into a round hole. When you know it won't fit but you try to jam it in there anyway, it may work for a short time, but eventually something is going to break—and usually it's your kid who will pay the price.

My father always told me, "It's not about what you want. *It's about what your kid needs.*"

He never tried to force me into that round hole. He gave me permission to be who I was—always. He understood I was a kid who wasn't athletic, who preferred to play nerdy geeked-out games, read comic books about Superman and Batman or watch my favorite TV shows. Dad never tried to push me into sports because he knew that was a setup for failure.

As I entered into my adult life, I took my dad's wisdom with me, though there have been plenty of times along the way I questioned whether or not I fit in. That is until one night I met record producer L. A. Reid, who has worked with everyone from Whitney Houston to

Mariah Carey. We were having drinks before a black-tie event. I was dressed in a light gray suit and feeling a little out of place because I wasn't wearing a tux. Sensing my discomfort, L.A. turned to me and said, "Just do *you!*"

What a cool cat L. A. Reid is—much cooler than me.

Still, when you boil it down, you want your kids to know that about themselves as they go out into the world. All they have to do is be themselves and be the best them they can be.

My dad gave that gift to me—and I hope I am passing that on to my kids too.

"Just do you," I say, smiling as I do. In the end, that's all any of us can really strive for.

4

Grace Under Pressure

AL

A Gown, a Tux, a Tutu and a Funeral

Back in May of 2006, Deborah called with exciting news: Our pastor, Reverend Brenda Husson, was hosting a dinner party at her home for Archbishop Desmond Tutu of South Africa, and she'd like us to attend. Naturally we accepted this invitation. After all, who wouldn't want to attend a dinner honoring one of the world's greatest spiritual leaders and an outspoken voice for civil rights—not just in South Africa, but around the world?

It wasn't until I went to put it on my calendar that I realized we already had an engagement that night, a black-tie charity event hosted by the Black Alumni of Pratt Institute at Lincoln Center.

"No problem," I thought. Like all busy New Yorkers, we could do both. First we'd swing by Reverend Husson's dinner for Archbishop Tutu and then we'd hit the charity event a little later.

Before we knew it, the date had arrived. Deborah looked radiant in a white-and-silver brocaded dress. I didn't look half bad, in my tux and a silver tie to play off my wife's dress. I don't know why, but it sometimes bugs her that I do this. It's not like I'm making us wear matching Hawaiian shirts. I would never do that to her! That's an embarrassment I would save for the whole family . . . on vacation . . . with lots of pictures. Still, I don't mind sharing a bit of color in common when Deborah and I get decked out for a night on the town!

Normally, we'd just grab a cab, but given that we needed to hit two places in one night and timing was critical, we decided to spring for a car service. I must say, we made for quite the dashing couple, and if we were overdressed for the first stop, well, we would simply explain we had another event to go to. After all, this is New York, where anything goes.

As we pulled up to the front door, I noticed a lot of other black cars in front of our pastor's apartment building, but hey, Archbishop Tutu was there, and no doubt there were a lot of dignitaries who wanted to pay their respects inside.

As we walked into the building, the doorman said, "Ah, Mr. and Mrs. Roker. I know why you're here. You just missed Mayor Bloomberg. First elevator on your right." So we walked to the elevator, duly impressed, and were whisked to the sixth floor of the building by the elevator operator.

The elevator opened onto a very large and beautiful apartment. It was more spacious than I remembered, but we had been to the reverend's apartment only once before, a few years earlier, so my recollections of it were a bit hazy. There was a lovely cocktail reception going on, befitting a person of Archbishop Tutu's stature, I thought, although the man himself was, by all accounts, very humble. A waiter took our drink request and hurried off as we wandered about the apartment, nodding and murmuring "Hellos" to several people we knew.

Some of the artwork on the wall caught my eye. If I didn't know any better, that was a Renoir . . . Wait, was that a genuine Matisse over there? I knew the reverend's husband, Tom, was an artist; was it possible he had painted these copies, or did they actually *own* such masterpieces? At just about that moment, Deborah came up to me and said, "I hope dinner is being served soon. We have to get going!"

Then she bumped into a couple of people she knew from the retail and fashion world, which was strange only because none of them belonged to our church. All the women commented on Deb's dress and how beautiful she looked. She demurred, something about "this old thing?" and explained we had another event to go to.

While Deb was talking to these acquaintances, I looked around. I hadn't yet seen our reverend, nor hide nor hair of the guest of honor. In fact, I didn't recognize any of these people from church at all. Deb circled back to me and said, "This is odd. The last two people I talked to I'm pretty sure are *Jewish*. Is that strange for a dinner celebrating an Episcopal archbishop?"

The fact is, not really. The New York Episcopal Church has a long history of interdenominational brotherhood that encompasses all religions. But before I could answer, Deborah was buttonholed by another pal. Deborah asked if she had seen Archbishop Tutu. The woman all but squealed with delight and surprise.

"Archbishop Tutu's here? Wow. I would love to meet him!" With that she took off like the Roadrunner with Wile E. Coyote in hot pursuit.

You know how you sometimes get a sneaking suspicion that something's not quite right? Like your fly might be down or the girl you're about to kiss might be your second cousin?

That's what this party was beginning to feel like.

That is until I stopped a passing waiter and asked, "Oh, are those lamb chops?" Deborah poked me. "I mean, is this the dinner for Archbishop Desmond Tutu?"

The waiter looked a little confused, even as I helped myself to three of the most succulent lamb chops I had ever tasted.

"Um, no," he replied. "This is Abe Rosenthal's shivah."

Then, instinctively realizing I was in the wrong place and protectively shielding the rest of his tray of lamb chops from me, he scurried away.

Abe Rosenthal?

The Abe Rosenthal?

The legendary editor of the *New York Times*? He was an iconic figure in New York City. I knew *of* him, but I certainly didn't *know* him.

Oy.

Deborah and I realized our mistake. The elevator operator had just assumed we were coming here, to the Rosenthal shivah in 6-A. We were going to *10-A.*

A difference of four floors was all the difference in the world.

A Jewish celebration of a life or a lovely sit-down dinner with a religious legend.

And we were way overdressed for both.

"We are in the wrong apartment! At a shivah!" Deb whispered. "We have got to get out of here!"

Well, at least we'd blended right in with crowd.

Not so much.

We were the only black couple in the room, and dressed to the nines to boot.

Nope.

Nobody was gonna think we were out of place.

Except us.

The ones asking for Desmond Tutu.

We had to get out inconspicuously and find our way to the right apartment, where there was a dinner party going on with two empty seats!

We casually made our way toward the door only to see that Mr. Rosenthal's widow, Shirley, was now standing there greeting newcomers and giving those leaving a fond farewell.

"Just act natural, say a few words and we're home free," I whispered to Deborah out of the side of my mouth.

"I know what to do. I'm not an idiot!" she hissed in reply.

To this day, my wife denies the following happened.

Trust me.

It did.

There's no reason to make it up.

In fact, there's no upside for me in sharing it with you. But I feel I have an obligation to tell you the rest of the story, so here it goes.

There was another couple ahead of us, saying something soothing and comforting to the newly widowed Mrs. Rosenthal. When it was our turn, I heard my wife say, "Oh, Mrs. Rosenthal. What a great man your husband was. *Congratulations!*"

Congratulations?

Hey, your husband's dead! Let's strike up the band!

I quickly jumped in, inserting myself between the two ladies, and said, "Yes, our condolences, Mrs. Rosenthal," as I grasped her hand, my hip pushing against Deborah's toward the door. "You know, my social studies teacher believed you couldn't consider yourself a true New Yorker unless you knew how to do the *New York Times* 'subway fold.' What a legacy!"

And with that, I hustled Deborah to the elevator.

"CONGRATULATIONS? The woman's husband just died. Were you wishing her well on cashing in on the insurance?"

Deborah looked at me like I was crazy.

"I said no such thing. I said 'condolences.'"

Just then the elevator door opened. "You let us off on the wrong floor," I said to the elevator operator. "We're going to the Husson apartment for the Desmond Tutu dinner."

"You didn't say where you were headed," he responded unapologetically. "You looked too fancy for the other thing."

A few seconds later, we were at the right affair, and as expected, dinner was well under way. It would have been awkward to sit down and join the dinner at this late juncture. Thankfully, our beloved reverend quickly ushered us in and, after some hasty introductions, we apologized for our tardiness and explained what had just transpired. Nobody laughed harder than Archbishop Tutu.

Of course, he was also the guy who, rather than engage me in a discussion about world affairs, said, "You know, I've seen you on TV. I thought you were a much fatter fellow." We offered our apologies for having to cut our visit short and made our way to the elevator once again.

But the elevator refused to arrive. After standing at the door for a good ten minutes, our hostess called down to the lobby. Hanging up the phone, she delivered the news. The elevator was on the fritz.

"You'll have to take the service elevator."

She showed us through the kitchen and into the hallway that led to the service elevator. It wasn't a total loss. Guess what was on the menu.

Yep.

Lamb chops.

I snagged a few for us on a napkin so we'd have something to nibble on in the car.

The service elevator arrived, and there was our old friend, Sol the elevator operator.

Our first stop?

Back down to six, to pick up some departing Rosenthal guests, who looked at us and said, "You're still here?"

"Long story," I replied around a mouthful of lamb chop.

Deborah and I exited the elevator, got in the car and collapsed into laughter.

What the heck had just happened?

It was something that could happen only in New York City and, in all likelihood, could happen only to *us*. As we drove off to what would now be our *third* event of the night, I thought, "There's nobody else I could have done this with except Deborah!" Despite the opportunity for embarrassment, she never lost her sense of humor or her beautiful smile throughout the evening. She is the definition of grace under pressure. I knew this would be a story we would remember for the rest of our lives. And *congratulations* to us both for that!

DEBORAH

Our Trials Have Lessons to Teach Us

There's no doubt that I am a blessed woman. I have two beautiful, healthy children, a warm and kind stepdaughter, a loving and generous husband and a fulfilling career that many would kill for. But what can I say? Even though I am fortunate to have the help of a wonderful caregiver at home, there are times I feel like any other stressed-out working mom who is trying to satisfy a dozen needs at the same time while itemizing the multitasks in my head . . . usually in the middle of the night.

Okay, I have a *GMA* segment at seven forty-five tomorrow—so I'll need to leave at six thirty.

Argh, I forgot to contact Mom's doctor to discuss her new medication . . .

Oh, and I didn't call my sister Tina back . . . for the third time . . .

Did I put out the thirteen dollars Nicky needs to buy a PE shirt?

I have to hound Leila to go over her reading for church this Sunday.

And, oh no, I have my annual mammogram tomorrow that I absolutely can't miss since I had a scare last time when they found a benign cyst!

I was especially agitated about this appointment, not just because all of us women hope for the best but fear the worst, but because immediately afterward I was scheduled to tape a video message to salute my dear friend Robin Roberts in her courageous fight against breast cancer! None of us ever wants to hear the words "You've got cancer," yet Robin, bless her heart, has had to endure cancer twice!

During weeks like this, which are most of the weeks of my life, I find myself feeling anxious, sometimes a little snippier than I'd like to admit, and usually frazzled. The world seems to be spinning too fast and I have no possible way of slowing it down. I occasionally take yoga and meditation classes to temper the fast-paced world I navigate, but clearly not often enough! Breathing and staying in the moment are fleeting and foreign ideas.

I can hear Sissy Spacek in her movie *Coal Miner's Daughter,* in which she portrays Loretta Lynn. On the verge of a breakdown, she turns to her husband and says, "I feel like I'm not running my life; my life is running me."

Some days I truly feel like life is running me . . . and I can't quite catch my breath.

Who among us hasn't felt that way from time to time?

Let's face it: Grace under pressure is not an easy achievement under most circumstances. But I have learned that if you simply pay attention, you don't have to look far to find examples of grace in your midst, people who are paragons of strength when you least expect it. One morning after a particularly stressful week of travel and appointments, I was cooking breakfast for Nicky with *Good Morning America* playing on the small kitchen TV, as I usually do on my mornings off. It was the day Robin decided to go public with her pre-leukemia diagnosis. She had shared this serious medical setback with me and a small group of trusted women friends weeks earlier, but I still found myself frozen in front of the television screen as I watched her stoically open up her personal world yet again to viewers who, like me, were in their kitchens sipping coffee before work. Through tears, Robin bravely and optimistically spoke about her plans for a stem cell transplant, thanks to her sister Sally-Ann, who was a perfect match.

In the midst of this frightening and devastating news, Robin was the one comforting others, including her colleagues and her viewers. She was an absolute pillar of strength, the epitome of grace under pressure. She was hopeful, grateful and strong. And even though I'd already known, I unexpectedly burst into tears. I have admired Robin for many reasons over the years and have treasured our friendship. But in this brave moment she was now my hero. I was overcome with respect for her courage in the face of such a mind-shattering diagnosis and felt deeply humbled that my "stressful life" paled by comparison. Suddenly everything was put in perspective.

The entire ABC family was shaken to its core by yet another blow inflicted on our steel magnolia. Like many, I was angry and hurt for her. It wasn't fair. Hadn't she suffered enough?

I never told anyone, but for many weeks after that I sobbed at night in the privacy of my home as I worried for Robin. She was not only a dear friend to me, but I had always been touched by the bond she shared with Leila over the years. Maybe it was the last name that we shared or Robin's heartwarming smile, but Leila adored her from the moment they met. Robin was the first woman she had ever known to battle breast cancer, and somehow my little girl was captivated by this woman who was a tower of strength, a living superhero. Of course we watched *GMA* in the mornings (shh . . . don't mention this to Al!), and Leila loved Robin's easy laugh, her folksy manner and her devotion to sports. Somehow she delivered the news in a way that a fourth grader could appreciate. So Leila often quoted Robin when talking about a news event and used her as an example in school during a discussion about strong, influential women.

So when I visited Robin during the 2008 Christmas holidays, while she was recovering from her breast cancer treatments, Leila wanted to come too. She brought chocolate chip cookies she had spent hours proudly preparing. We picked up Chinese food and had a fun and happy lunch. We were thrilled to watch Robin, bald, frail and thin from the chemo treatments, dig in and enjoy the food.

When we finished, Robin pulled Leila over and gave her a Christmas gift. My daughter's face lit up when she opened it to find a diary, which Robin explained was for journaling about her deepest thoughts, and a gift card to "buy whatever Santa didn't bring." Leila was blown away by the unexpected moment and kind generosity of the woman she had come to cheer up! When we got home, Leila began to weep, overcome that Robin had remembered her in such a personal way. I held her close as tears fell from my eyes too.

Now her icon was sick again.

I couldn't bear the thought of my daughter having to watch Robin suffer even more. We all thought Robin had won that battle, but now she was facing a second and much harder fight for her life—one no one saw coming.

As the months dragged on and Robin prepared for her stem cell surgery, she made time for our gal-pal lunch gatherings, which Tonya, Gayle, Theresa and I cherished more than any other we'd ever had. Though we couldn't meet as often, when we did, we still laughed and gasped and whispered private truths. Robin was bound and determined to live and love her life.

What she may not have realized at the time was that she was also teaching the rest of us how to live. In the midst of my stressed-out, "topsy-turvy" life, I was finding incredible strength, clarity and courage through the example of my desperately ill friend.

In August of 2013, just before she was scheduled to have her lifesaving bone marrow surgery, Robin's mom, Lucimarian, passed away—another cruel blow to this already physically fragile woman who was enduring more than her share of pain. Robin and I had shared many stories and stresses about our aging mothers over the years, and I had been blessed to spend time with Lucimarian. So I felt her passing deeply and hard.

I was touched to be invited to her funeral in Pass Christian, Mississippi. Nothing could have prepared me for this experience. First of all, practically the entire town attended the wake! As I pulled up to the funeral home, I couldn't believe my eyes: The line to greet the family wrapped all around the building. I took my place with the locals, who all seemed to have a story about Lucimarian's kindness and spunk. Hundreds and hundreds of people came to pay their respects to the once lively woman whose spiritual imprint was indelibly marked on this small coastal town. The outpouring of love was mind-boggling. It filled my heart knowing what this must have meant to Robin.

But for me the life-changing moment happened the next day, in the small family church where Robin and her two sisters, Dorothy and Sally-Ann, and her brother, Butch, said their final good-byes to their cherished mom. The funeral was simply a heart-stirring love letter written about a life well lived. Robin and her siblings shared tears, humor and spiritual lessons gained from their mom. I sat on a small wooden pew with George Stephanopoulos, Diane Sawyer and the president of ABC News, Ben Sherwood, overcome not with sadness but with joy and feelings of hope and happiness . . . all hallmarks of Lucimarian's legacy. Like the funerals I had attended in Perry, it was called a homegoing and was all about joy for a weary soul who was going home to God.

Though she was shockingly gaunt and no doubt weak from exhaustion, Robin stood firm and strong, gracefully enduring the harsh blows that had come her way during this past year or two, quoting a number of Lucimarianisms . . . simple sayings her mother famously uttered about humility, prayer and love of God.

Robin told how her mom often cautioned against hubris, saying, "If you strut, you fall." And there was her mom's view that bad things don't happen "to you" but "for you" so you can learn something and deepen your faith.

In death, Lucimarian was still the loving mom, offering me and everyone else the kind of warm, lasting life lessons that my mom, now suffering with dementia, is no longer capable of sharing. And even in her weakest moment, her youngest child, Robin, was extraordinary. Oddly, I left Lucimarian's funeral feeling blessed and happy, filled with unexplainable joy and hope. Somehow I felt at peace as I considered this beautiful woman's life of love and giving—the only things in life that truly matter.

Weeks later, Robin had her surgery. I remember the date, September 20, because it was my birthday. When I visited her in the hospital, somehow she always managed to smile and cheer up the rest of us, who were shedding a few tears behind the protective hospital face masks we were ordered to wear so we didn't risk getting Robin sick.

She had lost her hair and she appeared to be very weak, yet when

I saw her, she remained unbelievably positive and determined to beat her disease. In her heart, she knew that God was going to get her through yet another tough time. And somehow, I knew it too. She has a special angel looking after her.

Two years later, Robin is going strong, still helping all of us to laugh, love, learn and yes . . . live life to its fullest. Recently, during a tough week, I called and wondered if she had time for coffee.

I was feeling especially low.

My mom was sick with a respiratory illness, and I had been on the phone morning and evening with her caregivers. Leila, now a typical teenager, was often surly and angry. (That week we were at odds over her curfew.) And at work I was clashing with an exhausting and bullying male colleague (yes, they still exist in my business) and I had just been overlooked for a big assignment I'd desperately wanted. I was furious when it went to a less experienced reporter. Other than Al, there aren't many people I trust with such personal and professional frustrations. But Robin and I have shared many confidences over the years. Without hesitation she named a place and time, and as always, offered me her unwavering support and wise advice. She too had hit many bumps at ESPN and early on at ABC. "I know what you're dealing with, but hang tough," she advised. "You're talented and strong. That will win out. Life can be hard, but I guarantee if you poured your problems on a table along with everybody else's, you'd probably take yours right back." Of course, she was absolutely right, and in that moment, I knew her mother had passed those wise words of wisdom along to Robin somewhere along the way.

Sometimes I almost feel embarrassed to share my small struggles with Robin, who has truly seen some of the darker and more challenging sides of life. Yet she is quick to point out that there's no measurement on suffering.

I am grateful and blessed to have such a wise and generous friend in my life. Robin is a strong reminder that we all cope with burdens and trials. They often bring out our best selves, but even if they don't, they have something to teach us, if we pay attention.

AL

—————

Boots on the Ground

Back in the day, your family would gather 'round the television and watch the "boob tube" together. It could have been *I Love Lucy*, *The Diahann Carroll Show*, *I Spy* or *The Carol Burnett Show*. For us baby boomers, the blue glow of the television was the communal hearth around which we parked our "rusty dusty," as my mom called it, and let the entertainment wash over us.

One of the shows I most vividly remember was the annual *Bob Hope Christmas Show* on NBC. For much of my youth, it recorded his annual trip to Vietnam to entertain the troops. I loved watching him prowling the stage, firing off one-liners, swinging his ever-present golf club and introducing Raquel Welch or another hot actress of the day, saying, "Wanted to remind you boys what you're fighting to protect back home."

Bob Hope was the face of the USO tour for many years. Countless entertainers crisscrossed the country and the globe performing for our troops, but for almost fifty years, no one was as closely associated with the USO tour as Bob Hope.

I always wondered what it would be like to travel to a war zone and take part in one of those tours. My desire to do so was heightened when my buddy Matt Lauer and I did the *Today* show from Camp Eggers in Kabul, Afghanistan, back around Thanksgiving 2007. We saw firsthand the sacrifices our troops make, protecting our freedoms 365 days a year, twenty-four hours a day. It was there that I overheard a couple of soldiers talking about how much they were looking forward to an upcoming USO show.

After that it was my dream to shine a light on our military troops as frequently as possible, while also supporting the USO and its efforts to help our amazing servicemen and -women, as well as their families. We can never totally repay them for all they have done for us over the years, but what an honor to help the USO bring a little bit of home to our troops wherever they are.

In early October 2014, my dream became personal when the *Today* show launched its first *Today* USO Comedy Tour.

To make it a truly legitimate USO Comedy Tour, you need comedy. Someone who is instantly recognizable *and* funny. Someone whose name is synonymous with comedy. Once we had that, we knew others would jump on board.

As much as I like to think I can get off a powerful zinger every now and again, I'm certainly nowhere close to the likes of a Bob Hope and not even in the same room when it comes to doing professional stand-up comedy. If we were going to do this, we needed a giant in the comedy world. Someone in that same pantheon as Bob Hope. My producers and I batted around names, and then someone said, "What about Jay Leno?"

Jay Leno! Who's bigger than Jay? He was perfect! He is comedy, the stand-up comic's comic. Legendary *Tonight Show* host, car aficionado *and* a guy who'd already done a number of USO tours.

Surely there was no way we could get Jay. (I'll pause while you say, "Please don't call me Shirley.") (And now you know why I could never lead the tour!)

But I figured, you don't ask, you don't get.

I somehow got the number for the garage where he spends most of his time since stepping down from *The Tonight Show*. After the third ring, a voice familiar to millions of late-night audiences answered.

"Hey, it's Jay."

And Jay not only said yes, but he told me whenever we needed him, he was in and he was bringing his former bandleader, Kevin Eubanks, as well.

THIS . . . WAS . . . HUGE!!!!

With Jay in our pocket, everything fell into place.

One of the hottest comics out there today, Iliza Schlesinger, immediately said yes, and then movie star/TV star/musician/comedian Craig Robinson jumped on board as well.

With the talent lined up, I flew thirteen hours from New York to Dubai, where I met up with Jay, Craig, Iliza and Kevin. From there we flew about four more hours to Bagram Air Force Base in Afghanistan, to perform for more than twelve hundred American troops.

We landed early in the morning and deposited our belongings in the barracks, which stood behind twelve-foot-tall, three-foot-thick cement blast shields reinforced with rebar. Then we went to have lunch in the commissary with the troops. It looked like any other cafeteria except all the customers had automatic rifles and wore camo gear. Come to think of it, it sounds a lot like one of my family reunions!

After that we headed over to a giant hangar from where we'd be broadcasting the *Today* show followed by the USO Comedy Tour. For four hours, the gang shook hands, took pictures and kibitzed with the troops nonstop, taking breaks only to do some *Today* segments. We were just finishing that up and getting ready to do our USO show, when the reality of life in Afghanistan hit hard.

As shocking as it may sound, I had no idea what our soldiers' lives are really like in active duty until I saw it with my own eyes. Sure, I knew they battled these awful elements I didn't want to think about, and I knew they put their lives in danger every day, but I don't think I truly understood the hostile environment they face with such bravery until I was on the air base watching shells explode overhead.

When we first arrived, we were warned that if we heard one siren blast, we should hit the deck.

Two blasts, you run for the bunkers.

Three meant all clear.

Now this plaintive wail of a siren seemed to come from out of nowhere. The folks with us yelled out to hit the deck. We all dropped to the ground right where we were, and suddenly the deafening sound of a giant anti-missile gun started blasting. After thirty seconds or so, silence, then two blasts, and suddenly I'm being dragged up and out toward a reinforced bunker, where we waited for around ten minutes till we heard the all-clear sound.

Wow.

The soldiers told me that happened several times a week, sometimes more than once a day.

That's life at Bagram. And that's why we were there. To try to block that reality out for our brave soldiers for just a little while.

So then it was showtime. For the next two and a half hours, we brought laughter, music and joy to this amazing group of soldiers who deserved it more than anyone else I could think of at that moment. I never understood the profundity of the saying "'Tis far better to give than to receive" more than I did during that tour.

Giving of myself to those who put themselves in harm's way every single day was an absolutely life-changing experience—one I didn't see coming. I had patriotically and spiritually supported the troops for years. I always sought out military families on the plaza, for example, and put them on the air whenever possible as my small gesture of support for the troops. Yet, within hours of our arrival, I had a completely different understanding of what these brave men and women had done, sacrificed and given of themselves—for my freedom and *yours*. It was the kind of appreciation I could never achieve without witnessing it in my own boots-on-the-ground experience. Working in news for as many years as I have, I couldn't conceive the kind of understanding I now had of our servicemen and -women without the kind of eyewitness coverage that being at Bagram gave me.

I couldn't hold back my tears that first night as I crawled into my bed. I was incredibly grateful to all the fearless men and women who serve our country and unbelievably appreciative for the opportunity to be there. I was also feeling terribly guilty, knowing I would be going home in twenty-four hours to see my wife and kids.

You can bet I hugged everyone a little tighter than usual when I got back to New York. I was never in the military, but I would certainly have a different filter going forward whenever I'd hear stories about time people spent serving our country.

Age and wisdom don't necessarily come together, but perspective always follows experience.

Freedom comes at a cost.

The people who help pay that cost are the servicemen and -women of our armed forces and their families. Here at home and all across the globe, they protect us.

They serve us.

They keep our freedom secure.

One of the most visible parts of the USO is the USO entertainment tours. The smiles and laughs and appreciation on the faces of those servicemen and -women brought warmth to our hearts. After our first show, one of the soldiers came up to me and said, "God bless you. For two and a half hours, I forgot where I was."

And that to me was the definition of irony. They kept thanking all of us for taking the time to be there when in fact it was our purpose for being there—to thank them for all they do—that made our presence pale in comparison.

The whole experience gave me chills and an endless willingness to offer a hug in gratitude.

That is the point of the USO. Whether it's a comfortable place to be as they transit between assignments, or help figuring out a problem with family back home, for more than seventy years, the USO has provided a safe haven—physically and emotionally—for our troops.

By supporting the USO, we support our troops. And by supporting our troops, we support the mission to keep this nation and its ideals free.

That's why I made the "Rokerthon," a fund-raiser for the USO, during which I set the world record for the longest uninterrupted weather report broadcast.

The idea for the Rokerthon was born in October 2014, when Natalie Morales reported on a woman in Norway who'd allegedly broken the Guinness World Record with a thirty-three-hour live weather broadcast. When I heard the report, I flippantly said, "I can do that."

I didn't think anyone would take me up on it!

At the end of the broadcast that morning, our executive producer called a meeting and said, "So, you're going to break the record?"

At first I didn't know what he was talking about. But then I said, "Sure, why not? As long as we raise some money for the USO in the process."

We decided to start the Rokerthon at ten p.m. on Wednesday, November 12. It was on MSNBC at the top of *The Last Word* with Lawrence O'Donnell, and I hoped to break the record at eight a.m. Friday, November 14, during the *Today* show.

Little did I know what a major undertaking it would be—for everyone. We needed a special team of producers, social media people, crew, official witnesses from Guinness, and lots of other details no one had considered when we said we were in.

But we pulled it together. Dotted our i's and crossed our t's.

Well . . .

One little thing: I forgot to tell Deborah. Oh, sure, a month or so earlier I had mentioned I was thinking about doing this stunt to raise money for the USO, but neglected to share one or two details . . . like the actual date—or even that we were, in fact, doing it!

So the weekend before, as we're going through our calendars, I happened to just sort of toss out, "Oh, and of course I'll be live on the air from Wednesday till Friday, doing Rokerthon, so I won't—"

I never got a chance to finish my sentence.

Deborah went ballistic!

"YOU WHAT?

"When were you going to tell me this? What plans have you made? You can't just get up there and be live for three days straight. Are you insane?"

I wasn't sure which question to answer first. But I did realize a good rule of thumb: Before embarking on a potentially dangerous stunt on live TV, tell your significant other. They have this wacky idea that they want to be "in the loop"! You would think that after twenty years of marriage I would have known this by now.

Thanks to Deb's well-placed outrage, I actually sought some medical advice and got clearance from NBC's medical director, Dr. Tanya Bensimon. I was told to stay away from caffeine early on, stay hydrated, bank sleep leading up to the event. Try to keep carbs to a minimum and eat higher-fat and higher-protein snacks. Save a necessary caffeine jolt for the last hour or so if I absolutely need it. Of course I would need it! I was going to be on the air for thirty-four straight hours! I was thinking a jolt of caffeine wasn't going to be enough! Maybe a caffeine drip?

A few days before the event, we learned that the Norwegian record still hadn't been verified. That left the standing record at twenty-four hours, and I would have to broadcast for only twenty-four hours and one minute to set a new record. In fact, when I was covering Hurricane Sandy, I was on the air for forty-eight hours, but because of the very strict rules surrounding setting a Guinness World Record, that broadcast didn't qualify me for the record book. This time I wasn't taking any chances. If the Norway record somehow became real, I wanted mine to beat it, so I was going all the way.

As they say, go big or go home!

To officially set the record, the rules were very specific.

1. I had to talk *only* about weather for the entirety of my broadcast.
2. I could talk about current weather and weather seven days in the past or seven days ahead.
3. For every sixty minutes completed, I was given a five-minute break. The breaks could be carried over and combined, so if I went four hours without stopping, I could take a twenty-minute break.
4. Two independent witnesses had to be there at all times.

Once we were on the air, the only moment I doubted I could do it was after the first fifteen minutes. It was the same feeling I had in the first mile of the New York City Marathon. I remember thinking as I ran up the Verrazano Bridge, "What the *hell* am I doing?" And then I got past the midpoint of the bridge and started running downhill, calmed down and just kept going. The exact same thing happened to me during the broadcast. Fifteen minutes in, I thought, "I cannot do this. I have thirty-three hours and forty-five minutes to go! How am I going to fill the time?"

And then I did my first chat with a local television station, which settled my nerves and helped me to push onward. We filled the time talking to West Coast affiliates and even a station in Australia. Although I was allowed to take a five-minute break every hour, at one point I had such a rhythm going that I was on the air for five hours straight, banking enough rest minutes to take a shower and change my clothes!

Besides talking with local stations, the Weather Channel and MSNBC colleagues, I also had a lot of support from friends and family throughout my time on the air. Candice Bergen, Aaron Sorkin, Alan Alda, Sam Champion, Willie Geist, Tamron Hall, Diego Klattenhoff and Ryan Eggold from *The Blacklist* came by to chat about the weather, and my beautiful and understanding wife, Deborah, dropped in with hot chocolate for me.

By the end of the broadcast, my voice was reduced to a mere croak.

I could barely speak. (Deborah and the kids wished that would last for a while.) But even though the thirty-four-hour broadcast took a lot out of me, I *did* it; I set the world record! I can officially check this one off my bucket list. I assure you, I won't be doing it again!

After it was all over, I received a surprise phone call from Vice President Joe Biden, who reminded me that the only mistake I made during my marathon broadcast was leaving my microphone on during a bathroom break.

Well, I had to admit, he had me there.

"Yes, sir. It gave new meaning to live stream." Hey, it was the best ad-lib I had under the circumstances.

Thankfully, the vice president was kind enough to play along, admitting that he too had had a few problems of his own over the years with microphones he didn't realize were still on.

And that's why I love live television.

You never know what to expect. Even after thirty-four hours on the air!

Man, I love my job!

What made it especially worthwhile was having so many people pull together toward one common goal. We do that every morning on the *Today* show, of course, but it had been a while since there was anything that had snowballed like the Rokerthon did. (For reasons I can't explain, it was the hottest trending topic on Twitter!) But best of all, through our Crowdrise campaign, we raised $80,000 for the USO.

5

Don't Confuse the Wedding with the Marriage

DEBORAH

Don't Confuse the Wedding with the Marriage

I attended a cocktail party for a friend who was joyfully days away from her wedding. I was so happy to be celebrating this blessing with her, as she had been looking for Mr. Right for a long time. A strikingly beautiful woman with smooth dark hair and a quick, bright smile, she had finally discovered that the man of her dreams was actually a childhood acquaintance she had reconnected with. Her fiancé was handsome, charming and successful. I was thrilled my friend had found what she'd been looking for and was delighted to be part of such an intimate evening with friends.

As I was getting ready to leave the party, she and I were chatting about love, life and marriage, and I said, "Do you mind if I offer you some unsolicited advice?"

I know, shocking, right?

It's always risky to offer a friend unsolicited advice. While you know your heart is in the right place, sometimes people aren't open or ready to hear your thoughts even if you think they could be helpful. I never want anyone to feel judged or attacked, but I am the kind of friend who feels comfortable sharing life lessons I've learned along the way, especially with those I care most about.

Happily, she accepted my offer and listened closely as I began to talk.

"Honey, don't confuse the wedding with the marriage." I paused because I wanted her to *really* hear what I was about to share. "I know it sounds kind of strange, but it seems that so many hopeless romantics make that mistake. Take my word on this. *They're not the same.*

"The wedding is going to be a whirlwind of bliss, beauty and magic . . . everything fairy tales and dreams are made of. Marriage isn't always that way."

Okay, I didn't want to overdo it and scare the poor girl to death just before her long-awaited walk down the aisle. After all, I am a big believer in marriage! "Soon Al and I are going to celebrate twenty amazing years together. It has been fabulous, and I would do it all over again. But it is serious business. It's easy to go into it believing every day is going to feel like your wedding day—floating on air, embracing each other without a care in the world, not seeing anyone else in the room. And for a while it's like that. But sooner rather than later reality sets in. Life takes over, and there will be decisions to make. *Hard decisions.* You will face challenges that will test your strength, your commitment, your patience and perhaps even your love. The fact is, marriage is hard, and you have to make the choice to be there with that person and believe he is worth it and worthy of struggling through whatever crisis you face." I spoke softly, and I reached over and touched her arm so she would know I was coming from a place of love. I reiterated how wonderful it is, just in case she was about to freak out.

Then I mentioned a memorable piece of advice from a dear friend who got married just before Al and I did. It sounded corny and poetic at the same time. She said, "Marriage is like a long dance. Sometimes you are slow dancing in each other's arms and it is lovely and lustful, and sometimes you are pushing away and fast dancing. Sometimes you are doing a romantic tango, and sometimes you are strutting around doing your own thing in a different part of the room. The key thing to remember is that no matter what, you are always in the dance together."

I've never forgotten those very important words of wisdom.

My friend gave me a big, long hug and a smile signaling that she appreciated the advice.

I am far from an expert, but to me, marriage is about all of the challenges and tests you have endured and, yes, the tough times you pull through together. It is also about the decision you make over and over that it is worth continuing to do that. When I look at my husband, I think to myself, "Wow!" We've weathered fertility issues, health scares, Al's weight issues, our career ups and downs, competitiveness, disappointments, highs, lows, family illnesses, deaths and many other stresses and strains together.

T-O-G-E-T-H-E-R.

And that's the most important thing.

Sometimes when Al is upset with me or he's done something that has left me disappointed, after the dust has settled I think to myself, "*This* is what the marriage part is all about." We're not living a wedding. We are in a marriage. That means effort, love, patience, forgiveness, compassion and more love.

At our wedding rehearsal dinner, Al's mom, Isabel, gave *me* some unsolicited advice that I still remember clearly and have held dear. Al's mom was a power to be reckoned with, even at four foot three and about 110 pounds. She had a wicked sense of humor, and her cackling laugh was audible two floors away. But on that particular day, she looked us both dead in the eyes and in a serious tone said, "Communication is the secret to a long marriage. Talk . . . talk . . . talk . . . about everything. Marriage isn't easy, but if you talk you will avoid a lot of problems."

I have to admit, we both brushed it off in the thrill of the festive night. I remember thinking, "Al's mom is nothing if not dramatic!" But as the years rolled by, I came to realize that her simple words offered powerful advice based on experience and wisdom. John Gray was absolutely right in his famous book *Men Are from Mars and Women Are from Venus*. Men and women speak entirely different languages! When Al and I have had a frustrating misunderstanding, it's usually because one of us didn't fully explain our intentions or feelings. I feel annoyed when he throws out that wonderful half of a salad that I was planning to take for lunch the next day, but of course I didn't tell him not to. I just assumed he could read my mind. Or when he's steaming that I'm in an edit room working late even though he made a nice dinner for me and the kids, it's usually because he didn't tell me he was making dinner at a certain time and I neglected to let him know I wouldn't be home. Or there was the time when my sisters came to town and Al was quiet and a bit grumpy at dinner, far from the happy weatherman we'd seen on TV twelve hours earlier. I felt angry and embarrassed. But if Al had simply told me that he'd had two late-afternoon meetings after the show and was running out of steam, I would've understood. I wanted to show my sisters a good time and counted on Al to join me in it. Only after we discussed my expectations and his exhaustion did we understand each other. As Isabel said, talking to each other would help us avoid a lot of our troubles.

And though we have a healthy, strong marriage, we will both admit that as we close in on two decades of marriage, we are stronger and happier, thanks to couples therapy. Some might ask why I am choosing to share such personal details about our lives, but Al and I are proud that we have both been open to seeking help. A lot of people, especially people of color, don't want to admit to needing outside help in their relationships. Traditionally, especially in our parents' generation, the community has relied solely on the church or prayer to solve difficulties; anything more would be seen as airing their dirty laundry, a sign of failure or someone meddling in their lives.

We aren't saying it's the answer for everyone, but for Al and me, it has been our secret sauce to navigating situations we weren't capable of handling on our own.

The first time I saw a therapist was actually before Al and I were married. I did a story on the lifelong pain of sibling rivalry, for which I interviewed someone who, like me, came from a family of nine kids. And as in my family, the relationships were complicated now that they were adults. The child who was labeled "the baby" continued to behave that way, and the sibling who was "irresponsible" demanded a lot of energy and left her siblings feeling angry and disappointed. In talking with this woman, I saw myself. I too had strained relationships with some of my brothers and sisters. Some of us had grown apart over the years, and some weren't doing their share in helping with our parents, who were beginning to show signs of age. The woman I interviewed was having trouble expressing herself and feeling manipulated, and I was struck by how many issues were triggered for me. I soon made an appointment with a highly regarded therapist and felt so much better. I became a stronger woman. I was less hesitant to express my wants and needs and more capable of setting boundaries, which I was always fearful of doing. I began saying no when I felt one of my sisters was asking me to do something I didn't want to do. And I was feeling less guilty doing so.

Therapy was useful when Al and I began to get serious in our relationship and later, when we married. Since Al came to the relationship with an ex-wife and a daughter, we were destined for complications. I thought our happiness and love would cure any problems we faced, but that was wishful thinking, and of course, it wasn't the case. Al felt a tremendous amount of guilt about his daughter Courtney. I completely accepted that she was a part of his life and I struggled to include her in everything, but like any child of divorce, she was hurting and blamed me for her broken family. Of course, I wasn't the reason her parents divorced, but that didn't matter to Courtney.

Once when I traveled to Texas on assignment, I brought her back a cute blouse and a little doll. I expected a happy "thank you" and a hug.

But eight-year-old Courtney took the gift bag from me with a blank look. Al, embarrassed, chided her for not saying thank you. Meekly, she thanked me, but I was upset by her reaction—or lack of one. Moments like this began to tug at our relationship. There were times when I wanted Al's full attention and devotion and he was terribly conflicted—especially when it was time for Courtney to head back to her mom after a weekend with us. Al's happiness clearly dipped at those moments. It was as if he were being pulled on by two women in his life. We began to have small arguments while trying to figure out how to help Courtney fit in and feel comfortable. It was the classic struggle that so many blended families feel and deal with. We needed help, and fortunately, Al was open to the idea of therapy to talk out our problems.

Through friends, we were referred to a very experienced therapist who happened to be an African-American man named Henry. Originally from the South, he had a deep appreciation for subtle things that might be influenced by my black Southern heritage. He was a tall, lanky man with a booming voice, and when Henry spoke, which wasn't often, you can bet we listened. In fact, he said so little, we sometimes wondered if he was asleep during our sessions. Maybe he was, and honestly, who could have blamed him after listening to some of our mundane problems?

When he offered his opinion, it was filled with facts. It was neither hearsay nor hypothetical, which I always appreciated. He advised us to talk more and to discuss the hurt we each felt. But we also had to be willing to consider the other person's feelings. I had to put myself in Al's shoes and appreciate his pain. And he had to be sensitive to moments when I needed him and to learn to let go of the guilt.

By now you know I'm a say-it-like-it-is kind of gal and therefore I have a tremendous appreciation for anyone else who operates that way. So Henry really won me over. Al trusted him too. But it was one remark that truly sealed the deal for him. After talking about my guilt over this and that and my desire to please everyone, which leaves me feeling exhausted, Henry dryly said, "You know, Deborah, there's not enough room up there on the cross for you *and* Jesus." I don't know if it was his intent, but Al howled. (I smiled . . . a bit.)

Sometimes we saw Henry together, and other times we each went alone. With his guidance, we were able to come to our own understanding and acceptance of certain things.

While uncovering problems and pain is never a walk in the park, Al and I appreciated Henry and truly admired his insights. The more we saw him, the more we realized it was good for us to have a neutral third party to talk to, especially someone both of us respected and whose opinion we came to greatly trust. I think a lot of spouses go through a period where problems or feelings seem to be falling on deaf ears. But if it comes from a third party, suddenly, that same idea is crystal clear.

Seeing the therapist was an outlet, a place where we felt safe and secure enough to pour out our problems and give them to a person who was equipped to offer sound advice. He also helped us see ourselves and each other's point of view without judgment.

Al and I made a commitment to each other a long time ago that no matter what, we would be devoted to our marriage and family. As my mom famously told Al, "Once someone comes into this family, they don't step out!"

Two-thirds of all divorcing couples today never sought therapy before calling it quits, which means these couples would rather divorce than face the prospect of therapy. Al and I aren't willing to so easily throw away everything we have built together. The thought of going to therapy can be scary, daunting, overwhelming and disappointing— but it beats giving up. At least it does for us.

Like I told my friend, marriage—and even love—takes work. And it certainly takes commitment—a lot of commitment. Al and I are totally committed to each other and to our family. Anytime there are problems, we want to make things better before the only thing we share are our children and maybe the furniture. That would stink!

Even if you are reluctant to consider therapy, I strongly encourage you to take the time to check in with your partner every now and then, and if you have children, make it a point to spend some time together alone. It's important to talk about your relationship.

I can't deny that I hit the jackpot when it comes to life partners. Many people know that my guy is fun-loving and kind. But not everyone knows how romantic and thoughtful he is. Some years ago, he got me a rare edition of Shakespeare's sonnets for my birthday, and once when I mentioned offhandedly that I liked a certain necklace, I found it on my pillow a few weeks later—just because. Al is a man who *truly* listens, which is why I fell in love with him.

But if your relationship is anything like ours, it's an ever-changing work in progress that will require some fine-tuning along the way, and that's a good thing. Great romances don't happen overnight. They're built over a *lifetime* of love, adoration and the promise of "happily ever after!"

AL

Men Always Want to Have Sex

My dad taught me many things over the years, especially when it came to relationships and marriage. He said, "Son, marriage is a constant compromise. If you aren't working at it, you won't succeed."

I know my parents didn't have a perfect marriage and there were times when they fought, but they were very affectionate and demonstrative and I always knew they loved each other. They were open about their feelings. It was an extension of who they were as a couple—and it impacted me and how I view myself as a husband.

That being said . . .

I am going to talk about something that no couple really wants to discuss—*together*.

Because guys know you ladies talk about this with your girlfriends.

Yeah, I said it.

We know.

My wife thinks I always want to have sex.

Is she wrong?

No!

Am I unique?

I don't think so!

Every one of her friends' husbands or boyfriends wants the same thing.

I am no different from any of those guys.

And she knows it because she talks about it with her girlfriends all the time at lunches, where they devise very clever ways to get out of having sex with their men. I can picture these lunches in my mind, with Deborah and her perfectly coiffed pals sitting at a restaurant in Midtown Manhattan, sipping wine and laughing about how one of them made up some excuse the night before so they didn't have to make love to their husband.

Spoiler alert:

WE KNOW!

We know when you get into bed really fast and pull the covers up over your head and pretend to be asleep.

We know you secretly pray for one of the kids to come into the room, and when they do, encourage them to stay.

We know when you put on the same old, unsexy pajamas and loudly proclaim how tired you are that what you're really saying is, "Not tonight, dear!"

When exactly did "I'm so tired" replace "I've got a headache" anyway?

There aren't any excuses we haven't heard or Academy Award–worthy performances we haven't endured when you are trying to avoid the act.

WE ALL KNOW!

It's no great secret.

We also know that you love us, love our children, the family and life we share.

We know you want to keep the relationship going, the fire burning and your man happy.

We know we want more and you want less.

We know there are two days a year most guys can count on for sex—their birthdays and Valentine's Day. *Maybe* Christmas, but that too comes but once a year.

After that, we just hope.

I consider great sex any sex I have that doesn't require me to beg for it. I hate feeling like I'm holding a cash can in bed with a sign that reads, "Help me. I'm starving—for sex." There's nothing more pathetic, is there?

Thankfully, my beautiful wife knows this about me, and from time to time she will surprise the heck out of me with unsolicited and unexpected moments of bliss. And after more than twenty years together, we've learned that "moves" that once worked can sometimes fade over the years—or worse, turn into an irritation—so we try to shake things up, keep it interesting and make sure we aren't annoying each other (okay, mostly me annoying Deborah with my hints that I'm in the mood). As long as I'm smooth, romantic and not too crass, I'm usually "in like Flynn!"

While I hope my efforts will pay off with a passionate evening, afternoon, morning (I am not choosy) of lovemaking, believe it or not, every time I light a candle I am not necessarily trying to set the mood.

I like candles!

I also make my own bath salts out of Himalayan sea salt, eucalyptus, peppermint and lavender. That doesn't mean I'm trying to get my wife into the tub—though it wouldn't be discouraged.

To be fair, there are plenty of times I *am* trying to set the mood when I light candles around the house, but there are also times I am just looking to create ambience. Is there any prettier light than candlelight?

Especially in the bedroom?

And yet, just when I think Deborah is all on board, the mood feels right with soft music playing in the background and a couple of candles burning on the nightstands, she will lean over and blow them out.

"I know what you're up to!" she says.

Another attempt thwarted.

"Oh well," I think. "Tomorrow is another day."

But honestly, I am by nature a romantic guy. It really isn't difficult. Especially for guys, if you can show a modicum of effort, you'll be deemed romantic. It's a sad fact, but the bar is set a lot lower for guys than it is for women. Women are impressed when we think about anything besides nachos and beer. So there are times I make a move with no ulterior motive. Sometimes I might massage Deborah's shoulders because I know she has had a long day.

"That's okay," she says, trying to stop me, thinking I want more.

"No, sweetie. I'm not going to try to have sex with you. I just want to give you a massage," I say with the utmost sincerity.

To me, that is romance.

As a guy, of course I am thinking, "Maybe she will be so taken that she'll want to have sex . . ." but I am willing to accept the fact that she probably won't.

And there's the ugly truth that we guys have to face: As we get older, the spirit is willing but while the flesh may not be weak, it is tired . . . and stressed . . . and basically falling apart.

Let's face it—when it comes to just about anything, things you could do at thirty, or forty, or even fifty may become a little more difficult as you approach sixty. If you're like me and you work a long day, by the time evening rolls around, odds are just about even that if your significant other doesn't show interest relatively quickly, you are off to dreamland, counting those cartoon sheep you see in the mattress commercials.

That's why the romancing is so important. Sure, there are medicinal cures that your doctor can prescribe, but given the side effects, I'm not so sure the sex is worth it. Except for the warning about a four-hour erection.

I love the admonition. "If you experience an erection of four hours or longer, tell your doctor." Hell, if I have a boner for four hours, I'm telling *everyone*.

And while we're talking about the medications, what's with the commercial that always ends with the couple in the side-by-side tubs, watching the sunset? You're in separate bathtubs. How are you having sex if you're in separate tubs? And, by the way, how sexy do you think you are going to look after spending forty minutes sitting in side-by-side tubs? Either of you stand up, you are going to be seriously wrinkled. Well, if you've taken that magic pill, you'll have at least one part that's not shriveled!

All kidding aside, relationships do ebb and flow, especially as we get older. I'll admit there are plenty of nights when I am too tired to comply even if Deborah were to offer herself up on a platter; the moment I hit the pillow, I am down for the count.

So, sometimes, I'm not actually after the physical act so much as the reconnection, the reassurance that we, as a couple, are "all good." In a way, sex is an extension of connection—especially at a certain age or stage in life.

I remember many times when my mom was out of town for a few days and my dad was adrift. He'd come over to hang around, and as soon as Mom came back, he was gone. He needed to have some kind of connection to her while she was away, and I suppose as one of her kids, I represented that to him in her absence.

The act of intimacy is an anchor in a solid relationship. If it gets overlooked you become a rudderless ship.

And as a couple, if we aren't in a good place, we aren't going to be good for the kids. From my point of view, intimate time together is just as important as any school meeting or Little League game.

Doing anything you don't normally get to do together, even holding hands, shopping, walking around downtown, having a night out, can be as good as foreplay. Hopefully it will lead to something more, but it doesn't always have to for it to have a positive impact. I call my wife because I like to hear her voice during the day. For me that's a connection. When I put my hand on her leg and she grabs it and holds it, that's a connection. When I surprise her with flowers for no reason and she isn't expecting it—and I am not doing it for any reason other than to see her beautiful smile—that is a connection. It's so easy to get wrapped up in our harried lives and forget why we married or fell in love. It doesn't take a lot to remind ourselves that we are crazy about each other, just a few moments of stopping the noise from the outside world to reaffirm and reconnect.

And if you happen to get lucky in the process?

Then it was a great day!

Or night.

Or both.

DEBORAH

Weathering the Storm

Although Al and I both work in the fiercely competitive world of network television, for many years there was very little tension or competition between us, especially in the early years of our relationship when we were both at NBC. Work-related conflicts were almost nonexistent because Al and I traveled in clearly marked lanes. Back then he primarily did the weather and I did more hard news reporting, traveling to far corners of the country and the world. He was focused on the battle among morning TV programs, and I fought the good fight on the evening news and in prime-time news magazines, although occasionally I did fill in and did some sporadic anchor work on the weekend edition of *Today*. Al was my biggest cheerleader and I was his. All was peaceful at home, albeit chaotic at times. The only frustration between us was due to my travel, which often disrupted planned dinners and events.

The spring before our wedding in September of 1995, Barbara Walters called me, and I nearly fainted to hear the famous voice of my idol on the phone. She wanted to meet with me to discuss a position on the prestigious news magazine show *20/20*. I was flattered beyond measure! My lifelong dream was to be a reporter on the number-one-rated network!

I excitedly accepted the job at ABC. The idea of any type of rivalry with my husband never entered my mind since Al was happily working in morning television and I was assigned to Friday nights doing investigative reports. These were our dream jobs, putting us both at the top of our fields. It was unimaginable that a kid from Queens and a little girl from Georgia were riding that high!

Our jobs didn't define us as a couple, but if anything, I thought they made us stronger because we understood each other's worlds. He had his orbit and I had mine.

Within a few years, though, I started to expand my horizons, doing occasional stories on *Good Morning America*. It was the first time I did any type of work that directly competed with Al and the *Today* show. Around this same time, Al also began expanding his role at work, doing more mainstream interviews and feature stories that went beyond the weather.

For the first time, professionally speaking, we began stepping on each other's toes a bit. We never saw it coming, and neither of us knew how to handle this new wrinkle in our relationship. We had always unconditionally supported each other in our careers. It wasn't that we suddenly stopped, but now there was an unspoken tension—at least there was for *me*.

Things would get even more complicated during a shake-up at *Good Morning America*. Longtime anchors Joan Lunden and Charlie Gibson were out and the new team of Lisa McRee and Kevin Newman were in. The ratings were tanking, and the publicity around the show was vicious. During the rocky transition, I became the regular fill-in at the news desk—one of the few black women holding such a position. It was exciting and terrifying.

My profile at the network was growing, and viewers were embracing me. My job was beyond blissful, even with the long, grueling hours. And even more amazingly, I was being considered for the permanent gig. I was flying high. But there was occasional turbulence; with *Today* and *GMA* going head-to-head, I started to rankle a little if Al talked about the prowess of the *Today* show or how well they were doing. But mostly we shook off any personal rivalry; sometimes we even thought it was quite funny.

There has always been a certain cutthroat competition among the morning shows, and these were very trying times at both *GMA* and *Today*. Most people don't realize that the morning shows are the financial engines of their network news divisions. More than the evening news, more than the established prime-time news magazines, it's the daily battle for ratings between *GMA* and the *Today* show that defines the TV news industry rivalry.

Why?

The morning shows make the real money that allows network news to exist, paying for the multimillion-dollar salaries of the top news anchors and the high cost of worldwide news coverage. That's why every big interview or exclusive story is run to the ground by armies of bookers, producers and reporters. It's not unusual that anchors themselves are pressed into service to secure the big celeb "gets."

In the winter of 2010, Al and I would feel this network rivalry personally and face an excruciating career challenge that put our love and marriage to the toughest test ever.

When pop star Whitney Houston died a day before the Grammy Awards, there wasn't a bigger story in the news. Every broadcast outlet was scrambling to cover the story and telling their anchors, reporters, producers, bookers—anyone who had access to the family—to bring in an exclusive interview.

During a brainstorming session with my producers at *20/20*, I mentioned that I knew a particular music legend who was very close to Whitney and her family. Al had interviewed her once or twice, and we had been invited to intimate concerts and dinner with her. I felt we had a nice rapport. I had her phone number and felt comfortable reaching out to her even during this tragic moment. My executive producer, David Sloan, was thrilled by the prospect of landing such a huge get. Since *20/20* airs on Friday night, we had three days to land a powerful interview. Al wasn't covering Whitney's death for NBC, so I never imagined there could potentially be any conflict regarding my suggestion. In fact, he helped. I tried for thirty minutes to get the singer on her personal line, but I got no answer, not even voice mail, and I didn't have an e-mail address. The pressure was mounting. So I called Al, and he said I was using an outdated phone number. He happily gave me the famous singer's new phone number and her e-mail address. Al was thrilled at the thought of me scoring a huge scoop and wished me luck. I sent off a heartfelt e-mail and text message right away, expressing my condolences and explaining how awkward I felt about intruding during such a personal tragedy. I expressed my desire to do an interview with her and hoped she would trust me with her stories and memories. Much to my surprise, my phone quickly lit up with a reply from the singer. She graciously thanked me and said she was coming to New York later that week and would be happy to sit down and talk to me. She said it would be a wonderful way to honor Whitney and the relationship she felt she had with Al and me.

I was ecstatic! Getting an exclusive with this elusive megastar on everyone's list was a major coup. I conveyed the good news to David Sloan, who was beyond thrilled too and informed the executives throughout the network that I had snared the scoop of the week. *Good Morning America*, *World News Tonight* and *Nightline* were all happily anticipating a slice of this coveted interview.

I touched base with the singer one more time before she arrived in New York, and she assured me she was committed to doing the interview with me.

When she got to New York on Tuesday night, I called her as planned. Much to my surprise, she didn't call me back. This is never a good sign in journalism, especially the day before a big interview is set to air.

I was sitting on pins and needles, waiting for the phone to ring.

Nothing.

Unbeknownst to me, she had been approached by someone . . . from the *Today* show. And, astonishingly, she agreed to also do an interview for them, but only with Al.

I had no clue that this was happening and neither did Al! He didn't know that his producer had pursued the singer, much less that he was expected to interview her.

It only got worse. At three p.m., forty-eight hours before *20/20* was planning to air my big get, one of our show bookers called to say the singer had changed her mind and was *only* interviewing with Al.

I was devastated.

How could this happen?

I had her word!

The network was counting on my promise to deliver this get.

I frantically called Al, who was befuddled. He had no idea how this had happened. He was as rattled to hear this news as I was heartbroken.

I had a lot riding on that interview, and Al knew it.

I felt humiliated, angry and betrayed. My reputation, my credibility and everything I had promised to deliver was on the line. I wasn't going to give up without a fight.

I immediately made a distress call to the singer and left a distraught message. I phoned her manager and did my best to plead my case. I sent a beautiful bouquet of flowers to her hotel with a note begging her not to cancel. I called her manager again, who felt horrible but was at the mercy of her capricious client. I did everything except go to her hotel and camp out.

And still I got no response—until finally someone from her camp called to say she was so distraught and stressed by Whitney's death that she needed to rest. It was a passive way of telling me to back off. I had no choice but to accept that as her final answer and let it go. I was sick with disappointment. I finally had to call David Sloan, who was deeply upset.

How would we fill our program without an interview from someone in Whitney's life?

I was devastated because I felt I had let my show and my network down.

Al felt terrible about the situation too. He didn't know what to do. It wasn't his fault that the singer had bailed on me or that she wanted him to interview her. He must have called my office ten times that day, but I couldn't answer.

Finally I picked up and I told him, "You have to tell them no, Al."

I realize I was being selfish, but I reasoned that Al was at a big enough place in his career to decline without a penalty. I, on the other hand, needed a boost. It never occurred to me that I was not being fair to my husband, who was also under pressure in the ever-present and ongoing morning-show war we were now inadvertently fighting.

I spent the rest of the afternoon crying in my office.

Was my reputation damaged . . . my career over? What could I do to salvage this?

When Al came home that night, I was completely exhausted and overwhelmed. While we prepared dinner, I struggled to keep my cool in front of the kids, but they could tell I was very upset. My eyes looked puffy, and they could hear Al and me talking about the situation. We weren't fighting, but they heard us discussing it with some gusto.

Finally, Nicky came into the kitchen and blurted out, "Daddy, don't take Mommy's story away. She needs it for her job!" Of course, he couldn't possibly understand what he was saying, but he went on, "Don't hurt Mommy. She's sad." I could immediately see the pain in my husband's eyes.

That wasn't what I wanted.

I knew in my heart that Al was hurting too, but to hear it from his son must have been a blow.

I did my best to reassure Leila and Nicky that wasn't the case. That this was just work and it wasn't a big deal.

But when they left the room and we had a quiet moment together, despite the anguish I knew we both were feeling, I pleaded with Al to change his mind.

"You know what this means to me. You need to tell them you can't do this. This interview means far more to me than it does to you." That was the last thing I said about it that night. There was nothing more left to say.

Al and I silently fell into bed.

I hated being angry with Al, but I felt that this was a career-defining moment and he was somehow keeping it from me.

Maybe he cared more about his career than about me.

I wondered if I could look at him the same way after this.

The next day Al kept his appointment to do the interview. But first, as I would later learn, he did something that would forever change my feelings for him. Before he would allow the cameras to roll, he pleaded with the singer to do two interviews—a short one with him, then a short one with me. His producer nearly fainted, but it was an unbelievable gesture of love in the midst of a professional crisis. Unfortunately, the singer was stubbornly resolute.

"No. If I am going to give an interview at all, it's going to be one time," she responded. She explained that she was already on the verge of laryngitis and didn't have it in her to do this more than once. Al knew that if he didn't get the interview right there and then, she wasn't going to give one at all, and that would have been a total disaster for everyone. So he did what he had to do.

What my husband did that morning was above and beyond the call of duty and showed just how much love he has in his heart for me and our relationship. He selflessly put my feelings and my career needs above his own. He knew exactly what that interview meant to me, and had it been possible, he would have walked away from it. But his hands were tied. This interview was going to happen with one person only: Al. It wasn't his fault any more than it was mine that she decided to go someplace else. But that kind of unshakable support meant more to me than I could have ever expressed in the moment, and surely it spoke to the solid foundation on which our marriage sits.

While that was going on without my knowledge, I did what I always do when my back is against the wall. I dug deep and found my reserves, and I came out swinging—I still needed a story for *20/20* the next night, and I was going to get it.

As the saying goes, "When one door closes another opens."

I remembered that gospel star BeBe Winans knew Whitney Houston and might be able to help me find another personal friend to interview. I had met BeBe years before, at the opening of Oprah Winfrey's girls' school in South Africa. We had gone for a jog together and become friendly. When I reached BeBe, who was distraught over the loss of his friend, I got an amazing surprise. Not only had BeBe known Whitney far better than I'd thought, but he'd spent years traveling and hanging out with her. He had a treasure trove of intimate stories about the fallen singer.

As it turned out, BeBe was a true "get"! And, lucky for me, he was reluctantly willing to share his memories of their time together.

God is good.

Hours later, BeBe was sitting across from me in an interview suite, regaling me with happy, painful and poignant stories about his dear friend. He shared how Whitney bristled at being called a pop sellout and how he sarcastically advised her to "cry all the way to the bank." For an hour, the camera crew laughed and got teary listening to BeBe's riveting stories. I had scored a home run.

Everybody at ABC was thrilled, and my interview aired to rave reviews.

Though Al got the bigger star, in the end, I got the better interview.

Later that evening, before *20/20* aired, Al and I drove up to the country to unwind. It had been a trying week. We were both emotionally and physically worn to the bone. We were also still shaken from the intense experience of rivalry and competition between us. I could tell that Al still felt hurt by my insensitive take on the situation, and I definitely felt wounded by his decision to go ahead with his interview. Of course, I had no idea that he had already gone out on a limb for me by asking her to do a second interview.

We decided to record *20/20*, as we both were too weary to watch it that night. The next morning I went for a walk in the crisp, cold air of early spring. The sky was blue and the birds were singing. I began to think of all we had been through that week and quickly realized how fast everything at work fades away after the deadline passes.

As I walked among the glory of nature, I was reminded that I was home and blessed with peace and love and a beautiful family . . . and a remarkable husband who loves me in sickness and in health—for better or for worse—till death do us part.

No interview could ever be more important than that.

How could I have been so ridiculous to equate a score at work with my beautiful life?

This is what really matters.

No famous singer can steal that from me.

Ever!

I returned home and pulled Al in close for a long embrace.

"I am so very sorry," I said. "You matter more to me than any story. And I know the same is true for you. Forgive me for ever doubting that."

We smiled and held each other tightly.

Later, after we watched my interview with BeBe, Al turned to me and said, "You know, I thought my interview was good, but it wasn't *that* good."

God bless my husband. He always was and always will be my biggest cheerleader. I realized that we were on the same page: What we have together is far greater and more powerful than any outside force that seems monumental in the moment.

Landing a great story and beating that deadline are a thrill and a victory for a journalist. But jobs will come and go. Our real success as a couple is being together forever—and we have this great family, life and relationship to cherish.

Al is fond of saying, "Always keep your eye on the prize," meaning, don't focus so much on the little things that you lose sight of the big picture. Boy, did that resonate for me that day. It doesn't mean you're not going to have moments where you feel thoroughly upset with each other or totally stressed out in your relationship. Believe me, you will.

Lots of them.

When you do, it's important to cling tighter than ever to each other and the love you share. Remember, your relationship is far more valuable than anything else you will gain outside of it for the sake of work or career.

AL AND DEBORAH

Sometimes You Have to Get Away

We know a couple who have a daughter Leila's age who, as of a few years ago, had never taken a vacation without their child.

NEVER.

They felt such guilt at the mere thought of leaving their only child behind that they simply didn't.

Whenever we shared stories about romantic getaways we had taken, we could see that the wife was hesitantly taken with the idea. But the husband seemed to find the whole thing beyond the pale, so we stopped trying to coax them.

But we're convinced it's the magical glue that holds a marriage together. For career couples with children, alone time isn't a luxury; it's a necessity if you have any hopes of keeping the passion alive. Now that our kids are older, they accept the idea of the parental getaway, but they still can't quite understand it. Once when we couldn't arrange an actual out-of-town trip, we planned a weekend staycation at New York City's fabled Carlyle Hotel. When we told the kids that our last-minute get-away was ten blocks from home, Leila asked why we were spending good money on a hotel.

"You just want to get away from us," she suspiciously opined.

"Bingo!" Al said.

We think it's healthy for our kids to know that Mommy and Daddy need Mommy and Daddy time, even when Nicky asks, with those big puppy-dog eyes, "But without us . . . ? Why . . . ?" As much as we love being with our children, there is tremendous value in having a few hours of uninterrupted time to actually hear what the other person is saying. Imagine finishing a sentence or story for once! No whining or fighting in the background. Even though Deborah struggles with a lit-tle mom guilt, whenever we get away, we both realize that it's a good thing for us to do from time to time.

Sometimes we have the time and luxury of flying off somewhere. Other times we head to one of the many country inns within driving distance of New York City. And then there's the bliss that can be found just a short cab ride away, once we made the huge discovery that people living in the city can actually book rooms in those fabulous hotels we read about. So now and again we reserve a hotel room and maybe get tickets to a show without any worry about getting home to let the dog out or scolding one of the kids about staying up too late.

Just last year we made another brilliant discovery. We actually have a weekend house that still functions even when kids are not scampering around! Our house, tucked quietly behind acres of pine trees, is our getaway spot from our otherwise hectic and overscheduled lives. Since both of us travel so frequently for work, it is a joy to have a retreat to spend quality time with our children and each other without the pres-sure of being social if we don't want to be. We get to sleep late, play board games and watch movies without any obligations or commit-ments other than being together as a family.

It had never occurred to us before that the most obvious getaway location was our charming house in upstate New York, because we always went there with our kids. Well, one particular summer weekend, we had made plans to go up with the kids when it turned out that both of them had activities they desperately wanted to do in the city. A light-bulb went off. What if we got our babysitter to come in for the kids and headed up there alone?

Alone!

We suddenly became giddy with excitement. It was as though we had been given a last-minute trip to Paris.

Since the day Leila arrived, we'd never been there without children. We'd bought the place about a year before she was born, anxious for a serene spot to escape the city madness. Nestled in the woods just off a gravel road, the house was an oasis of calm and tranquillity for two people who traveled and worked under the stress of deadlines. We'd sit and read, cook, watch movies, swim or just be. It wasn't until we got there that weekend that we realized how much we missed that time together there.

The car ride up was strangely peaceful. No backseat hoopla, no arguments, not even a jab about Al's driving.

We were so used to the kids running around the house, dashing in and out, us yelling at them to close the doors or stay away from the pool, that it seemed suspiciously quiet when we first arrived. But there was something so liberating about being in our own space without having to worry about the kids, their needs or anyone else's schedule. We put on our sweats, plopped on the sofa, and stayed put for the first few hours like shut-ins.

We made plans for the next night: a romantic dinner out and a symphony performance at Tanglewood, a wonderful outdoor venue just a few miles away in Lenox, Massachusetts. This was beginning to feel like a deliriously romantic vacation.

Suddenly, the realization that it was just us sank in.

And it was lovely.

Al cracked, "1998 called and they are happy to have us back!"

And that dispelled any angst or guilt we may have been feeling for the rest of the weekend. We both let out a big, relaxing, cleansing sigh!

As we eased into the freedom of being alone for the weekend, we both found ourselves letting go of our stress. Al's daily alarm was draining him, and Deborah had been busier than ever at work, traveling and juggling deadlines on *20/20* and also sometimes reporting stories on *Good Morning America* at the crack of dawn. Deborah felt the emotional toll of the decline of her eighty-seven-year-old mom, who was slipping deeper into her Alzheimer's disease. We were also in the throes of Nicky's applications to middle school. Deborah simmered with resentment that, like many women, she shouldered the bulk of the kids' issues. Al disagreed, given that he's a deeply involved, hands-on dad. Distracted and exhausted, we'd been on edge, snapping at each other over small things and feeling disconnected as a couple. If Al forgot to run the dishwasher before going to bed, Deborah was annoyed. And when Deborah forgot to call to discuss who was taking Nicky to tae kwon do, Al was irritated. The smallest and seemingly most insignificant things suddenly felt huge and insurmountable. Each of us felt the other simply didn't understand our frustrations. As the months dragged on, both of us secretly wondered if our marriage was in trouble. Romance wasn't even a thought as we made it through each day. So here we were, alone, staring at each other as a summer breeze blew through the empty hallways of our home.

We made dinner, laughed, talked and went to bed early, falling into each other's arms. *"Ahh, now we remember this person lying next to us in bed—the person each of us fell in love with."*

The next morning, though there was no room service, we were able to have a leisurely breakfast in our kitchen, enjoying our coffee in the comfort and privacy of home.

It was a brilliant summer day. With a little Barry White playing in the background and a dip in the pool together, anything was possible!

When Al peeled off to Guido's, our local grocer, for salmon, asparagus and salad greens, Deborah lit a couple of Diptyque orange-blossom candles and cut some fresh flowers from the garden to set the stage for a romantic lunch at home.

An hour later, Al cheerfully returned from the store, bursting into the house with a fistful of sunflowers and another fistful of gladiolas. In the background, the Luther Vandross song "I'd Rather" was playing, which brought us both to tears.

I'd rather have bad times with you than good times with someone else . . .

We basked in the glow of a stolen moment. The flowers were a beautiful gesture . . . a reminder of how thoughtful and romantic Al has always been. In that moment we were reminded of the love we feel for each other. Family responsibilities can suck out all of our attention and energy, and by the end of the day, we're so tired, we fall asleep before we can focus on us. But now, with the smooth and sexy sounds of Luther as our guide, we were finding each other again.

We both grew up with parents who couldn't afford regular family vacations, much less romantic getaways. Any vacation was usually a road trip of some sort to visit relatives. Not exactly romantic. It simply wasn't part of the culture we grew up in.

Deborah's parents, busy raising nine kids in the segregated South, weren't outwardly affectionate, but Al recalls plenty of romance between his mom and dad. As a result of seeing his parents show their affection, Al is the more classic romantic. He leaves cards and heartfelt love notes on the dresser or hidden away in Deborah's suitcase for her to find when she arrives at her assignment. And Deborah will sometimes leave a string of candles on the darkened stairs to greet Al when he returns late at night from a trip, to let him know she missed him. But we both agree that it is Al who is the true-blue romantic in the relationship. While being unpredictable and full of surprises is not necessarily a good trait for a weatherman, it has been wonderful for our relationship. Keeping romance alive is important, but just thinking about it is important too.

This might sound weird, but if you are thinking loving thoughts or just cuddling your spouse without any expectation of anything else (if you get our drift), that goes a long way.

In our hectic lives there's one thing about our relationship we've learned for sure. We're better partners and better parents by taking time here and there for each other. It's something we happily own with our children. We want them to understand that as much as we love them, Mom and Dad are stronger and more available when our bond is intact. Twenty years so far . . . and here's to twenty more!

6

Family Is Forever

DEBORAH

Choices We Make as Parents

I think any parent would agree that we all make sacrifices we never contemplated before having children. In fact, for me just getting pregnant was in and of itself a struggle and a major life adjustment, one that I don't regret for a second.

When Al and I got married, I was in my midthirties, so I knew that we needed to get cracking if I was ever going to hear that magical word "Mommy." To our surprise, within a year, Al and I were ecstatic to learn that I was pregnant.

We were reluctant to make a big announcement since my obstetrician, Janice Marks, warned us that the first twelve weeks for a woman in her thirties could be dicey. But that very first weekend, I was substitute hosting the weekend edition of *ABC World News Tonight* and couldn't contain my excitement! I pulled aside my executive producer, Kathy O'Hearn, an accomplished and kind woman in the tough world of network news who was also a friend. "I'm pregnant," I whispered gleefully. Kathy knew how much I wanted a family and gave me an excited hug.

Days later, Al and I shared the great news with a few close friends and family and began making plans for our new bundle. Then we had a sonogram that stopped us in our tracks. Something didn't look right. Dr. Marks, usually spirited and happy, looked ashen as she revealed an unthinkable prognosis. The fetus wasn't growing and barely had a heartbeat. We were likely to miscarry. My throat went dry. Al and I were devastated. We prayed and hoped against hope that the doctors were wrong. But days later, I began feeling intense stomach spasms. We had lost our baby.

Months later, barely able to discuss our gut-wrenching pain, Al and I met with Dr. Marks. The good news was that I had healed and would be fine. The tough news, she added, was that in the world of reproduction, I was no spring chicken. She strongly advised us to consider fertility assistance if we truly wanted to begin a family now. Still a bit numb, we were dumbfounded and in denial. "We don't need medical help," we thought. This was only one miscarriage. But after meeting with a fertility specialist who determined that I had mild endometriosis and that Al had, shall we say, reluctant sperm, we concluded that in vitro fertilization was probably our best hope of getting pregnant.

It was not an easy proposition, to say the least. I had to have hormone treatments, including injections that Al had to give me in my butt. This was slightly comical, at first, but became annoying when he discovered that slapping my bum numbed me temporarily and gave him the courage to jam the needle in. Remember, this was a daily event! The whole process was painful, humbling and tiresome—and for an added dose of fun, the progesterone, Lupron and estrogen made me cranky, bloated and emotional.

Each weekly visit to the fertility clinic was a roller-coaster ride. There was blood work, pronouncements about the quality and quantity of my eggs and lots of emotional ups and downs. I began to feel like a lab experiment. At the end of each day, who could consider romance when my plumbing was under renovation?

Every night I looked at my flat abdomen and prayed for the gift of pregnancy—and patience, as I knew it could take time to conceive. After years of smooth sailing in my career and in the romance department, I was hitting some serious potholes in the road of life. I began to wonder whether I was meant to give birth and if all of this pain and stress was worth it. One month we were excited to begin the egg fertilization process only to discover that I had missed my ovulation period during an overseas reporting trip. I often found myself in tears.

Then, after several frustrating and painful misfires . . . a miracle. I was indeed pregnant! Al and I were having a baby.

God is good.

This was a treasured pregnancy. I could feel the radiance emanating from this pea-size ball of hope and light within me. I cherished every flutter and twinge I felt. Kathy and other colleagues at work joined us in our joy. I even shared the news of my pregnancy on *Good Morning America*. The good wishes and excitement filled us with unimaginable joy. And just as thrilling, my career was on the ascent.

I was gradually moving into the prestigious world of news anchoring, filling in on *Good Morning America* and the weekend edition of *ABC World News Tonight* while of course remaining a regular correspondent at *20/20*. While my belly grew, so did my stature at the network. I was known as a dependable and seasoned journalist; now stardom was just over the horizon. I owed a lot to Amy Entelis, the company's vice president for talent relations. She believed in me and she was also becoming a trusted adviser and friend.

At the time, things were a bit rocky at the network. The ratings for *Good Morning America* had been slipping, and longtime anchors Joan Lunden and Charlie Gibson had left the program, leading to a game of musical chairs. It was somewhat dizzying and uncomfortable to be sure, but it was also an opportunity for someone new to the scene like me. ABC was turning to me often, and I was becoming a big part of the family, especially at *Good Morning America*. The further along I got in my pregnancy, the more we incorporated it into on-air conversations as a way for the audience to get to know me. I began referring to my unborn baby as "Pookie" on the air, having fun with hosts Lisa McRee and Kevin Newman during this magical time in my life. I was excited about everything in front of me, from my exploding career to my expanding belly. I couldn't wait to be a mom. At the same time, I was also secretly feeling vulnerable and uncertain about how having a baby would affect everything I was working so hard to establish. I wondered if I was prepared to juggle this long-awaited miracle baby with a grueling work schedule. Could I bear to leave her in the arms of someone else and race off to the studio or jump on a plane for the next assignment? I had always thought that this decision would be logical and easy, but it was now weighing heavily on me.

Al, on the other hand, was completely and deliriously ready for our bundle of joy. His career was secure and he already had his morning routine well in place. His alarm would go off at four a.m. and he was out of the house by five. On the many days I was appearing on *Good Morning America*, I was keeping a similar schedule. Long before reality TV, we were a perfect fit for our own show, both of us bleary-eyed and bumbling around in the darkness for an early-morning call. Then we'd hop on the elevator and step into the predawn light together, get into our respective cars, and head to competing morning shows. Sometimes we even showed up on the air at the same time, much to the amusement of our families. As a couple, it was fine and manageable. We both had dinner at six and fell asleep by eight thirty. But what if this was a permanent arrangement? What would it mean to our newborn baby if we were both gone before she even woke up? Could I handle that kind of emotional tug-of-war?

Could I hit pause and postpone my career trajectory?

After trying for so long to get pregnant, what was I willing to sacrifice for the well-being of my child?

Amy had asked me point-blank if I could see myself on the morning show. I knew she was taking my temperature in case the network wanted to offer me the prized job as news anchor. Like any ambitious reporter, I told her, "Of course I could."

I was flattered and thrilled. I was also terrified! I should have been honest with Amy, but I was worried it would be career suicide. Instead, I spilled my guts to a senior producer at ABC whom I trusted and admired very much. I wanted his opinion because I knew he could be neutral and nonemotional, plus he had worked on the morning program and knew the rhythm well.

"Deborah, are you sure you want to sacrifice your personal life for a program that is still under construction and isn't stable or secure yet?" he said. "I predict there will be other changes before this is all over."

That was the first time I had considered whether I was walking onto a sinking ship and might lose my footing in the process. Maybe he was right. Maybe this wasn't the time to sign on with so much at stake professionally and personally. Would I sacrifice precious time with my daughter only to end up dismissed from a troubled program, just as others had been? I wrestled with this idea, playing out every possible scenario in my head.

One Saturday, just before my daughter was born, I received a call from David Westin, the head of the news division. He said he wanted to talk to me about becoming news anchor. Even though I'd known it was probably coming, I felt completely unprepared! Ordinarily, anyone would jump for joy at the prospect of what he was offering. In fact, if I got that same call today, I would be thrilled. But at the time, I was so petrified about the uncertainty of what I was facing, personally and professionally, I wasn't sure how to respond. I was paralyzed by fear of the unknown. Instead of being excited and appreciative, I was hesitant and a bit aloof. I asked if I could get back to him with my answer.

I spent the weekend discussing the pros and cons with Al and my agent, Richard Leibner. There was a lot to consider. I was about to have my first baby, a baby I'd struggled to conceive. I knew if I signed on to the troubled morning show, I would need to hit the ground running immediately—no maternity leave—and give it my all. I also knew I would never get those first few months of bonding time with Leila back. I didn't want to regret that, and I didn't want to resent the network if they later decided to rearrange the morning lineup again, at my expense.

Richard understood, but cautioned that it could be awkward. "The network hates to hear the word 'no,'" he gently offered. I was torn and confused. I was certainly not intending to take on a lighter workload after becoming a mother, but did I want to *increase* the pressure and the hours? In retrospect, I wish I had called Amy for a heart-to-heart mom talk, but I didn't. In the end, I came to the conclusion that it was not the right time for me to take the job.

On Monday morning I reluctantly passed. David Westin was visibly surprised. Who would turn down such an opportunity? It was a defining moment that I now realize was a career torpedo. Although I had imagined it as a worst-case scenario, I didn't expect to be an exile to the land of "mommyhood." But when I returned to work, things were slightly different. Suddenly the assignments I had been used to getting dried up. Any ascension toward the anchor world came to a halt. I still filled in on the weekend nightly news from time to time and continued with my regular segments on 20/20, but other specialized assignments no longer came my way. The buzz of excitement had quieted. I'm not going to lie—it was painful.

But I was able to bond with my daughter in a way I wouldn't have if I had gone that route, and for that reason alone, I wouldn't change a thing. I was able to spend three carefree months at home with Leila, breastfeeding her on demand, strolling through the park with her on long walks and getting to know my little Pookie. It was sheer bliss.

Do I ever wonder how things might have been different if I had taken the anchor job and had gone forward on that path?

Sure, sometimes.

In fact, I confess that I had second thoughts about my decision for months—okay, for years. But I ultimately made peace with my choice.

Every woman—and I hope every parent—has to weigh what is best for the family as a whole. After years of thought and prayer about moments gained and lost, I now know one true thing. When we make decisions, we must own them: no second-guessing or what-might-have-beens. I have faith that God guides our decisions and puts us on the road we're supposed to be on. Happiness is contingent on accepting our choices.

AL

What Do Soupy Sales and Drake Have in Common?

AUGUST 1965

"Mom! Mom! Soupy Sales is playing at the Singer Bowl! Can you take me? Please?"

I was eleven years old and I was desperate to see Soupy Sales at the World's Fairgrounds in Queens, New York. Soupy Sales was a master of slapstick comedy, a descendant of the baggy-pants comedians of vaudeville and burlesque. It might be hard to imagine today, but when I was a kid, Soupy was a huge star who could get away with hitting guys like Frank Sinatra and Sammy Davis Jr. in the face with a pie. People actually lined up to get hit in the face with one of his pies!

I was what you might call a hard-core Soupy Sales fan. Like any devotee, I collected his fan magazine and even had all the Soupy Sales comic books, published by Archie Comics. I had all his albums, and played his three hit songs, "The Mouse," "Your Brains Will Fall Out" and "Pachalafaka," over and over, making my parents nuts. To me, he was a rock star. I watched his show every day on WNEW, Channel 5 in

New York. If Soupy was eating grilled cheese and tomato soup for lunch, you can bet I was too! I'm not exactly sure how big his demographic was with preteen black kids, but he had me.

In short, I was obsessed with the guy, and once I found out he was coming to Queens, I was relentless in my pursuit to get tickets to his show.

My mom didn't exactly have a great appreciation for slapstick comedy. She didn't like Abbott and Costello, didn't get Laurel and Hardy and hated the Three Stooges. To her, Soupy Sales fell into that same category of entertainment. The idea of a pie in the face wasn't funny to her—or most women, whose first thought is usually, "Who's going to clean up that mess?"

Despite feeling like she'd rather have a toothache than see Soupy Sales, Mom could see how much this meant to me—or I wore her down with my begging—and she agreed to take me and my friend Keith Morgan to the show at the Singer Bowl. When the day arrived, all of Queens seemed to be out in the streets. The World's Fairgrounds were packed and the buses and subway trains were too. When we got off the number 7 train, we walked for what felt like miles among the sea of people.

Mom kept asking, "Is Soupy Sales really this popular?" She didn't have any idea that the Beatles were playing nearby, at Shea Stadium!

Our tickets were in the nosebleed section, but it didn't matter. I was there to see my hero and, deep down, I secretly believed he would somehow see me. Knowing I could barely see the stage, Mom bought me a pair of souvenir binoculars with Soupy's face on them. For an hour and a half, Keith and I laughed at his jokes and sang along to his hits. I was in heaven. To this day, I fondly remember this as one of the best nights of my life.

Mom, on the other hand, paid absolutely no attention to the concert. She spent the ninety minutes reading a book.

Many years later, when Soupy was the midday radio host on AM 66 WNBC, I finally had the chance to meet my hero, just like in my childhood dreams. But it was even better: We became friends, and he was my sponsor into the Friars Club, the renowned show-business fraternity.

"Dad, Dad! Drake is playing at the new Barclay Center in Brooklyn and at the New Jersey Performing Arts Center too. Is there any way you would let me go?"

I'd love to tell you this was my first experience taking one of my kids to a concert I didn't want to go to, but it wasn't. My older daughter, Courtney, somehow figured out a way to get me to take her and some of her friends to their first Jingle Ball—an annual concert at Madison Square Garden where twelve or more acts perform a couple of songs each—for four hours! The sheer pandemonium of it had me thinking I had actually found hell on earth. As I sat there enduring the pain, every minute feeling like an hour, I flashed back on my mother taking me to Soupy Sales that night and thought to myself, "Oh, right. This is what we do as parents . . . Now I get it."

It still didn't make being there any easier.

The following year Courtney asked me to take her to the Jingle Ball again. Being a little older, though, she said, "Dad, do you *have* to sit with us?"

I understood where she was coming from, so I got a ticket for myself a couple of rows back. I packed an itty-bitty night-light, foam earplugs, headphones and a book and thought, "This time, I'm ready!"

The band Smash Mouth was onstage singing their hit song "All Star," and despite myself I found myself singing along. I never once lifted my head up from the pages of my book—until a roar began to build from the crowd. When I looked up, I realized that someone thought it was a good idea to flash a shot of me on the Jumbotron!

Ugh!

I knew in my heart that Courtney was mortified. Nobody else would know she was my daughter, but I knew she would think seeing her dad up on the Jumbotron was horrendous.

In that moment, I said to myself, "I am done with this." I never wanted to put one of my kids through that kind of embarrassment again.

But when my daughter Leila came to me with such passion, such hope, such desire to see her beloved Drake—what was I supposed say?

"No," I told her.

Are you kidding me? I've listened to this guy's music. There was no way I would let my fifteen-year-old daughter go to a Drake concert.

But, of course, I then thought back to my mother and the sacrifice she made for me when she took me to see Soupy Sales, and I realized I had responded without thinking about it first. I didn't want to be the dad who was always saying "No!" so I changed my answer to, "Okay . . . if I take you."

The look on her face was a cross between disbelief and abject horror. I could see her processing the concept. "I want to go to this concert more than anything, but the thought of being seen with my old-fogy father is so depressing. Yet I want to go sooooo badly . . ."

"Leila," I said, interrupting her reverie, "do you want to go or not?"

"I guess so. Can you sit in another section?"

I didn't want to take a gaggle of girls to Brooklyn, because the Barclay Center is very large and overwhelming, especially on a Saturday night. The concert in New Jersey was on Sunday night, which somehow felt more, well, tame, but it was a school night, which meant by the time the concert was over, we'd have no choice but to hightail it home and we'd still get in past midnight—not ideal for a kid who has to get up for school and a dad who has to get up even earlier for work.

I looked up other options and saw that Drake was playing Hartford, Connecticut, the night before Brooklyn. Hartford was only a couple hours away by car. Bingo! Since the show was on a Friday night, we could have a father-daughter getaway. We'd make a road trip out of it.

I booked two hotel rooms—one for Leila and her friends and one for me. It took the girls *two hours* to get ready for the show. Thankfully, I had planned for the primping in advance and got us to the hotel early.

Let's not even talk about the transformation of Leila and her pals from clearly fifteen-year-olds to young women whom guys were going to be ogling. I do not like this part of the job. But I've seen girls her age wearing far worse, and so I held my tongue as we drove to the venue.

Other than the parking-lot attendants, a few of the food-concession workers and security guards, I was, by far, the oldest person there. And also the only guy in the audience wearing a sport coat. Hey, I had never been to a rap concert before.

There were three—yes, three—acts, all with only one name each.

Future.

Miguel.

Drake.

Weren't any of these guys given a last name?

Sting, I get.

Cher, I get.

But these guys? Get over yourselves, sheesh!

Someone buy a last name—please!

My next problem was, why have a concert with three acts doing the exact same thing?

Okay, maybe they did do slightly different things. Future jumped around a lot and had another DJ mixing beats for him. Miguel jumped around a lot, but also played guitar and ripped his shirt off.

And, of course, there's Drake, from the mean streets of . . . Toronto.

Are there mean streets in Toronto?

It didn't take long for the people around us to start noticing that Al Roker, their friendly morning-show weatherman, was at, of all things, a Drake concert. My general rule of thumb when I am out with my kids is to keep my focus on them. I never want to appear to be a jerk and refuse to sign an autograph or take a picture with a fan, but when I am with my family, it's about my family. Fortunately, Leila was amused by the reaction I was getting, which made it more palatable for all involved. That is, until three white dudes sat in front of us—obviously college students, obviously half drunk, with their pants halfway down their butts, trying to look like they're black rappers.

All I could think was "No! Stop it! Stop! You're not black or rappers! Pull your damn pants up!" as I tried to shield my daughter's eyes from the awful sight. To make matters worse, one of them turned around and actually tried to hit on Leila and her friends.

"Pull your pants up and face forward, got it?" I said. "They're in high school, pal!" He never turned around again.

About halfway through the concert, one of the security guards finally took pity on me. He came over and handed me some bright yellow foam earplugs. I'd like to tell you they helped, but my hearing was already shot.

Four hours later, I understood exactly how my mother felt the day she took me to see Soupy Sales. I was awakened from my pounding, bass-induced state of semicatatonia by a transparent circle that detached itself from the stage and transported Drake skyward about seventy-five feet off the floor of the XL Center. While a DJ played sexy beats, Drake started pacing around the circle, talking to the girls in the audience from his lofty perch. "I see you . . . and you . . . Hey, you, in the leopard suit . . . I see you. Ooooh, pretty mama in those hot pants . . . I see you."

He did this *for twenty minutes*. Leila and her friends were ecstatic, hoping and then believing that Drake was pointing right at them.

In fact, the crowd was going nuts. I'll admit—he held them in the palm of his hand for that entire segment of the show. It was around this time I decided to take a video on my iPhone and upload it to Vine. It's pretty much a still shot of me looking like a miserable zombie, while everyone around me is enjoying the show. It was like I was frozen in time while everyone around me was moving, dancing and having fun. My expression conveyed what I was thinking: "Why am I here? I am way too old for this!" This wasn't a concert to enjoy; it was a test of endurance.

But then I realized I was wrong.

You see, I got to spend some quality time with my daughter doing something she liked. Plus, Leila and her friends were having a wonderful time. And the more I watched her smile and dance, having fun with her girls, the more I realized that none of this was about me. These experiences are all about my kids.

My parents' passing left me thinking about my mortality a little more often than I used to. When you have parents, there is a symbolic buffer between you and the abyss. But now I was much more grateful for every moment. And as a parent, this is what I'd signed up for—concerts, Disney On Ice, amusement parks, school plays, dance recitals and all of the other things that we sometimes moan and groan about having to do—especially someone like me who is a slightly more "mature" father. "Why am I here?"

Because this is what we do.

We sit through the recital—watching other people's kids dance right alongside our own.

We spend weekends at soccer games and horse shows and yes, even concerts.

Not because we have to.

Because we want to—because we don't know how long we have to share those moments with our children or how long they will want to share them with us. If I didn't take Leila and her friends to see Drake, another parent would have, and those memories would be someone else's to hold on to. When I weigh out the options, the truth is, there's no other place I'd rather be than watching my kid have the time of her life.

After the show, the girls were so excited, laughing and being silly, like young girls can be. I will admit, that made me feel pretty darn good. And then I heard, "Thanks, Pappers!" That's what Leila calls me. In that moment, despite the fact I hadn't fully regained my hearing yet, my heart was full of pure love. I had forgotten all about my misery and replaced it with her joy. I smiled, knowing I had done something good that night. It was worth it. And so what if I've lost a little bit of my hearing? It'll come in handy when Leila asks me to go to another concert.

DEBORAH

Mom Guilt

I am an overscheduled, goal-oriented, people-pleasing, career mom who just can't seem to say no. Here's how life generally works for me.

The minute I hear of a hot story, I'm on it, lobbying to do it for *20/20*. If a producer pitches an intriguing idea, even while I'm on a plane in the midst of another shoot, I am quick to say, "Let's do it!"

When Nicky asks for pancakes at six thirty a.m. before school, I am whipping up the batter by six forty-five.

At least two days a week we find ourselves racing from the breakfast table to the garage so I can drive both kids to school across town and hopefully dash back in time to squeeze in a two-mile run.

If a friend asks me to swing by a charity reception, I vow to make my way there, even if I'm still in the audio booth at six p.m., the event starts at seven and I still need to get home and change clothes and I'm freaking out in Manhattan evening traffic to get there.

If Al suggests a long-overdue romantic dinner, I feel I should accept his sweet gesture even though I've got a bad case of acid reflux and I've promised Leila I'll watch *Pretty Little Liars* with her. I quickly snuggle up with her when we return, to squeeze in a dose of what's left of Mommy.

Whew! I'm exhausted just thinking about it! But I'm also riddled with guilt, because I can't be everywhere I want to be all of the time. Oprah Winfrey, who's been an acquaintance for many years, calls this the "disease to please," and boy, do I have a bad case of it.

The worst kind of guilt is Mom Guilt. Like so many mothers with demanding jobs, I feel that I need to sacrifice myself for my children. In order to be more there for them, I have to give up time for me.

If Nicky is feeling anxious about a test or has a tae kwon do competition, I want to make sure I am there for him. When I missed Leila's basketball game or her beloved hamster Buttercup died while I was at the airport, I worried about whether I let Leila down by not being there.

I kick myself when I have to tiptoe out of the house before my kids wake up, or when I'm traveling somewhere for work and can't tuck them in at night, or when I'm working on a weekend and miss out on going to church or to the movies with Al and the kids. I realize that I am there more often than I am gone, but somehow that rational thought is suppressed by the dreaded *Mom Guilt*.

I am determined to change this because I understand it's wasted energy that doesn't make life better or happier for anyone—most of all me! As women, we too often beat ourselves up for never being in the right place. If I'm at work, I feel like I should be at home doing more. If I'm home, I'm e-mailing and trying to figure out how I can get more work done. Like so many others, I'm constantly wondering if I am a good enough mom.

Did I say the right thing when Leila dissolved into tears after a disappointing audition?

Was I too harsh on Nicky for sneaking his iPad to school?

I know I am not alone here.

Please tell me you're nodding your head in agreement.

No matter how well things seem to be going at home, I constantly wonder if the grass is greener on the other side. Recently, I had lunch with Karen, a dear friend who exited off the career freeway to stay home with her four kids. Whenever we meet, she breezes in looking serene, and I secretly and enviously wonder, "Should I do that?"

I never stop to wonder, "*Could* I do that?"

If I did, the answer would probably be, no way—at least not long-term. I am too driven and career-minded. Last winter, when a snow-storm closed New York City schools for a highly unusual two days, Al was stuck at work, reporting the weather for nearly forty-eight hours straight. I stayed home with the kids, thinking it could be a treasured bonding experience. I imagined us playing games and doing homework together before baking cookies and eating them in front of the fire.

Instead, Leila and Nicky were at each other's throats within hours, and I was haranguing them to walk Pepper, make their beds and turn off the TV. I was exhausted by lunch (which I made, of course).

The next morning, itching to get to work, I decided to keep my appointment to do an interview downtown. The acerbic comedian Gilbert Gottfried had been fired by Aflac after making some controversial remarks, and I was going to ask him how comics know if they're going over the line. It was straightforward enough, so I decided to take Nicky with me. "I can be a mom and a reporter at the same time," I thought.

Wrong!

As the cameras began rolling, we could hear Nicky cheering and jeering as he played Angry Birds on my phone. Gilbert, himself a dad, good-naturedly shouted, "Shut up!" And then laced it with an obscenity.

Oh, that Gilbert!

We all laughed and soon finished the interview, but I learned a big lesson. Assuaging my guilt by bringing my son to work only made me feel more stressed and, in the end, guiltier!

I often assume the kids are feeling slighted and are suffering emotional erosion when I am at work or not entirely focused on them when we are together. But I am slowly learning that it isn't always the case *at all*.

In the midst of another guilt trip, after a shoot that required me to work the previous weekend, I decided to spend a Saturday alone at our weekend home with Leila while Al and Nicky stayed in the city for a birthday party. I was in the throes of a complex three-part story for *20/20* about a father who had mysteriously vanished and the piece was due in a few days. My producer, a smart go-getter named Alyssa, who was also a mom, offered to begin in the edit room and work with me by phone for the day so I could keep my plans with Leila.

Leila and I were looking forward to snuggling together on the sofa, eating some popcorn and enjoying an afternoon movie. Just as we pressed play on the DVD player, the phone rang. Alyssa wanted to talk through some concerns about the script. I grabbed my iPad and began rewriting a few paragraphs. Then, as often happens when I'm engrossed in script writing, I had a new thought and then another. I carefully and specifically gave her directions as we rewrote a page or two. We said good-bye. Ten minutes later the phone rang again. Ever the careful journalist, Alyssa wanted to confirm a date in the story that seemed questionable.

Half an hour later, I hung up, feeling guilty that I had shortchanged Leila on "our" weekend.

I apologized to my daughter because I wanted her to know I respected our time together and didn't take it for granted. But before I could finish, Leila threw me a serious curveball.

"Mom, you're really cool," she said.

Huh? I didn't see that coming.

"The way you juggle everything and the way you always try to balance your work life with your family life means a lot. And your patience with your producer was amazing," she added.

Wow! I was floored!

Here I was thinking that thanks to my career, I was wrecking a beautiful memory and providing fodder for therapy one day, and Leila made me feel like a million bucks.

It took my teenager to drive home a serious message. I was so busy feeling guilty, I never once stopped to consider that I might be successfully setting a good example about being flexible, accomplished and nurturing toward a coworker. I knew I *wanted* to be that kind of mom. I was *trying* to be that mom. I just didn't realize that I *was* that mom. Al often tells me that women should take a page out of the guys' handbook and feel less guilt. I think he's right!

When it comes to parental G-U-I-L-T . . . *Guys Understand It's Less Tricky!*

Somehow they have a way of feeling half full about life rather than half empty. Al doesn't dwell on whether or not he missed Nicky's school assembly three days ago; he focuses on how he raced home in time to take him to swim class today. Somehow he holds on to what he accomplished and lives much more in the moment—and for the moment—than I do. A few weeks ago, as we were lying in bed after a long, exhausting day, I asked Al if he ever feels like he is screwing up as a parent, or not doing it right.

"Nope, not really. I made Nicky's lunch this morning and sat in on his tae kwon do class. I feel pretty good about how I'm doing," he said with great confidence.

Granted, he has been through the parenting thing before, raising his daughter Courtney, so he had a little experience under his belt.

Look, I am not saying that my husband is immune to guilt, but he doesn't carry it around like a weight around his neck. Why fret over what he didn't do last week? He reminds me that he can't do anything to change the past. Similarly, my mom used to quote Old Testament scripture that essentially says, "Once you put your hand to the plow, don't look back."

That lesson also applies to parenting. I am trying every day to take it to heart and to teach my children that no matter what happened yesterday, we are now focusing on today and what lies ahead. Feelings of regret and guilt are wasted emotions.

Thankfully, I am blessed to have a supportive husband who understands that. He also seems to recognize when I need to step away from the stresses to reclaim myself.

When my good friend Jerri moved to London a few years ago, she invited me to come hang out for a girls' weekend. Now and again I mentioned it to Al, and for months I came up with dates that worked and then excuses for why they didn't.

"I should go check in on Mom down in Georgia and see how she's doing" or "Leila needs help with that project" or "Nicky really needs a new winter coat."

Before I knew it, a year had passed and we still hadn't booked our trip. Finally, Al took matters into his own hands.

"Let's book this trip once and for all!" he said as he took out his iPad and began searching for flights.

Al was forcing me to do something wonderful that I felt slightly guilty about doing for myself. He knew I needed this getaway more than I did! A weekend away from the kids, with no stress, no pressure, no one pulling at me and *no guilt* was a gift beyond comprehension.

I boarded my evening flight with a joyful ease that I rarely feel when leaving home. My thoughtful, kind husband had booked me in business class. Woo hoo! When the flight attendant offered a glass of champagne and eye shades, any misgivings I felt soon melted away.

Soon I felt like a giddy teenager playing hooky. Jerri and her husband, Gregg, gave me a beautiful weekend getaway. We enjoyed shopping, sipping English tea and long, beautiful walks around London. What a joy to sleep late and worry about absolutely nothing except which hot new London restaurant we should try next! When I called home, Leila quickly remarked that I sounded so *relaxed*.

"You should do things like this more often!" she said.

At that moment, both she and I understood the power of taking a deep breath . . . even thousands of miles away.

I hung up with a happy smile—and best of all, *no guilt*!

Since I came home from that trip, I've strived to remember and hold on to that relaxed feeling.

Of course, it doesn't always work. Oh well. Maybe another trip will help. I hear Paris is nice in April! As they say, practice makes perfect!

AL
_____

The Opposite of Mom Guilt

If your life is anything like mine, you're in constant motion, doing your best to keep up with your obligations at home and at work. The idea that you could actually stop and take a breath every once in a while sounds pretty good, though most of us don't give ourselves that much-needed break. When we do get free time, we feel like it should be spent with our kids or doing things around the house, to make up for the time we spend away from home.

That's why I love business trips. I am a firm believer in the value of getting away from the home front for a period of time, leaving a little early and taking an extra day or night to relax. I don't fill my time away with unnecessary dinners or meetings that merely fill empty space. I am busy enough. I look at these windows as an opportunity to slow down and take a breath.

Deborah is the complete opposite.

I think it's her Mom Guilt—which is what moms get by putting the weight of the world on themselves.

I have the opposite of Mom Guilt.

Would I rather be home? Absolutely.

But I don't feel like a bad guy because my job takes me away from time to time. It's part of the gig. Working in morning television is like belonging to a small fraternity. There are only a handful of people who have the same experiences that I have, not to mention the hours. While there are definite perks, there are, of course, drawbacks. I go to bed early and am awake well before the crack of dawn. I am often in bed before my kids and can't be at home in the morning to put them on the bus to school. On the other hand, I can be there to pick them up at the end of their day, help them with their homework and make dinner. I'm usually home before Deborah, which means I'm waiting for her with a glass of wine in hand and a home-cooked meal waiting on the table. It's a bit of role reversal that I rather enjoy.

Matt Lauer and I don't sit around trading parenting tips, but we do talk about what we do in our off time, such as traveling to horse shows because his wife and his daughter ride. We're just like every other dad who wants to attend every swim meet, chess tournament or spring concert we can. I can recall one occasion when Matt couldn't make his son's baseball game because he had to do a big interview, and I could see in his eyes he was disappointed. I think it's great that today's dads are much more involved. When I was growing up, fathers weren't expected to be at parent-teacher conferences or art shows. Now when I go to school during the day, at least half the parents there are dads. Even President Obama finds the time to attend his daughters' school and sporting events! He has the weight of the free world on his shoulders—if he can make the time, anyone can! The problem is that dads get a big pat on the back when they come and often get a pass when they don't. Moms are expected to be there, and when they can't make it, they feel guilty about it! Even when no one else is putting that pressure on them, they put it on themselves.

Whenever Deborah has to travel for work, she prefers to leave the morning of her interview, rushing to catch her plane and then rushing right back home, getting back late at night, long after the kids have gone to bed.

Not me.

I prefer to leave the night before, get in a workout, have a nice dinner, get a good night's sleep, do what I need to do the next day and take a decent flight back.

Whenever I suggest going early, getting a massage, having a glass of wine, pampering herself a bit, Deborah says it sounds good in theory, but her Mom Guilt quickly creeps in before she can say yes. She always has a long list of things that have to be done, and have to be done by her.

Sometimes less is more. I think Nancy Reagan was ahead of her time when she came up with the motto "Just Say No."

I have a good buddy who just can't ever seem to say no!

No matter how hard he tries, he just can't say it. He's such a nice guy, he doesn't want to let anyone down, so he overcommits and spreads himself so thin that he's exhausted all of the time.

I don't understand why people can't just say no without feeling compelled to give a reason. Unless you are my wife or my parents, I don't feel the need to justify myself—not even if you are my kids!

"Because I said so and I am your father" is the only reason they need. I accepted that answer from my father, and I totally expect my children to accept it from me. Truthfully, it doesn't always work, but hey, sometimes it does! Why is it we can say yes to things we want without providing a lengthy explanation, but somehow "no" has become something we feel the need to rationalize? When you think about it, "no" is the most powerful word we can speak. "Yes" is a good word, but "no" is better. "No" says you are taking control—or better yet, you are actually *in* control.

People say yes to things they don't want to do all the time, because they feel guilty saying no.

Not me.

I know what I don't want to be a part of and I am quite comfortable saying no. I often think of the Snickers candy bar commercial where you are not yourself when you are hungry. Well, you can't be you when you're exhausted, tired and crazy because you've spread yourself too thin. Learn to say no and you will actually have a little time for yourself. Nobody is going to give it to you but you.

At the end of the day, I know I am a better husband and father because I have taken "me" time instead of giving that time to things I don't care about.

When Steve Harvey came out with his book saying women should think more like men, I liked the idea, but I think he missed one important point. I believe moms need to think more like dads. They need to stop feeling guilty about allowing themselves time and space. They need it as much as we do. We all do.

And guess what?

Your husbands are capable and even happy to help out so you can have that.

My coanchor, Natalie Morales, who is a great woman and married to a great guy, once told me she can't let her husband dress their kids.

"What would happen if he did?" I asked.

"He would have them wearing gym pants every day!"

"Are people going to stone them? Are they going to be shamed? Are people going to point at them on the street and post pictures on the Internet?" I asked.

"Well, no . . ."

Of course not! She knew I was right.

Look, as hard as it is to say no, sometimes it's even harder to say yes to help, or to just loosen your grip enough for your partner to chip in.

Dads are not incompetent, despite the premise of most great American sitcoms, from *The Flintstones* to *The Honeymooners* to *Everybody Loves Raymond* to *The King of Queens*. All of these shows were based in truth. You're supposed to be the king of the castle and the fact is you are not. (At times I feel more like the court jester, but it's okay.) Our wives still run the home and we just get to live in it. On the rare weekday that I'm off and have the chance to get Nicky ready for school (Leila is her own girl, with her own fashion sense. I have nothing to do with that), this is what I hear when he walks through the door at the end of the day.

"You sent him out of the house wearing that?"

Never mind that Leila doesn't own an outfit that covers her midriff. It seems I'm the only one in the house who has a problem with that.

I've had some memorable disagreements with my wife over my buying the kids' clothes or making their school lunches. These are things she feels are the mother's role or responsibility. What she really means is that she doesn't trust me to do as good a job as she would.

"Is this 1955?" I said when Deborah shared her feelings with me.

I liked the idea of packing the kids' lunches; I saw it as a way to be a part of their morning routine even though I leave the house long before they wake. Making their lunch gave us a nice little connection. Unfortunately, I had to make the lunches at four thirty a.m. and Deborah worried that the food wouldn't be fresh by the time they ate it at noon.

What? I put it in the refrigerator. People aren't salting their meats to preserve them anymore. We don't need a guy with a block of ice coming up a flight of stairs to put it in a wooden case. Refrigerators run on electricity these days! I know a lot of people make their kids' lunches *the night before*, but it was still a losing battle. Deborah started worrying about the portion sizes I was giving the kids. In her mind, I was putting fifty-five-gallon drums of sugar in their lunch boxes, when in fact I was giving them snack packs of Oreos or granola bars along with a piece of fruit. It's true that I wasn't packing carrots and celery sticks, but I had found those were the items that routinely came home uneaten. Call me crazy, but why bother?

And so you know what I did? I stopped making lunch. I said to Deborah, "It's probably better if you make lunch, since you know how you want it made and it'll save us a lot of stress and strife. I love you too much to argue about lunch."

Suddenly, my early mornings got a lot less hectic. I wasn't worried about what bread to use and whether we were out of raisins or where's the mayo? Deborah, on the other hand, started complaining that the extra workload was becoming a pain.

Ohhhh. Really?

Eventually, I took pity on Deborah, and now I'm back to packing lunches and she's staying out of it, letting me pack what I want. She even admitted that my making lunch makes her morning a little easier.

One of my favorite movies of all time is *Indiana Jones and the Last Crusade*. At the very end of the movie, Indiana has fallen into a gap, trying to reach the Holy Grail, and his father says, "Let it go."

His father spent his entire life looking for the Holy Grail, but when it became a choice between that and his son, there was no contest. When it comes to keeping peace in your home, sometimes you need to just let it go. The true Holy Grail is what is around you—your family, your happiness. If your kids are happy and healthy and they want to hang out with you, and your wife is happy and healthy and wants to hang out with you, stop looking for the Holy Grail, my friend—you've found it.

AL

Kids (and Dogs) Invading the Bedroom

When my kids were younger, I used to feel a tinge of rare dad guilt for not spending more quality time at home with them. I tried to convince myself that it wasn't about the quantity of time spent, but the quality. It turns out, I was wrong. It comes down to both.

I always wish I had more time to spend with my kids. I'm not there when they wake up and get ready for school, and one of the downfalls of getting up so early is finding myself dead tired at the end of the day. I can't remember the last time I slept late. Even when I have the opportunity, Nicky wakes up at the crack of dawn, so I find myself getting up with him by five or six a.m. But because my chance to see the kids is in the evening, I try to stay up as late as I can possibly manage in order to spend some quality time with them. I'll offer to help with homework or we'll cook something together, but honestly, by seven p.m., I am beat. People are talking to me and suddenly my eyes are closing.

"DAD!"

"Wha . . . what is it?" I mumble, half asleep.

"You're falling asleep—again," they say.

"I'm not sleeping. I'm just resting my eyes!" I can't help but think of my father every time I give that answer because that's exactly what he used to say.

Sigh. I may as well give it up. Sooner or later we all become our parents, and my day has come.

Admittedly, my perpetual state of fatigue has become something of a running gag around our house.

You see, by the time my kids finish all their homework and we have dinner, I have come down from my day and am ready to hit the sack.

Leila will say, "Why are you so tired?"

And before I can answer, Nicky will chime in with my usual answer. "Do you know what time I get up?"

"Every day I have to wake up at three forty-five in the morning. I work a long day, so of course I'm tired by the end of the day . . ." Leila will continue, as if it were a well-rehearsed monologue.

It's like their version of Abbott and Costello's Niagara Falls bit . . . "Slowly I turned . . . step by step . . . inch by inch." As soon as you hear the words "Niagara Falls," you launch into the routine.

Same in my house. They sure know my spiel by heart.

Well, they should.

I've been saying it for years!

And it isn't just at home where this can happen. I have been known to doze off in restaurants, at the theater, in cabs and just about any-where I can catch a little shut-eye. Sometimes Deborah tries to get me to sit up straight as a way to revive me, but it doesn't help when all I want is to get horizontal.

Yet just as I'm ready to call it a night, Leila comes in and sprawls at the foot of our bed and starts to download her day. It's literally an information dump. She begins to talk and doesn't take a breath for ten minutes. Mean-while, Nicky comes in and snuggles up, and of course, Pepper, the World's Greatest Dog, will not be denied and takes up her position. When we got Pepper, I always said that no matter what, that dog wouldn't be allowed to sleep on the bed; *that* is where I draw the line.

Well, you can see where I rank in the pecking order, because this is the usual scene that greets me as I come out of the bathroom, freshly shaved and showered and ready for bed.

Noooooooooo!

I may have mentioned I am a bit OCD about certain things. My bedtime routine is one of them. I like my pillow cool and untouched. I like my side of the bed cool as well. I love the feel of slipping into those crisp, unrumpled sheets and settling in. When there are two kids, a wife and a dog in there, my pillow and sheets are anything but. They are warm, rumpled—and occupied! So not only is there no room at the inn, but the inn is as hot and bothered as I am.

Now I must wriggle in and find a spot to settle on, while my children and dog, wide-awake, want to engage their dad.

Believe me, I want to be engaged.

I try to keep my eyes open.

I do everything I can to not fall asleep.

But usually I fail.

"Dad, I want to—" Leila says before noticing I'm drifting off. "DAD!"

"I've got to go to sleep," I sheepishly say.

Deborah often reminds me that we don't know how long Leila will want to continue sharing the details of her high school life—that we should cherish it, embrace her presence and let her talk. I agree. She's right, but I'm really tired!

I'm trying to get better, but it's hard.

Besides, I come from a generation where you didn't spend any time in your parents' bedroom and there was no expectation of it at the end of the day. I did my homework, took a shower, put on my pajamas, kissed my mom and dad good night and went to bed. I never even went into their room unless I was summoned, sick or absolutely had to bring something to them. And if I did enter their sacred space, I knew enough to stay for a brief moment and then get out.

The only time we spent any significant time in their room was to watch their color TV. We had a black-and-white television in the basement, which we could watch whenever we wanted. The color TV was reserved for special occasions, such as the World Series or the Knicks championship game.

Deborah and I go back and forth about whether or not these same standards and expectations still work in today's world of cosleeping and family beds. Call me crazy, but I like the idea of taking a shower and not having to worry about covering up before walking from my bathroom to my bedroom. And while you're at it, knock on the door and wait for me to say "come in" before you enter. That's why we close the door in the first place! For privacy! A door should be knocked on if it's closed.

That said, one of the things I admire about Deborah and am trying to emulate more is her ability to engage the kids at bedtime. She gives them all the time they need to unwind, unload and unburden their souls. (Pepper just needs her belly rubbed. So do I, but that's another story.)

Kids' lives are much more programmed and scheduled today than mine was growing up. Homework looms over them in a way I never felt. Even though we talk at the dinner table, I find that to be a very different kind of conversation. Everyone is still in their "on" mode, thinking about what still needs to be done before calling it a night. The only chance we all get to let out a sigh of relief is at bedtime. Those fifteen or twenty minutes spent hanging out in our bedroom allow our children to decompress and just *be*.

And so now, when I come out of the bathroom expecting a chance to snuggle with my wife (and these days, as tired as I am, a snuggle is all I want!) and then a quick visit from the Sandman and find my kids camped out, I just smile and say, "Kids, start your mouths. I'm all ears."

Sure, I wish they'd stay off my side of the bed, for Pete's sake . . . Okay, nobody under the age of seventy-five says that anymore but I can't say what I'd like to say, so I smile and climb in, looking for a little room, offer an inviting ear and with a little luck, a quick rub o' the belly.

Is it an exercise in patience?

Sometimes.

Do I struggle?

It's harder for me when I am tired.

When I don't have to work the next day, the burden is certainly lifted.

But I always try to remind myself of my father's sage advice: It's not about *your* needs; it is about what *they* need.

Yeah, I know I've referred to this advice a few times throughout this book, but it does seem to cover a lot of territory, especially when it comes to parenting.

Although my children don't necessarily realize it, it's our job as parents to know they need that connection with us, just as I need my connection with Deborah and she with me. Connecting as a family is a priority for us, and I will take it any way I can get it, because I realize these nights of gathering on the bed won't last forever. Sometimes I hear Harry Chapin singing "Cat's in the Cradle" in my head, especially on those rare nights one of the kids *doesn't* pop in. Kids grow up fast, and you have to make each day count. Strive for both quality *and* quantity in your time together. That's what creates connection.

7

Actions Speak Louder Than Words

DEBORAH
_____

CEO of the Home

I think it's fair to say that women are generally the emotional glue that holds a household together. And most of us would say we are the logistical support too. With no disrespect to our mates, if our homes were a business, we'd be in charge. You may as well call us the CEO!

Now, to be fair, I have a fabulous, capable co-CEO in Al. He often catches a glitch in the kids' schedules before I do. But even *he* would admit—if he's smart—that the brunt of our day-to-day life falls on my shoulders. Ask any woman, from any walk of life, and she'll tell you that's usually the way it goes. Whenever I get together with a girlfriend, we inevitably land on the subject of how stressed we are. Though most of my friends have spouses who pitch in, one complains how her husband aspires to do as little as possible around the house. He wouldn't begin to know where the pancake griddle is, what time school lets out or where their child's best friend lives. Thankfully, I don't have that situation. (Well, at least Al knows where to find the pots and pans!) But seriously,

I am truly blessed to have a husband who not only looks forward to being home with the family but also cooks most of our meals and is deeply involved in the kids' lives (sometimes a little too much).

Even so, if Nicky forgot his lunch or Leila's frantic because she left her PE clothes on the bench in our hallway, Al isn't fielding that call at work.

I am.

If Nicky is throwing up at school or the piano teacher can't make it, guess who races to the school or reschedules the lesson? You got it.

Me.

Even if I'm in a Texas jail about to roll on an interview with an accused murderer, somehow I'm the one who gets that call from home about how someone's day is unraveling. Somehow everyone at my house seems to think that Al's work couldn't possibly be disturbed. Maybe it's hard to imagine phoning the man you're watching on TV warn the country of an impending nor'easter about missing gym clothes or a dentist appointment after school. Yet there seems to be an assumption that men are busy and unavailable but women . . . moms . . . not so much. I don't think this situation is unique to our home so much as it is a social stereotype that all moms face.

Make no mistake—I love it when Leila confides in me about things going on in her personal life, whether it's about a problem at school with one of her teachers or how her once-close friend has changed and drifted away. We moms are often privy to shared moments of tenderness with our children that dads miss out on. But we also carry a lot of the burden in child-rearing, which can leave us vulnerable. If you are a working mom, you are probably weighted down by the details in the day to day. Aside from schoolwork, there is that added pressure of activities. Nicky is passionate about martial arts and swimming. Leila loves theater. But one year I insisted that she try sports. She fought me, but ultimately she played on both the volleyball and basketball teams, and guess what—she enjoyed both! I felt victorious; I'd pushed her beyond her comfort zone and it paid off. But of course I'd managed to add more activities to our already hectic lives!

Certainly there are plenty of dads who push their kids to excel, but they don't seem to obsess over their kids' activities the same way a mother does.

To be fair, I plead guilty to being more competitive than Al and also more socially aware. Al couldn't care less about the dance class or ice-skating lessons, although I know he wants whatever is best for our children. He's a big fan of downtime. But he's usually supportive as long as I don't drag him into each and every activity.

Like many women, I am the social planner in our house. I am the reason we go to the opening night of the ballet, or the theater, and other important cultural events. Anyone sitting next to us has probably seen Al dozing off during a production of the *Radio City Christmas Spectacular* or a Broadway show. In fact, the only reason he goes with me to the opera at all is because he knows he will get in a good nap! But he gets a pass since he gets up at three thirty a.m.—and he did go with me.

We both admit, though, that our lives would likely fall apart without a reliable babysitter. When Al's mother died, we no longer had a relative we could turn to for help, so our caregiver Bibi has become a godsend. She picks up Nicky from school unless Al can get away to do it himself. She also spends the night when one—or both—of us travels on assignment for work, which is more often than we'd like to admit. We are indebted to Bibi, a mom herself of grown children, who has a warm smile and a kind touch. For six years she has been my stand-in when I have to catch a flight at six a.m. or if Al and I want to grab a rare night out. Sometimes she is my saving grace.

I didn't always have such support. After giving birth to Leila, I wasn't prepared for how vulnerable I would feel. There's an old expression that "to have a child is to forever know what it is to have your heart beating outside your chest." No truer words have been spoken about parenthood. That little bundle of joy changes everything. So for me, like so many women, handing my child off to a babysitter was beyond difficult. I didn't grow up with babysitters and neither did Al. My aunts and cousins pitched in whenever Mom needed to go somewhere. But today life is so different, especially when you don't have close family living nearby. I accepted that I would need help after having children, especially if I wanted to work, but I still wanted to be the glue holding the household together. I'd had a C-section and needed quite a bit of help around the house, so I turned to a sitter to guide me, someone who could hopefully help me figure out how to keep all of the moving parts together without falling to pieces. My first babysitter was loving and smart. She had a son of her own and was happy to share her wisdom. And I was all too happy to accept it! I was a nervous new mom, not yet comfortable in the role, who had great appreciation for the love and care this woman showed Leila. After all, she was looking after my life's treasure. I was so grateful for her help, and of course I depended on her. So even if I didn't like something here and there, I was reluctant to say anything for fear of upsetting her.

Red flag!

I should have recognized that immediately as a problem in the relationship, but I didn't. Al was oblivious to it, so it made it challenging to talk to him about how I was feeling.

Over time, as I eased back into the demands of my job at ABC, things slowly began to change. I noticed how my otherwise charming and warm babysitter could be very controlling. She'd brag to others about what a great dad Al is and how involved he is, while pointedly remaining silent about me. Even when I was around, she rushed to take charge of the kids. When Leila accidentally locked herself in the bathroom, our sitter raced to save the day before I could sort it out.

One day, my colleague and friend Cynthia McFadden was visiting, and she pointed out something that I had been glossing over.

"You know your sitter doesn't always have your best interest at heart," she quietly said. Cynthia's son, Spencer, and Leila often played together, and she had noticed other instances of subtle sabotage. She had put into words a vague feeling I'd been having. Her next words shocked me, though. "She sees herself as Leila's second mom and acts like you're just Al's wife who comes and goes."

At first I thought it was overdramatic and ridiculous, but I soon recalled many instances when the sitter had inserted herself in a family moment. And even stranger, this woman kind of resembled me. We were similar in size and stature. I had offered her some clothes that I was giving away, and when she wore them, from a distance she was a dead ringer. It was kind of eerie. It reminded me of the movie *All About Eve.*

Women can smell another woman who is being competitive. Guys don't always see it, but women do. Al thought everything was peachy keen, but it was far from it. I could feel the tension growing, and it was getting frustrating for me. I had a gentle talk with the sitter, and for a while things seemed better. I consoled myself with the fact that she was reliable and honest and Leila adored her. And let's face it, I traveled and needed the help.

A couple of years passed, and although the situation was far from good, I was afraid to let our sitter go. She had the household running like a top. And Leila cherished her. Once when Leila fell down, she ran into the arms of the babysitter first. That stung! But leaving aside what I now regarded as subtle condescension toward me, I trusted this woman with my children. Our second baby had arrived, and I craved a familiar routine. I overlooked it when she criticized the breakfast I made Leila or stepped into a family photo uninvited. Some of my friends told me that it was time to start fresh, to find someone who would better understand boundaries. When I broached the subject of firing that longtime babysitter, Al did his best to understand how I felt, but he thought we could make it work; he worried that making a change would be upsetting to the children. That was true, but his reluctance bothered me deeply, because it felt like he wasn't supporting me. I am his wife and I was being disrespected. I didn't understand how he could defend the behavior of a dismissive babysitter over my feelings. I know Al was thinking about the kids' well-being, but what about mine?

When I shared the situation with my girlfriends Agenia and Tonya, both savvy moms who also had babysitters, they had one response. "It's time to start over."

In my gut I knew they were right, but I was afraid. How would I manage without someone who'd been there from the start and knew the kids and the house like the backs of her hands? Here I was, incredibly blessed to be able to afford daily child care, which many working moms cannot. So maybe I should just "suck it up"! And besides, everything might fall apart without her, making me even more stressed and leaving me unable to travel for my next assignment.

What was wrong with me? I am a strong, accomplished woman who can stand up to the most hardened criminals in interviews or powerful network bosses for what I believe in, and yet I couldn't fire a babysitter?

I realized that at the end of the day I share a common trait with many women.

My children are my weakness.

I will suffer slings and arrows when it comes to them. In this case, I was blinded by the fear of shaking up their world.

Then one morning the blinders came off. I unexpectedly came home to drop off a package and overheard my babysitter in the kitchen, bad-mouthing me to the plumber. She was mimicking my voice and disparaging me. My jaw dropped! When I rounded the corner, her eyes widened in surprise and my hands began to shake. This betrayal was the final straw.

"You need to get your things and leave," I said sternly.

I'd had enough. I had been enduring moment after moment of insubordination from this woman, and I'd hit my threshold of tolerance. There were no second thoughts this time. I couldn't have someone in my home blatantly showing me disrespect in front of someone else. Period. I had no idea how I would manage the next few days—or even the next few hours—but I knew I was making the right move. There had to be someone else out there who would be happy to work with a warm and caring young family.

The next few weeks were tough. Leila cried and cried for her babysitter, and I felt terrible that we couldn't work things out. But I knew that it was impossible. We all needed a clean slate. And I needed to know that I was back in control of my own home. It wasn't easy, but I learned two powerful lessons from this experience.

First, my children's most valuable assets will always be Al and me.

Second, life is all about change. It's up to us to make that change positive and powerful and to believe that God will make a way.

Al was fully supportive of the decision. We juggled our schedules, and within a week we had found Mila, a lovely, soft-spoken new babysitter who had a gentle way about her. I laid out the details of her duties with newfound authority, creating a relationship of respect and friendship from the very start. And soon the positive impact of the change was clear. My children quickly learned that no matter what, their mommy and daddy will always be a constant in their lives. Losing a lifelong caregiver was harder on Leila than Nicky, since he was a baby, but she got through it and she understood that in life there will be little bumps and unexpected changes. This would be the first of many blips in her life. It wasn't an easy time for any of us, but we grew stronger as a family because of it. I learned how to be more honest about my feelings, and Al learned how to listen more. Now I have no doubt that he will step up and support me whenever I need him.

AL

Lessons My Father Taught Me

Dads were different in the 1950s and 1960s than they are today. There were more defined gender roles, and when people pictured a dad they probably pictured a man showing his son how things worked. That was us. I could happily sit and watch my dad work on his car, changing spark plugs and checking the oil, replacing the distributor cap or doing any number of other guy things that dads did, and find it fun. Fathers and sons probably still do this, except now you need a computer, a hydraulic lift and a physics degree to work on a car!

One of my favorite movies of all time is *A Christmas Story*, with the great Darren McGavin playing the dad. It's set in post–World War II Indianapolis, but it was shot in Cleveland when I was living there! At one point in the movie, the "old man" and his son Ralphie, the boy who narrates the story, go out to get a Christmas tree. On their way home, they get a flat tire.

"He had always pictured himself in the pits of the Indianapolis Speedway," Ralphie says. (The dad doesn't have a name; he appears in the credits simply as "the old man.")

"Four minutes! Time me!" the old man says as he hops out of the car.

Then he shows Ralphie how to change a flat. When they lose one of the lug nuts, Ralphie accidentally uses the F word. No, not "fudge." "I said the mother of all curse words," Ralphie admits. These are the moments between fathers and sons that create the kind of bond that can never be broken. The physical act of changing the tire together brought Ralphie and the old man closer together (of course, dads didn't have AAA back then).

Not long ago, Leila, Nicky and I were driving in the Berkshires in Massachusetts when I felt our compact car shimmying. I pulled over to see what was going on. When I got out of the car, I discovered I had a flat tire.

"Oh man," I thought.

I did what every red-blooded American dad does in the new millennium. I hit the red aid button on the roof of my car and summoned roadside assistance.

"We can have someone out to you in an hour," the man said.

To be fair, we were in a rural area.

I pulled the car over to park under the nearest tree because it was 93 degrees out and I didn't want to leave it running. About five minutes into our wait, with the images of the tire-changing scene from *A Christmas Story* dancing through my head, I turned to Nicky and said, "You know what? We can change this tire. C'mon, son!" (Of course, I hoped neither of us would drop the F bomb!)

We opened the trunk, grabbed the spare (which resembles a doughnut more than a tire these days) and the tire iron. It took us thirty minutes and a lot of sweat, but we changed that tire! And for those thirty minutes, for the first time in years, I was reminded of what it might have been like for my dad so many years ago—to be engaged in a physical act with my son, showing him how to do it just like my dad would have done.

Although I'm not as handy as my dad was, in so many ways he inspired me to become the father I am today. For example, he was never afraid to show his emotions, positive or negative. He was a big hugger and kisser at a time when men were very macho and didn't embrace like they do today.

I remember visiting relatives and going in for a hug and a kiss with my uncles only to be stiff-armed; they'd keep me at arm's length with their left hand while thrusting their right hand out to shake. In the sixties and seventies, real men shook hands. End of story. Not my dad. He was the original "Bring it in here, hug it out" guy.

Dad enjoyed life. He played on the softball team at work, wore bell-bottom jeans and from time to time went out for drinks with his buddies. He was the kind of guy who got a little tipsy and put his arms around everyone. It wasn't unusual for him to give his friends a great big bear hug or a peck on the cheek. He demonstrated that you could be a caring, gentle, loving person and still be a man. That there was nothing wrong with showing people how you felt.

It's no secret that I wasn't an athletic child. My interest was in animation—especially cartoons and movies. My father never once pushed me into sports just because he was passionate about playing. You see, when it came to his children, my father's philosophy was "Don't do what you want; do what your kid needs." So instead of tossing the ball around, we watched *The Flintstones* together and talked about cartoons and comic books. He nurtured my interest in the audiovisual by giving me a 35mm camera, a reel-to-reel tape recorder and a movie camera. His goal wasn't to push me to do what he liked but to share in my interests and to provide whatever I needed for support.

I've never forgotten what that felt like as a kid and have carried that into my role as dad, whether it's spending time cooking with Courtney, talking music with Leila or doing anything that involves electronics with Nicky—it's all about connection.

My number one job as dad is to make sure my kids know I will do everything necessary to make them safe and whatever they need in order to *feel* safe. I never once doubted for a moment that I was safe as long as my dad was around, and I want to pass that security on to my children.

My dad retired from his job when he was fifty-five years old. He enjoyed his job, and the minute he wasn't enjoying it anymore, he knew it was time to leave. I think a lot of people hang in there and stay a little too long—often because they need the money, but sometimes because they just aren't quite ready to move into the next phase of their lives, whether it's a career change or retirement. My dad wasn't that guy. The second he wasn't enjoying himself anymore, he quit and never looked back. He didn't need to stay until he turned sixty-five—fortunately, as it turned out, because he passed away when he was sixty-nine years old.

When my dad retired, the person who took it the hardest was my mom. She was not ready to have him at home. The first couple of months were rough. I heard "I am going to kill your father" a lot before they found a happy balance. A lot of couples don't realize that while you might be ready for change, your partner may not be. The change in routine was hard for Mom to take.

Watching my dad in retirement, I learned something else from him: Never stop moving. Never stop evolving. Right after he retired, he started a mentoring program at a local middle school. He deepened a nascent love of jazz. He indulged in his passion for deep-sea fishing, and he got a posse of fellow retired transit workers together for a twice-weekly walk for exercise around the local mall, followed by coffee and cake at their favorite coffee shop—thereby negating the effects of the walk. God, I miss him.

That feeling of safety my dad gave me as a boy lasted until the day he died. I suppose that's why losing him hit me as hard as it did. No matter how old I was, as long as he was alive, I knew there was this other person around who was my safety net. Sure, I have my wife and family, but my dad—well, there's nothing like the bond between a son and his father. He was my rock—my touchstone. Even when I visited him in his hospital room in his final days, I felt safe being in there because he was there too.

I always want my kids to feel that.

We lost my mom only three months after the passing of my father. I have always said that the worst thing in the world is that they went quickly and the best thing in the world is that they went quickly. I mean, it was horrible to lose both of them in quick succession, but I'm glad neither suffered for long. A day doesn't go by that I don't think about them and miss them. I would do anything to have them back. But that being said, I feel incredibly blessed that they were my parents.

There was a legendary journalist in New York I got to know over the years. At his retirement dinner, his son got up and spoke.

"With Dad, we always knew his job came first," he said.

I'm certain his son meant those words in the best way, but I thought to myself, "I never want my kids to feel that way." I have always made them my first priority—and will always reassure them they are my number one.

Finally, I have to say that losing my parents has made me a lot less likely to sweat the small stuff. One life is all you get, so enjoy it! None of us knows how much time we have—and we never know if it is time for us to get off the stage or just change theaters. At this point in my life, I face challenges and change with one single question: "What's the worst that could happen?" If the answer doesn't come back "DEATH," I'm confident I can always figure something out.

DEBORAH

Many Ways to Say I Love You

My mom had many ways of showing her affection but she was definitely not a warm and fuzzy parent. I wish she'd felt comfortable saying the words "I love you" a little more often. Even so, I still felt extremely loved and cherished and was always grateful for Mom's loving actions.

So I want my kids to understand there are numerous ways to say "I love you." So often, actions speak louder than words, and what we show through our behavior is what our kids will learn. Someone once told me that *your kids may not hear what you say, but they surely watch what you do.* While my kids have watched me interact with my mom, as she has declined over the years, I hope the tenderness and concern between us means something to them. I hope they store away the memories of our many visits to Georgia and know that no matter how busy and chaotic their future lives may be, they need to make time for the people they hold near and dear. I hope they'll be there for them as I have tried to be for my mom during the twilight of her life. I hope I have infused in them a sense of strength, love and compassion toward the elderly, and I hope they've come to understand the true meaning of being a multigenerational family—taking care of one another.

I also want my children to remember where they came from and the history of our family. I want them to recall my small childhood home with its one bathroom for eleven people and always remember my humble beginnings. I take great pride in reinforcing that memory every time we go back to Georgia to visit my relatives and friends—God-fearing people with thick Southern accents and simple lives.

Most of all, I want to show my children that faith is the bedrock of everything in life. My mom taught me so much based on her strong faith. Her love for God guided her in all things. Mom believed that no matter how high or how low you are in life, you are first and foremost a child of God. I think about that a lot—especially the importance of staying humble and putting my relationship with God ahead of everything else. I find myself walking down a New York City street singing a gospel hymn I learned so long ago in the New Hope Baptist Church: "Blessed assurance, Jesus is mine! Oh, what a foretaste of glory divine! . . ." just like we sang it in the church choir. I remember hating choir rehearsal and Sunday school, but here I am forty years later singing "Blessed Assurance" or "The Old Rugged Cross." Mom got us all up every Sunday, all nine of the kids, and made sure we were fed and dressed for church.

"You owe something to God," she would always say.

God was always a strong presence in our home. We said grace before every meal and knelt beside our beds to say our prayers at night to give thanks to God and all his glory for our blessings. Whenever one of us lied about something, Mom reminded us that "the Lord is watching," and you can bet that if we ever mistreated someone, we'd get a lecture about the Golden Rule—"Do unto others as you'd have them do unto you" was one of her favorite lessons to pass along to each of her children.

As I grew older these valuable lessons resonated deep inside of me. Like any kid, I sometimes fought with my younger sisters or acted selfishly when I wanted something. But more and more I'd ask myself, "What would God think of my actions or my words?" Whenever I felt hurt or afraid, I felt the Lord's presence to guide and comfort me.

I took Mom's admonitions to heart and never dreamed of swearing or drinking. In high school, when some of my friends managed to get a six-pack of beer or sneak into nightclubs on Friday nights, I wanted nothing to do with it, because Mom and Dad would be disappointed, but most of all, so would God. Yes, sometimes I felt like a Goody Two-shoes, but my faith had taken root and was my ever-present compass.

Today I still cling tightly to my Christian faith even as I race around in a high-pressure city juggling family and career. Or maybe I should say I cling to my faith *because* I am racing around in a high-stress life. Whenever I am discouraged or anxious, it is always prayer that brings me peace. I remind myself that work, while satisfying, doesn't define me. When I am at an airport late at night and one of the kids is on the other end of the phone sick or crying, I take a deep breath and pray. I know that through God's grace they will get through it. And when things seem to be falling apart, I trust that God has a greater plan. I place my trust in him and know that everyone will be all right.

When we were worried about something growing up, Mom would always say, "It's in God's hands. The Lord knows what's right." Somehow, knowing that always made me feel safe, secure and certain that life was unfolding exactly as it should. No matter what was happening in that moment, whether I was stressing out about a test or hurt by kids teasing me about my dark skin, knowing God had a plan helped me to shrug off the problems of day-to-day life; I had the solace that he would set things right.

Mom was raised in a religious home, but after losing her mother and father too young, she found even deeper comfort in her faith. We went to Sunday school every week at the New Hope Baptist Church, and by the time we were in grade school, we were expected to participate in church, such as joining the choir or being an usher. Not my brother Ben, though; he just refused. He often tried to slip out of church when Mom wasn't watching from the choir stand, but she would promptly send an usher to go outside and get him.

She wanted all of her children to know God's love and make it a part of our daily life. She taught me the importance of having a connection to a higher power and the impact it would have on us later in life. I owe my sense of spirituality to my mother and feel so lucky that she passed this gift on to me. Whether I'm about to do a big interview or make a speech or help one of the kids with a problem, I never begin before asking for God's guidance and blessing.

I am appreciative that Al's parents gave him a strong spiritual foundation too. His mom spoke of her faith daily, which influenced Al in his beliefs. If we called with exciting news of a new contract or an upcoming vacation, she always replied with a glorious "God is good!"—a saying I will admit I have adopted because I feel it praises the Lord in such a positive way.

Al and I are both determined to pass these lessons of faith on to our children because we know how wonderfully influenced our lives have been by having the presence of faith and God in our lives. Of course, like most kids, they sometimes complain about it, but we go to church nearly every Sunday. I was raised Baptist and Al was raised Catholic, but we have found a wonderful Episcopal church not far from our home that is a comfortable middle ground. St. James' Church has a dynamic kids' program and a female rector. From our first Sunday service, we immediately felt at home there.

My husband and I are proud to have savvy, smart kids who are able to make good decisions and will no doubt have an impact on the world someday. But we're even prouder to be raising spiritually minded children who care about their community and who also consider God in their decisions. Whenever we sit down for dinner, Nicky is the first to offer prayer for our meals, and bedtime prayers are part of our nightly ritual. It's a delight to see some of my childhood traditions being carried on through my children. In her quiet way my mom taught me to give thanks to God for all things. I hope and pray my children will someday do the same—and maybe even exclaim to my future grandchildren, "God is good!"

DEBORAH

Coping with an Ailing Parent

Once I left the comfort of small-town Perry, Georgia, to begin my career, I never imagined returning there to live someday. I had a loving and nurturing upbringing, and I have beautiful memories. But my sights were set on conquering the great big world out there and making my parents proud. They never demanded it of me, but being successful fit into my childhood desire to make everyone happy. It meant a lot to me to know my parents could be proud of what I was doing with my life. They were thrilled when I went to the University of Georgia and proudly wore the Georgia Bulldog shirts and hats I gave them. After graduation, I landed my first television job as a general assignment reporter in Columbus, Georgia. I felt that I was on my way. I had my own apartment and felt as fabulous as Mary Tyler Moore. I would even hum her famous end line from her television theme song: "You're gonna make it after all." All I needed was a beret to toss up in the air. I still remember my first yearly salary: $11,500. Believe it or not, that wasn't bad for a twenty-two-year-old gal in the early eighties. That *I* was able to accomplish this in my life was both gratifying and fulfilling.

As soon as I settled into the working world, I started sending Mom little gifts for no reason and flowers on her birthday, my way of giving back to her and celebrating my success. She loved the attention. When she called to thank me, she often said, "I like getting my flowers when I'm living and can smell them . . . not when I'm dead."

Mama and Daddy beamed whenever I had a report on the air, even if it was about a county commission meeting. And when I joined NBC News around eight years later, they were beyond ecstatic. Their little girl was a *national* newswoman. Whenever I came home to visit, Mom would proudly declare to the insurance man, the grocery store checkout lady or anyone who would listen: "This is my television girl . . . my celebrity!" I cringed every time I heard her say that, but I also realized how much it meant to two people who'd never graduated high school. Mom also boasted about my sister Annette, who was a successful manager with the Enron energy corporation (before it went belly-up, devastating her and thousands of others), my brother Jackie, who had traveled the world with the air force, and my sisters Janet and Bennie, who had moved to Miami to pursue careers in fashion and music. But my job in television left my folks feeling like mini celebrities.

One fall I was invited to be the grand marshal of the Perry farm festival parade. My parents got to ride behind me in a convertible Ford Mustang, waving and smiling to the crowds. To this day it remains one of my proudest moments. Al, a product of New York, immediately noticed the irony. My parents, who had once been denied opportunities because of their color, were now front and center, leading the parade— something neither of them would ever forget.

After some years of distance, Dad and I grew steadily closer. He had a deep respect and steady curiosity about my work. And boy, did he get a kick out of meeting Barbara Walters at my wedding. (Barbara couldn't have been sweeter to my parents!)

Daddy also loved talking about my trips around the country and abroad. He was the one who encouraged me to take an assignment in Kuwait covering the lead-up to the Persian Gulf War. Mom was petrified and in tears, afraid that I would be killed there. But Dad got on the phone and said, "I'm going to pray for you every day. I know you will be all right." That was the most tender moment I had ever shared with my daddy.

And soon there would be more.

Thanks to his prayers, I made it home from Kuwait, and the next time I visited my parents, they were anxious to hear all about the Middle East. Daddy even began sharing a few stories about his World War II experiences, including the Normandy Invasion.

But Daddy was about to be diagnosed with colon cancer. Katie Couric, a former colleague and a friend, had done much to make us all aware of colon cancer after losing her husband, Jay, to the disease and I'd even done a bit of reporting on the disease myself, so we pretty much knew what to expect: a grueling treatment. Daddy was game to fight for a while, but two years later he began to grow weak and weary, often staring into space for an hour without saying a word. I think he was making a decision.

You see, Daddy was proud. I soon realized that he wasn't the type who'd want to linger on and spend years trying out the latest possible treatment with debilitating side effects. My sister Tina, who dived in, bringing Daddy to doctor appointments and taking notes, tried to be upbeat for everyone. But soon after a surgery to remove part of his colon she noticed a change. The fight was taking its toll and he'd had enough. Though I'd called a doctor I'd met at Dana Farber Hospital in Boston who consulted with Dad's doctor about his drug cocktail, the struggle against cancer was still difficult. At the age of eighty-two, Dad was growing tired of the weekly doctor checkups and the chemo drips. His six-foot-two frame was becoming alarmingly thin. And, no doubt, he was living with pain that he privately held. Finally, he chose not to fight on. I respected that decision. He'd lived a proud and good life and had watched his children grow up and have their own children. He felt connected to God and at peace.

Ever since he passed, I have been especially emotional about watching my mother age. Whenever something has been slightly wrong, I've jumped on a plane and flown down to Georgia so I can be by her side.

Although Mom had been showing some signs of decline before my dad died, she really started to go downhill after he passed. She seemed to detach from everyone and everything, and it didn't take long for me to notice that she was cognitively slipping too.

Whenever I called, she would ramble on, telling me the same stories over and over, often losing her train of thought or not remembering what I'd told her in our previous conversation. This went on for a couple of years.

But then one day I called her and for a moment she had no idea who I was.

My heart was shattered.

When I hung up, Al asked what was wrong, and I sobbed in his arms. My family was losing our sweet mom somewhere in the darkness of dementia that would eventually become Alzheimer's.

I immediately grew concerned about Mom driving. During one visit to Perry, I took a ride with her to the grocery story that would prove to be scary and quite revealing.

Within minutes, Mom ran a red light and almost sideswiped a car.

Then she made a sharp turn around a curve.

When I told her what she had just done, she was in complete denial. That's when I knew her reflexes weren't what they used to be and that she should definitely not be driving.

Naturally, Mom disagreed with my assessment.

Not long after, I got another frightening call from Tina. Mom had been in a car accident. She pulled out from a stop sign and hit an oncoming car. Fortunately, nobody was hurt. Thank God! It could've been so much worse.

Her car was totaled. My brother Jackie, in a call from his home in Ohio, declared this to be good news, that this could give us the opening we were looking for to take her keys away without a big fight. We didn't want her back on the road anytime soon.

For Mom, like any elderly person, driving was part of her independence. Simply driving the two miles to the grocery store or post office in downtown Perry represented freedom. Without a car, she would feel virtually marooned at home.

Unfortunately, the accident took that decision out of her hands. Jackie soon convinced us all that we could get someone to drive Mom where she needed to go. Well, Mom didn't take the news well. She fell into a debilitating depression for several weeks. No doubt she was mourning the loss of her self-sufficiency. The woman who had always advised her daughters to be independent and take care of themselves would now be dependent on someone else to take care of her. I don't think there was anything worse in her mind.

My sister Tina lived nearby, but she couldn't take care of Mom 24-7. We began to talk about an assisted-living facility or getting in some outside help.

I couldn't bear the idea of putting her in a nursing home. I had reported stories on nursing-home abuse and thought of them as harsh warehouses for the elderly, even though I had aunts who were well taken care of in Perry's Summerhill nursing home. I felt Mom was now stripped of some of her dignity by losing her ability to drive; at least she should be in her own place, where she could do whatever she wanted.

Al and I talked about it and agreed that since we were blessed to have a solid financial situation, we would pay for whatever assistance Mom needed. Tina agreed to do some research. I knew Mom would be happier in her own home, even though, as time went on, she was less able to communicate.

Making these types of decisions for a parent can be challenging for anyone, and they can cause a lot of unexpected family turmoil, especially in a large, far-flung family like mine. We were scattered about in Ohio, Texas, Florida and New York. My siblings and I decided to divvy up what each of us was reasonably able to do and how each of us could help our mom to the best of our ability. All of us had something to contribute to make Mom more comfortable and were happy to do whatever we could. We also made a commitment to make this about her well-being and not about who was doing more or less. We had to put Mom front and center or there would be petty arguments and problems none of us wanted to contend with during this trying time.

Caring for aging parents was a subject Diane Sawyer, my colleague and close friend, was deeply interested in; we'd had many conversations about our elderly moms and how heartbreaking it is caring for them from afar. In her brilliant way, Diane knew that many people were dealing with the same thing and encouraged me to do a report about it for *World News Tonight*. What a lifesaver for me! It gave me some great specific ideas of how we could all help one another deal with the emotions and logistics of caring for Mom.

Tina soon found the perfect caregiver. An old classmate, Doretha Lester, was a home health aide who was looking for a new job. Doretha, a cheerful, outgoing woman with a quick laugh and a sensitive manner, was a dream. She treated Mom beautifully and made life happy and healthy for her. She took great pride in making sure Mom was eating vegetables and dressing every day. She took her out for drives, shopping and even peach picking. Mom was completely happy. But then her knees began to give out, which made it hard for her to walk or get in and out of the car. She eventually needed to use a walker, which slowed her down even more. With this loss of mobility came a loss of self-esteem and positivity that Mom would never recover.

This went well for a few years. Then one afternoon I received a frantic call from Doretha. Apparently, she had gone into my mother's bedroom and discovered that the bedclothes were covered in blood. Doretha had nearly fainted at the sight. She told me an ambulance was on its way.

I had no idea what to think but the worst—my mom was surely dying.

I needed to get to Georgia as soon as possible.

I hung up the phone and headed to the airport.

I was a wreck, but I also knew I had to get ahold of myself in case decisions had to be made.

All I could pray for was that I would get there in time to say good-bye.

By the time my plane landed, I had more information. Mom had ruptured a bowel and they were operating on her.

She'd had no symptoms; it just happened suddenly. It's often unclear what causes a bowel rupture, and Mom's doctor couldn't tell us why it happened, but it can be fatal, especially if you lose a lot of blood, which my mother had.

Mom was eighty-six years old and was having major surgery; under the best of circumstances, this would be a dicey situation. But Mom's health wasn't perfect to begin with, so I was gravely concerned. Tina was there at Mom's side, with Doretha holding down the fort, but I wanted—needed—to be there too.

As I got into my rental car and headed to the hospital, I called Ruhanna Neal, a dear friend since college. Ruhanna is the most spiritual and positive woman I know. She's the one I call first during a challenge, and I needed her now. I asked her to pray with me as I drove to Perry.

For ten minutes she soothed me with her words. "You are going to get there and see your mom. You need to believe that you are going to get there to hold her hand and that you have done the best job a daughter can do. You have been there in ways that others wish they could be there with their moms. You go there in peace, knowing you have taken good care of her and given back to her in so very many ways over the years. Don't think about anything else."

After we hung up I found myself talking, crying and praying to God for a miracle all the rest of the way to the hospital.

When I arrived I learned that my mom had come through the surgery and was miraculously doing very well. Naturally I was thrilled at the wonderful news, but my joy quickly turned to panic when I walked into Mom's room. She looked absolutely helpless with tubes down her throat, surrounded by wires and monitors, unable to talk, heavily sedated and bandaged. I fought back tears. But when she saw me, she reached out for my hand, held it and squeezed me tight. On some level, she knew who I was, why I was there! Even if she couldn't say my name, she knew I was someone who loved her, and I knew she loved me.

I leaned in close and whispered, "I'm here, Mom, and I love you."

I wanted to scream it from the hilltops. I needed her to know she wasn't alone. I was there to hold her hand, rub her cheeks and just be with her. That brought me peace, and I hope it gave her something too.

I stayed by her side until the surgeon came in to give me an update.

"She's one tough bird!" he said.

"Yes, she is."

She had made it through the surgery and was expected to make a full physical recovery. But her mental capacity was never going to be what it once was.

I sent Tina home and clung by my mother's side for the next several days, making it a point to get to know her doctors and nurses and talk to all of the people who were taking such great care of her. I wanted them to know how appreciative I was of their kindness and compassion.

I spent each night in Mom's room, waking up every couple of hours when the nurses came in to check on her. I kept thinking about all the times my mom had been there for me and the myriad ways she had contributed to me as a person, as a woman. I thought of her those many years ago wiping my nose and making me feel special. Even though I was exhausted, I was filled with contentment and love. I felt like this was my opportunity to give Mom all of the love I have for her in the sunset of her life. These are moments I rarely get, being so far away.

During the day I took on the role of advocate and became her voice since she couldn't speak. I could see she was in pain. Whenever the nurses moved her, she would wince and moan. The trachea tube down her throat bothered her and therefore it bothered me. I became Shirley MacLaine from *Terms of Endearment*. (Well, I never had to ratchet it up quite like she did in the movie, but I would have if it had become necessary!) I badgered and complained and hounded the nurses and doctors . . . until finally the doctors removed the tube. Mom instantly become calmer and looked relieved. I felt like I had shepherded her to the summit of Kilimanjaro—accomplishing something for her that she couldn't quite do for herself, getting her to a place where she could now begin to heal.

It was the day before Christmas Eve and I called Al to let him know I thought I'd be coming home soon. I felt as if I had been able to minister to my mom during a difficult time and the sun was slowly peeking over the horizon. It was time to get back home to my own family, who needed me too.

Throughout, Al was loving, patient and inherently understanding of my need to be by my mom's side. He assured me the kids were doing well and gave me peace of mind so I didn't feel torn about where to be. I needed this private time, uninterrupted and undisturbed. When Tina offered to relieve me at the hospital, I declined. I needed this time with Mom. Tina had always been there for doctor visits or emergencies; now I wanted to take a turn. I felt like at any moment it could be time to say good-bye; either way, it was a chance to be there for my mother in a time of difficulty, pain and crisis. And Al was my rock back home, making it possible.

I stayed at the hospital for seventy-two hours, leaving her room only to get a bite to eat or to take a quick shower at my hotel. Otherwise, I was right there, holding Mom's hand, telling her I loved her.

A few months after she left the hospital, we finally made the difficult decision to move Mom to a nursing home. She has remained in good hands at Summerhill for the past five years. Doretha and Tina are always right there, so Mom is never alone.

It has been beyond difficult. No matter what I'm doing, each day is filled with a bit of heaviness, thinking of Mom. Doretha keeps me updated, often texting me sweet pictures of Mom sitting in the morning sun. I smile, often through tears.

I steel myself for visits and minister to Mom as best I can, wheeling her into the nursing home garden, watching old reruns of *The Andy Griffith Show* in her room or taking her to the rec room for a game of bingo. I often bring Leila and Nicky with me. We'll bring Mom flowers or a new blanket or nightgown, little things that hopefully bring her some pleasure. Our visits can be long and boring for them, but I hope they're learning the beauty of caring for loved ones without expecting something in return.

At times Mom looks at me blankly, unsure of who I am. But other times, when I grab onto her soft, wrinkled hand, she will squeeze my hand back, and I am convinced she knows I am there. Her warm touch is . . . healing. These quiet moments feel quite powerful. I feel the true closeness I always craved from Mom. As she looks deep into my eyes, I feel that finally I have found that soul-to-soul connection I always longed for. Though she speaks very little now, Mom communicates her love for me. Words aren't necessary.

8

I Am Who I Am

Everyone Has Their Kombucha

Every guy has that one thing they obsess over, whether it's sports, the remote control or their car. For me, it's an amazing elixir called GT's Gingerade Kombucha. What is it? you ask. Kombucha is a fermented tea, thought to be Chinese in origin, that's said to be an antioxidant, probiotic, anti-inflammatory, digestive superfood. I can't attest to all that. All I know is . . . Daddy likes!

While Kombucha comes in a whole raft of flavors, my favorite is the Gingerade. It's naturally carbonated, like a pungent ginger ale, or maybe I should say ginger beer—there are actually trace amounts of alcohol in each bottle. In fact, early on GT realized the fermentation process was running amok and the beverage had as much alcohol as a low-alcohol beer! Can you imagine knocking back a couple at work? "Man, I feel great! Where has this Kombucha been all my life?" Meantime your coworkers are talking about you behind your back as you get wasted at your cubicle. Of course, it would cease to be funny if you had one or two bottles, then got in a car to drive home or pick up the kids at soccer practice.

Well, they stopped production to get a handle on the problem and a month or so later resumed making it. Interestingly enough, they've taken lemons and made lemonade . . . or hard lemonade, to be precise. The company now bottles the high-octane Kombucha in black bottles for purchase by those twenty-one years and older.

To liven up its ginger flavor even more, I like to add my own fresh ginger. I started with a tablespoon or so per bottle. Little by little I added more, so that today, I combine about one quarter cup of chopped ginger with a twelve-ounce bottle of Kombucha. I drink an average of four bottles of Kombucha a day and go through about ten pounds of ginger and two cases of Kombucha a week. Did I mention I like Kombucha?

For whatever reason, and I can't explain it, my love of Kombucha has caused quite a stir in our family. While I know they're very supportive and happy to see that I have taken control of my health by changing my diet, now they tease me about being addicted to Kombucha, like an addict who gives up drinking but takes up smoking!

DEBORAH

Everywhere we go, Kombucha comes with us. Al and I were at a parent-teacher conference and he pulled a bottle out of his bag and *pop*, twisted off the cap. It is an unmistakable sound, like a cork coming out of a bottle of champagne.

As soon as we get in the car, Al automatically opens a bottle. It's almost Pavlovian. His car has a cup holder, so I don't mind it as much, but my car doesn't. Whenever I hear that *pop*, I quickly say, "Not in the car!" because I don't want it to spill.

While he started off putting a little fresh ginger in to fortify the taste, he now adds so much ginger it's like "Have a little Kombucha with your ginger!"

It's a running gag in our house. It's like watching Al walk around with a pacifier; every time we look at him, there's that bottle. It's fine that he loves his Kombucha, really, but maybe he could rein it in—a little?

AL

My feeling is that if what I am doing isn't hurting my health or causing harm to my family, what's the problem?

I don't gamble, don't smoke cigars, stay home instead of hitting the links or the bars with the boys.

I have one vice.

One!

Kombucha.

Deal with it!

There are far worse things in life to worry about. If it makes me feel good and I'm not hurting you guys, just let me have my Kombucha!

And yet my love of Kombucha continues to rile everyone up because, of all things, it takes up too much space in the refrigerator. Why can't my bottles of Kombucha be lined up with the other, lesser liquids like juice and milk? And even if I move my Kombucha out of sight to the vegetable or fruit bin, just the *thought* of the Kombucha residing in the communal fridge drives my family to distraction.

So what did my dear wife do? She ordered a refrigerator just for my stash of Kombucha and fresh ginger and put it in the basement.

THE BASEMENT!

Seriously?

Now I'm like the guy who has to go out on the porch to smoke his cigars. Which, as I mentioned, I don't do!

Why should I have to go down a flight of stairs every time I want to quench my thirst just so my wife and children don't have to see my bottles of Kombucha?

Then it dawned on me. Just like the fine folks at GT's Kombucha took lemons and made lemonade, I suddenly saw this basement fridge as my new best friend. Why? Now I have *two* places to keep my beloved drink! I use the basement fridge to stock up on *more* Kombucha and *extra* ginger.

Maybe Deborah hit on something. Since we live in a four-story brownstone, maybe I should have a fridge on *every* floor, Kombucha within reach, no matter where I am in the house. Maybe I'll get one of those flying drones to deliver it to me, straight from the fridge.

Yesss!

And though I know my love of Kombucha grates on my family, for the most part, they have learned to back off and just let me have it—as long as they don't have to see the evidence in the form of bottle caps left on the kitchen counter or excess grated ginger. It isn't a lot to ask, so I do my best to be conscientious and oblige.

There are lots of things I can overlook and have been willing to bend on throughout my marriage.

Kombucha isn't one of them.

In many ways, we all have our "Kombucha."

For my wife, it's clothes and shoes.

At the end of the day, I am not going to change her obsession for shopping or hitting sample sales with a passion. She's not harming anyone, so what am I going to accomplish by coming after her for it?

Nothing.

I could easily go into her closet and pull out mounds of clothes she hasn't worn for a couple of years.

Me, I have two rules when it comes to clothes and shoes. For every one thing that comes in, one has to go out. Ties, shoes, suits, shirts, underwear (yes, contrary to popular belief, guys do buy new underwear at least once a decade, whether we need it or not)—all fall under that rule. The outgoing gets donated, while the incoming finds a nice, neat, orderly home. The other rule is, if I haven't worn it in a year, I don't really need it. Once a season I have the urge to purge.

Deborah, on the other hand, says that she becomes attached to the clothes, the shoes, the handbags. How can she get rid of them? It's like abandoning her children. Okay, that might be a bit of an exaggeration, but she does have attachment issues with these clothes. Although I could harp on her, make her feel guilty or barrage her with nonstop commentary on her fashion "hoarding," I don't.

Is that going to promote marital harmony?

What do you think?

Is it worth scoring some cheap jokes at my wife's expense if it will come back to bite me when I am trying to score that night?

Learning to accept, tolerate and love your partner's foibles maintains peace and harmony in your relationship. Those quirks are still going to grate on you, but don't let them break you. Instead of focusing on the negative, remember to look at the whole package—the big picture. There may be a couple of things that bug the crap out of you about the person you share a bed with, but guess what. At heart they're good—and anyway, no matter how much complaining you do, they're unlikely to change. And you wanna know something? You're no walk in the park either. So maybe, just maybe, if you cut your spouse some slack, they might return the favor.

THE ROKER FAMILY

Does This Sound Familiar?

LEILA

My dad is a really slow driver, which makes everyone in our family a little crazy. And my mom likes to tell everyone how to drive—even New York City cabdrivers. If they're not going the right way, you can bet she will let them know. And if she doesn't like how you're driving, she will correct you.

You see, my mom believes in short honks of the horn and Dad believes in one long honk. That pretty much sums up my parents in a nutshell.

Little things happen during most every family outing that inevitably create a silent car ride because my parents are mad at each other over their driving differences.

"Well, do you want to drive?" Dad asks.

"No, it's fine," Mom replies, even though we all know she's seething inside.

"Then I don't need to hear your comments," Dad snaps back.

DEBORAH

Whether it's Al driving too slowly or his aggressive response to other drivers, his behavior behind the wheel makes me nuts.

If another driver cuts you off—and I don't mean threatens your life, but maybe moves over—Al feels the need to beep the horn in that long, crass New York way—*HOOOOOONNNNK*. I know I am splitting hairs, but if someone does that to me, I simply go, *beep-beep*.

To me there is a difference.

Beep-beep means "watch it," as opposed to *HOOOONNNKK*, which means "I'm really pissed off."

I will say, "Honey, why did you do that?"

"That guy was about to kill me," Al dramatically replies.

When, in actuality, the car just moved slightly over into our lane.

AL

I have come to the simple conclusion that it's easier not to drive, especially if it's Deborah's car. I just don't want to drive anymore.

DEBORAH

Don't say another word!

AL

We fight every time I drive and therefore, you know what? I give in!

DEBORAH

Fight? We don't fight. I'd say . . . it's more of a skirmish.

AL

It annoys me.

LEILA

Pappers, you need to learn how to tune it out like I do. You internalize your feelings, and you shouldn't do that.

AL

I have to keep my mouth shut because it never stops. The picking is a constant part of my life. The only way to avoid the endless "tips," "suggestions" and gentle "corrections" is simply not to put myself in that position.

LEILA

Or you can just nod in agreement, say okay and do what you want anyway, like I do.

AL

No. That doesn't work when you're in a car. You see, when you're in a car, you've got no place to go. You're stuck. You can't walk out of the room, close your bedroom door and hide.

DEBORAH

Oh, Al. It's not like I'm yelling at you!

AL

No! It's worse. If it was only a moment of yelling or mere silence, it would be fine. It's the constant pick, pick, pick that never stops that I can't take!

LEILA

But you feel like that with everything! You think everyone does that to you. If someone brings a comment up more than once, they're picking on you.

AL

Exactly! The irony is that when I do it to you guys, you get upset and I stop and back off. You, on the other hand, keep coming at me and never let up.

DEBORAH

We're joking! Kidding around.

AL

Not when it comes to my driving!

LEILA

You just don't get our jokes.

AL

I'm a very funny guy. I have a great sense of humor! But when it comes to my driving, I *don't* get your jokes. "Why can't you speed up?" *That's* not funny!

LEILA

But you do drive really slowly! What I don't get is why you're always the one getting pulled over.

AL

Thank you, Leila. Way to have my back!

LEILA

You're like *Driving Miss Daisy,* whereas Mom could be in *The Fast and the Furious.*

AL
———

So, I take a little more conservative approach in the city than your mother does because I know how crazy the other drivers can be. I don't tailgate or push—

DEBORAH
———

Are you saying I tailgate?

LEILA
———

It's kind of embarrassing when you tell cabdrivers how to drive. I mean, it is *their* job . . .

DEBORAH
———

I'm giving them tips, suggestions.

LEILA
———

Have you ever seen a suggestion box in a cab?

DEBORAH
———

There are plenty of drivers who are *very* open to it. Some even say to me, "Sounds great!" or "That worked out very well."

AL
_____

Oh yeah? How many times?

LEILA
_____

Once.

DEBORAH
_____

A few.

AL
_____

A few? I don't think so! You're always coaching them to go, go, go . . . make the light, turn left, go through the park, don't go up Madison. . . . The drivers are usually a wreck by the end of the ride.

LEILA
_____

We did get into a wreck one time.

DEBORAH
_____

Yeah, the one time I was quiet in the backseat! Leila and I were both looking at our phones instead of paying attention to the driver.

Look, I am not abrasive with my tips. I am very friendly. Like today at Macy's. I made a suggestion to the salesgirl. I told her they needed a better system. She said, "You're right."

AL
_____

What is she going to say? She was trapped! She wanted to make sure you got out of the store and never came back!

DEBORAH
_____

I think she appreciated it.

LEILA
_____

Mom, nobody appreciates your tips except you.

DEBORAH
_____

As a citizen of the world, I feel it is my responsibility to help my fellow p—

LEILA
_____

A citizen *of the world*? Even you know that sounds ludicrous!

NICKY

Can you all please stop fighting?

DEBORAH

Nicky, we aren't fighting. We are just having a lively family discussion. . . .

NICKY

Well, it's a LOUD discussion!

AL

Ahhhh . . . Welcome to my world. When we get in the car, I turn to Deborah and hold out the keys and say, "Here you go . . ." I'm a much better passenger. Happier too. At least there are no arguments.

DEBORAH

Maybe I should try a day of no suggestions?

LEILA

I've never had one of those.

AL

Ooooh, listen . . . Is that a chorus of angels?

Anyone who has ever been in a relationship or who has kids has endured this kind of banter at one time or another. Being busted on by the ones we love just goes with the territory. When your relationship is strong and healthy and sits on a solid foundation, these types of exchanges won't create disharmony or bigger issues. They're rooted in love—deep love and appreciation for who we really are, flaws and all. You see, we all have our flaws. It's what makes us human and, yes, vulnerable. There's great strength in allowing that vulnerability to show from time to time. It's an unwritten rite of passage as a parent that your kids will make fun of you no matter how cool you think you are, how hip you try to be and how hard you work to hang on to the good ol' days when they couldn't (or wouldn't dare) tell you what they really think.

On the other hand, we want our children to go out into the world able to speak their minds—have a voice, share their opinions—even if we don't like what they have to say about our driving, how we dress, the music we listen to . . . They're expressing themselves in ways that will make them stronger, happier and better-adjusted young adults as they enter the real world. So like it or not, you're the litmus test that allows them to find their voice and discover their boundaries. Yeah, we know it's not always fun to be the guinea pig—but hey, someday they'll be in your shoes, as parents with kids who make fun of them, and you'll have the chance to just sit back, smile and think, "Ahhh . . . payback . . . it's a lovely thing!" Or as Al's mother and just about every other parent on the planet used to say, "Someday yours are going to do to you what you've done to me."

9

Can You Hear Me Now?

DEBORAH

How Do You Work This Thing?

It's no secret within my family and circle of friends that I am not entirely comfortable with technology. Given that, it was rather ironic that ABC News assigned me, along with the octogenarian Barbara Walters, to the digital committee and charged me with helping the network move forward in the digital age. Barbara had recently begun tweeting and was building a huge following. With the help of my energetic and sunny assistant, Laura, I was also beginning to tweet and had joined Facebook as a way of connecting with viewers who are now getting more and more of their news from their iPhones and tablets instead of their televisions.

Like so many of you, on any given day I am snapping pictures of an interview I am doing or of a snowstorm in New York and tweeting my thoughts on it, or doing my best to create Facebook posts that entice viewers to watch my upcoming stories on ABC. The idea, of course, is to connect with our viewers and make them a part of the story. It's also a way to stay relevant and to communicate with the younger audience these days. And according to my sixteen-year-old daughter, Leila, it makes me look hip and with it.

But the truth is, I am not all that interested in being hip or with it! I must confess that my participation in the digital world is somewhat against my will. I know I sound like an old fogy, but I find new technology exhausting. Yes, I enjoy sending my family a video of Nicky getting a new tae kwon do belt just seconds after he got it. And yes, I love checking my electronic calendar to make a doctor appointment while I am on the phone with the receptionist. But all the texting, apps and programming often leave me confused and stressed.

Life used to be pretty simple. TVs had only a few channels to choose from, people actually talked to one another on the phone and technology was something I found fascinating and possibly helpful—not draining!

I grew up bursting with excitement and feeling like endless possibilities were in front of me. But now, when everyone seems obsessed with the latest cool app or game and Leila complains in no uncertain terms that my Instagram pictures are so yesterday and that I need to check out Vine, I can't help but feel like I am living in the wrong era.

Okay, I will admit that I like getting reviews of a new restaurant or ordering a car service with the click of a finger, and as a mom of a tween and a teen, it makes life a lot easier! I can text Leila to remind her to take the dog for a walk if I am running late, or discreetly send Al an e-mail from a crash editing session for *20/20* to let him know I can't meet him as planned. When I hear the *swoosh* from my iPhone, I know my life just got a lot easier. That's the beauty of the digital age.

But while I accept the power of technology, I haven't totally embraced it. Let's start with the glitch factor, like when you think you've canceled a meeting and later find out that somehow your phone froze or the message bounced back and no one got the message you wouldn't be there as planned. And who hasn't accidentally pressed send before thoroughly checking the content of the message—or worse, without taking a beat to think about it? This can be embarrassing—or even close to disastrous.

Not long ago I was working with a producer on a story about children orphaned after losing both parents to HIV. We had traveled to Africa and back to interview kids who were bravely carrying on with their lives despite poverty and the heartbreak of losing their parents at such a young age. It was a powerful story, and I wanted to make sure we struck the right tone. My producer and I wrote the piece together, putting in long hours in the edit room to weigh in on the shots and the interviews that would be used.

There are some correspondents who leave the production work to their producers. But I like to be involved at every stage. I was feeling especially proud of my work on this particular story, so I decided to toot my own horn a bit when replying to a quick e-mail from my executive producer. I wrote how pleased I was with the piece as it was shaping up and then reminded him that I wrote a good portion of the story he was about to see. In no way did I mean to dis my producer, a talented and capable veteran at the network. I simply wanted to be recognized for my hard work on this major undertaking. Let's face it—women are often more reluctant than men to take credit for their work projects. So at that moment I was determined to own my efforts. Unfortunately, I realized that I had chosen "Reply All" rather than "Reply."

Ugh.

Not only would my executive producer receive my e-mail but my producer would as well.

Too late.

I had already pressed send.

It took only a couple of minutes before I had my first reply.

Yup. You guessed it.

It wasn't from my executive producer.

It was an angry e-mail from my producer suggesting that I was undermining and backstabbing him. My face burned with embarrassment as I realized that he was on the e-mail chain.

Stupid me!

Argh.

I spent the next thirty minutes on the phone with him, trying to undo this unintended damage.

The next day I even took him to lunch, apologizing profusely for how my words had sounded. It took some time, but we eventually got past the incident. To this day, I always double-check the "To" line on my e-mails . . . and even count to three before I press send.

Although I realize mistakes happen, all of the pressure can sometimes get to me. That's when I want to go home, put my feet up and just relax in the comfort of home. I miss the good old days when I walked into the house and saw the blinking red light on the answering machine in the kitchen announcing that I had messages waiting. There was something warm and cozy about knowing that with the push of a (clearly marked!) button, I could hear, "Hey, this is Mom. Just calling to say hey and see how ya doin'. Call me back."

Now I don't know how to retrieve messages on our home phone, so I never know who called or when! That's because it is a combination phone, clock, intercom system and maybe calculator too.

I secretly long for the early days in our marriage when I bought a VCR that I could program in the dark and that responded to "play" and "fast-forward" at the drop of a hat. Now I'm lucky to be able to turn on the television with the massive remote. I call our audiovisual system the "Starship *Enterprise*"—except in space, no one would be able to hear me scream. There are no machines, no tapes. We still have a few rogue DVDs lying around the house, but mostly we rely on Apple TV these days. And now add Netflix to the equation—just one more thing to make me feel like a high-tech failure. Turning on the TV has become a scary thing for me in our house, which is pretty embarrassing since I work in television!

Some days when I have a picture but no sound, I beg Nicky to come help. From the age of nine he could troubleshoot the system faster than a cable technician. There is an episode in the television comedy *Modern Family* where Claire Dunphy, the high-strung mom, is coming unglued because she can't figure out how to work the new remote control. The small gadget with its innumerable buttons could just as easily control an unmanned rocket as far as she's concerned. She can't get the TV on, and once she does, she can't figure out how to adjust the volume. She soon tosses the remote at the TV and storms out of the room in frustration. I am Claire.

Al just had our remote consolidated into an iPad. "This will be easier and cooler," he said.

Of course, deep down, I knew it wouldn't.

On the very first day after we made the transition, I wanted to watch *Good Morning America* while doing a short workout before heading to the office. I love catching Robin and the gang before work. I grabbed the gleaming iPad from the console table and swiped with confidence. Myriad icons popped up.

"House," "Local," "Audio," "Apple TV," "DVR," "DVD."

I just wanted an "on" button.

There was none to be found.

I tried several combinations, thinking, "It can't be this hard."

Suddenly the big-screen TV was ablaze with family vacation photos. "Aww, there's Nicky smiling on the beach."

Nice, but I wanted to watch *GMA*, not reminisce about family vacations.

So I tried another random combination of swipes and pokes.

Now I was faced with a blank screen—no icons at all.

Uh-oh.

Finally, I spotted a small button labeled "Power."

Bingo!

There was Robin laughing with George Stephanopoulos.

All right, I thought, maybe technology isn't so bad.

After my workout, when I attempted to turn off the TV so I could get to work, pressing the power button didn't work. Then I realized the iPad battery was running low.

Argh! Maybe that was the problem.

I quickly plugged it into the charger while I showered and got dressed. When it was time to try again, I searched the icons, looking for the almighty power button—but it was now gone.

No!

After a few frantic moments I was prepared to launch the iPad, Claire Dunphy–style, at the TV. I gave the iPad one last desperate swipe and finally found the power button. The TV was finally off. I'm not sure I will ever want to turn it on again.

My kids are embarrassed that something so simple can be so hard for me and that I don't speak their digital language. They roll their eyes and tell me I am holding on to the past. Yes, I am . . . by my fingernails. But come on, life just felt calmer a few years ago. Their world is all about choices . . . so many choices.

Should I order the skirt on this site or that one?

Want to download a movie on Apple TV?

You're wrong about that, Mom. . . . I know 'cause I just Googled it.

Argh!

Call me a Luddite, but when I listen to music, I want to put in the CD and play the whole thing.

Today, Leila wouldn't be caught dead without a playlist on her iPhone. Even Nicky is strutting to One Direction, Katy Perry and Usher on his iPad!

How about Alicia Keys or Barry White, anyone?

For a full forty minutes?

Growing up I liked talking to my friends on the phone, and it never seemed like a burden to have to call them up if we wanted to get together. Plus, it meant we had to learn how to talk to adults if we wanted to talk to our friends, because their parents always answered the phone first. Yes, sometimes I hung up when Mrs. Ingram answered . . . or I hemmed and hawed uncomfortably for thirty seconds before she put Denise on the phone . . . but I learned how to exchange a sentence with an adult.

Leila only texts her friends.

I once asked her to actually call one of her friends instead of text.

"Why would I do that?" Leila asked. "Then I would have to speak to her mom."

My point exactly.

Al has less trouble with the digital world than I do. His iPhone is practically glued to his head. Even when he goes to the bathroom in the middle of the night, I can see the soft glow of the blue light while he checks e-mails. Am I the only one who finds this crazy? He tries to disconnect and unplug from technology when we are together as a family, but truthfully, he has become obsessed with his phone and being connected at all times.

My husband is an information addict. He likes to know things for the sake of knowing, whether it's important or not. He sleeps with his phone next to the bed and even if he's sleepwalking, he will pick it up in the middle of the night to see if he has missed a headline or a breaking news story. If it's weather related, I get it. But if it's another YouTube cat video or a headline about an actor who was just fired from a movie . . .

Put the phone down!

I've never been bold enough to actually swipe Al's phone, but I've been known to "accidentally" place the newspaper over it once or twice, making him less aware of where it was for a while.

Lately I have been trying to persuade my family to try "unplugged Sundays". . . or at the very least rally behind an electronic-free zone during the dinner hour and actually have a conversation with one another. Leila has a blinking strobe light that alerts her every time she gets a text—which is about every twenty seconds or so. Nicky just got his first phone. We held off for as long as we could. And of course there's the iPad. And when we haven't seen him for an hour or so . . . guess where he is. In a corner texting or playing some game! I know we can't fight the future, but I want my kids to know that life can be satisfying without gadgets on all the time.

Whether it's schoolwork, rushing to activities or just normal teenage angst, kids seem to feel a lot of stress today. So as they make their way into adulthood, I am determined to help my children learn to slow down and quiet their minds. Leila says I sound too New Agey sometimes, but I am convinced they can find a different level of happiness if they learn not only the value of technology but the value of escaping it too. Even President Obama has mentioned the need to unplug—so I know I'm in good company.

Not long ago I did a story for *World News Tonight* about the brain-soothing effects of nature. Diane Sawyer loves stories on emerging science and was excited for me to explore a new study that suggested reasons to put down our devices. It seems that dopamine, the happy chemical in the brain, is released during even a short, fifteen-minute walk amid nature. Yes, an infusion of trees and chirping birds can substitute for an antidepressant! Our brain, frazzled by all the multitasking, actually calms and sends positive feedback when we make time to turn everything off and go for a walk in a garden or in the park. Even a walk among pictures of nature scenes showed a release of dopamine in the brain!

So, clearly I am not completely out of my mind to nag my family about silencing the phones and tablets for a short time here and there. I am convinced that I am happier and more focused with my family when I step away from my devices too. My mood lifts and I am more patient. I even feel better physically when I am not in the midst of information overload.

Wouldn't life be a bit more peaceful and pleasant not knowing every single development the second it happens? This may sound crazy coming from a journalist, but I am as stressed as everyone else, and the influx of constant information hypes me up even more. I will learn about the latest murder, political scandal or plane crash soon enough. But for a couple of hours here and there, I want to free my mind. I think our lives would be more peaceful, relaxing and interesting without all of these interferences.

Somehow this burning desire to always feel connected has created a giant level of disconnection that has infected so many of us like a sweeping virus. I look around restaurants and see tables of friends or a family sitting together and not saying a word to one another because they all have their noses in their phones. No one even looks at each other! And worse, no one seems bothered by it. Whatever happened to actually talking to people at dinner?

Genuine communication is about the words we speak—not the words we type or the sentences we can tap out in 140 characters or less. I am deeply proud of my Twitter followers, and I appreciate a quick text to say "I love you," but I hope it doesn't come to replace the beauty of actually hearing those words from the person who is sending them. I want my children to know the difference between the two. In the meantime, I keep lobbying for "unplugged Sundays," when we all agree to put down the phones, iPads, and any other distracting technology and focus on books, museums and simply being with one another . . . but so far I don't have any takers.

AL

Antisocial Media

I saw a sign at a café the other day that said, "No Wi-Fi. Talk to Each Other! Call Your Mom. Pretend it's 1993. Live."

Pretty good advice when you think about it.

In a sense, I am a schizophrenic lover of technology. I embrace it and yet I'm annoyed by it too. Once you open the box, you can't close it.

I still love the way turning the page of a book feels as opposed to the finger swipe across the screen of my iPad or Kindle. I know it's often easier and more convenient to read on a device, but I don't think you comprehend the material in the same way as you do when you physically connect with the paper. (Studies support this!)

There's just something kind of special about holding a book in your hand or putting a pen to paper rather than connecting to an electronic device. Somehow, you are transported to a time and dimension electronics can't take you.

We've come to a place in society where our communication has been limited—if not stunted to 140 characters or less, certainly condensing emotion and meaning to a minimum. As a result, we've inadvertently created a world of Short Attention Span Theater.

What's the rush?

Is everyone so busy and important in their own lives that we've lost our ability to actually talk to the people who matter to us—whether coworkers, friends or family?

We are living in a weird time.

People no longer talk to one another.

We "chat."

We "text."

We "Instagram."

Not long ago, I drove Leila and two of her friends to a party and none of them said a word the entire way. They were all on their phones. This seemed odd for a car full of teenage girls. In my day, girls were giggly, chatty and always talking. As I drove in silence, I simultaneously felt very current and very old.

God only knows what is going to be out there in the next ten years. If you have kids who are five or six years old right now, good luck to you. I have no idea what you will be faced with and I'm glad I won't have to deal with it because my kids will be out of my house by then. They will probably have ocular implants giving them displays on their retinas. Phones will be grafted into their ear canal, and they will be able to make a call just by touching their temple. And Lord knows where the paper will come out when they blink "print" on their retinal display.

I can barely deal with the social media outlets we have today!

As the dad of a preteen, a teenager and a millennial, one of the most important lessons I try to convey to them is that the Internet is forever. Once something's posted on the Web, it is there for all time, whether true or false. And believe me when I say that your prospective colleges and employers will be Googling your online presence. Do you think those Facebook or Instagram photos of you on spring break that your folks don't know about are going to help advance your cause? And you'd better hope no one sees those shots of you on bootycall.com!

It's great that there's a lot of information out there in the world readily available and accessible at our fingertips. My daughter's teachers all have their own Web sites and use them to give homework assignments. Schools are pushing kids to the Internet to study, research and explore.

But here's a news flash for you.

Just because something is on the Internet doesn't mean it's true!

Here are a couple of gems about me!

I am a big amateur jam maker.

No!

David Letterman gave me my big break.

NO!

Yet these two tidbits appeared on my Wikipedia page for the longest time as *fact*.

The possibility of removing something once it's online ranges from very, very, very difficult to flat-out impossible. So, if you post a photo of yourself looking like a fool, just remember, it will remain there for everyone you work with today, might work with tomorrow or may work with in the future to see! And just in case you thought everything was safe in the cloud? Forget about it. Think about how many celebrities have had their sexy photos hacked from the cloud! Nothing is safe. My best advice is not to post anything, ever, that you wouldn't want your grandma to see!

Speaking of work, if you're on LinkedIn and you want to connect with me . . . please don't!

Leave me alone.

I know that experts tell you to reach out to people you don't know and ask them to connect with you, but don't! They're wrong! I don't want to help you. I would rather have enough time to help people I know. It's not that I am being rude or that I don't care about you—okay, maybe I don't care about you; but I don't know you!

And for those I do know: stop e-mailing so much. If you want my help, pick up the phone and ask for it. I don't want to spend time reading an e-mail, which you obviously think is very important to me.

IT'S NOT!

Like I have nothing else to do with my day than read your eight-paragraph e-mail about your career woes and then take the time to respond?

And then you have to respond back to me.

And then I respond back to you.

And before you know it, we are in a pitiful Ping-Pong match of e-mails!

No!

Don't do it!

CALL ME!

We can take care of whatever it is you need in ten minutes.

And while I am on this roll, let's talk about Twitter.

I like Twitter because it's efficient and to the point. It's also why I like Vine. Six seconds and you're out. But don't mistake this for communication. I still prefer a good old-fashioned phone call. I prefer hearing the sound of a friend's laugh over reading "LOL." There is no comparison between real emotion and a symbolic emoticon.

Deborah would rather text than talk on the phone—at least with me. My father used to take breaks in his day as a bus driver, stop at a phone booth and make it a point to call my mother and check in a couple of times a day, so I was raised with the mentality that this is what good husbands are supposed to do. But whenever I make superfluous check-in calls to my wife, it annoys her.

To be fair, I usually call about the time my day is done and she is smack in the middle of her day. I get that she is busy working and my intention isn't to bother her. I am merely letting her know I am thinking about her.

"Just text me," she says. So now, that's what I do.

I get it. I myself hate feeling like I have to respond to a text just because someone sent one to me—especially right away. I get a text from one of my kids, and if I don't respond immediately, I get a second text that says, "Hello???" Sorry. Life doesn't work that way. I am not on your schedule. I am not your monkey trained to respond every time you text.

And I can't stand all of the abbreviations.

I've taken the time to decipher them so I know what my kids and their friends are saying; I just hate them. It's a truncating of language that is already in danger of disappearing. If you send me a message with letters instead of words, I will not respond. *BRB, TTYL, IRL*—none of that works for me. I don't want to decipher what you mean. Speak English—because I have paid for a really good education and I don't want to feel like an idiot! We are already suffering from a diminution of the English language, and kids are having trouble writing essays because they can't think beyond 140 characters anymore.

While I will admit that I actually like taking pictures—with a real camera—if I ever find the guy who put the camera in the cell phone, I am going to kick his ass. I don't care how old he is—I am going to beat the crap out of him.

People are missing out on so much of life because they're too busy documenting every last second of it through the camera on their phone.

"This is what I had for breakfast."

Click.

Ooh, thanks for sharing that picture of your bacon and eggs with me. LIKE I'VE NEVER SEEN THAT BEFORE! If you're going to share a meal, it had better damn well be spectacular or really out of the ordinary.

"Here's the view out the window of my airplane."

Click.

Wow. There had better be aliens or unicorns out there on the wing, or at least a beautiful sunset or amazing cloud formation. Come on, people.

"Here's a picture of my daughter's first poop!"

Click.

REALLY?

Too much information!

When we host concerts on the plaza at the *Today* show, I am always amazed by the number of people who watch the concert through the three-inch screen on their phone (or even worse, their iPad. How stupid does that look? And thanks for blocking *my* view with *your* iPad!). They're recording it instead of actually being in the moment and taking in the show that's happening right in front of them. It's as if they're not even there. Somehow, the advent of the camera in our phones has created a social disconnect that worries me. Take your face out of your phone and look at me.

LOOK AT ME!

Don't hide behind your phone.

I hate it when people use their phone as a shield of protection.

I've got news for you. No matter what material your phone is made out of, it isn't going to protect you from the wrath of a pissed-off father—ever.

Listen, texting is great for some things, like "Can you pick up milk on your way home?" I've even grown to appreciate it for sending an occasional "I love you" when Deborah or my kids aren't expecting it. But recently, my oldest daughter's boyfriend sent me a text.

"Mr. Roker, I would like to talk to you about Courtney and me moving in together."

"Dude, NOT A CONVERSATION FOR TEXT. PLEASE CALL" was my response.

About a minute later, my phone rang.

It wasn't the boyfriend. It was Courtney.

"Dad, why are you yelling at Anthony?"

I explained that I wasn't yelling. How could I be yelling OVER TEXT!

I suppose to some people, texting in capital letters means you're yelling, but to me it's just emphasizing. I told Courtney it would have been nice to get a little heads-up from her that she was thinking about moving in with her boyfriend before I heard it from him—through a text.

Here's a little advice for anyone out there who thinks texting about important matters is okay.

If you plan to:

quit your job

ask for your girlfriend's hand in marriage

ask for time off from your boss

ask for a divorce

fight with your wife, girlfriend, kids

anything that is life-changing or important . . .

Don't do it over text.

Take my word on this.

You will regret it.

Hiding behind a text or an e-mail has not only killed personal communication but facilitates passive-aggressiveness. How many times have you sent a text or an e-mail to someone knowing they weren't around so you could avoid the hard questions or a conversation you just don't want to have?

We've all done it!

I had an agent who was in many ways a wonderful guy, but he was pretty old-school. While he had embraced technology, as he got older, his crotchetiness had taken on a strident tone and his e-mails could come off like drone missile strikes. There was one so devastating that I feared for my career at NBC. It so infuriated my then boss, Jeff Zucker, that I thought I was going to lose my job. Jeff was livid, and I couldn't blame him. When I saw the e-mail, all I could think about was the famous *Seinfeld* "Shrinkage" episode, where things get taken out of context. The tone and nuance he was trying to convey were completely lost. And that's the biggest problem with any type of electronic communication; lacking tone of voice, facial expression or context, they're incredibly subject to misinterpretation. That was the closest I ever came to being fired (that I know of!). Everyone involved in my career needed to get together for a face-to-face meeting to address the e-mail and clear the air. Thankfully, we were able to calm down the situation at NBC, but I realized it was time to move on when my agent didn't really see the error of his ways. He couldn't grasp that what might be acceptable in a phone call just comes off differently in an e-mail.

We all have a tendency to respond to e-mails quickly—like there's a race to see who can reply the quickest. When you do that, there's great potential for misinterpretation.

Bam!

You knock out a knee-jerk response and the person on the other end, who might have understood if you'd spoken face-to-face, is now royally pissed.

I have learned that with e-mail, as in life, it is always best to take a moment, an hour or even a day before responding to something emotional. Come back, take a look at the e-mail and make sure it reads exactly right—that it responds the way you really want to, with the right words and the right tone. There have been many occasions I've come back and reread my saved draft and said, "Never mind."

What might feel good in the moment usually becomes a lengthy period of regret for just a morsel of satisfaction, an unnecessary zinger or getting in the last word.

Life can't be expressed in 140 characters. As much as we have all come to rely on the convenience and ease our electronic devices offer us for communication (I'm guilty of it), there will never be a better way to connect with loved ones than being with them. Show them how much they matter through your words and actions, not your emoticons.

10

Learning to Slow Down

DEBORAH

Taxicab Therapy

#MiamiMornings Cabbing it out round town since 8 am because I'm bored! On some "taxi driver be my shrink for the hour, leave the meter running" type s**t #WhereAmIEvenGoing

Rihanna Tweet August 12, 2013

By now it's probably clear that I have a special bond with New York City cabdrivers. If I am not involved in some kind of conversation with them, the ride just feels sort of empty.

Over the years of living in New York, I've discovered that cabdrivers are some of the greatest psychiatrists and philosophers. That twenty-minute ride can be better than a therapy session, and cheaper too. Many a time have I gotten into a cab driven by a great conversationalist with provocative views on politics or life. We might talk about the driver's home country or what it's like to be a female cabdriver, or who should be the next president or the mayor of our great city. Cabdrivers are often a kind of touchstone—straightforward, plainspoken and honest. As a reporter and a Southerner, I appreciate that.

Once, I was running very late for a lunch meeting and the driver could see I was agitated in the backseat; I was looking at my watch every few seconds and straining my neck to check the traffic. I could see him staring back at me in his rearview mirror, which made me even more uncomfortable. Finally he said, "You've got to breathe, because at the end of the day, it's not about this stuff."

He told me about his children who were now in college and how happy he was to have come to this country from the Middle East, where he could work at often backbreaking jobs in order to make a better life for his family. Suddenly my lunch at an expensive Manhattan restaurant didn't seem so important. As we talked, I found myself relaxing with every click of the meter.

"You've got to breathe. I can see you back there. You're not breathing!" he'd say periodically while telling me his story.

Twelve minutes later, as I reached my destination, I left the cab feeling so much better. I felt more gentle, compassionate and grateful for my life, pressured as it is.

You never know where you will find little pearls of wisdom or moments of inspiration throughout the day. They're hard to come by in New York City, for sure—but they do come. It all boils down to your attitude and openness to receiving these messages of positivity.

Life is fast.

Especially if, like me, you're a career mom juggling family, deadlines and travel. On any given day I am getting children off to school, working logistics for school plays and competitions, doing interviews and editing, maybe giving a speech and, if I'm lucky, squeezing in a run through Central Park or a quick workout at the gym.

Whew!

Like most people, I need reminders from time to time to slow down and check myself.

If not, life will pass me by—and what a shame that would be.

And usually, just when I need it most, God offers a moment of humility. Not long ago, I rushed out of my office to flag a cab because I was late to do an interview.

"Excuse me," a woman's voice said. "Is this Columbus Avenue?"

I noticed her white guide stick and realized she was blind.

I said, "Yes," and offered my elbow to help her cross the street.

"Thanks a lot," she said with a smile, and was soon on her way.

Suddenly my stress over being late didn't feel as important or urgent. I truly believe that God puts people or circumstances in our path to keep us in a spirit of grace.

Even jarring New York moments like the angry man who banged on my window because he didn't like the way I was driving on Sixth Avenue, or the homeless man who is always plopped on the sidewalk near my local coffee shop with a sign saying "Will make you a hat for money" or the news of a colleague who was laid off in a round of downsizing—there are so many events in life that remind me to be in the moment and to count my blessings. I am aware that for all my stresses and disappointments, I have a good, fulfilling and happy life and that so many people have it much harder.

As my wise makeup artist Nancy said one day when I was complaining about a babysitter, "Those are *uptown* problems."

And she was right.

Not a single day goes by that I don't realize how blessed I am. Reporting the news means focusing largely on the negative, on episodes of violence or evil in this world. But there is often something redemptive to be found. I've interviewed a despondent mom whose son was killed in an accidental shooting, an African teenager who lost both parents and yet found the strength to excel in college, and a brave woman who lost her leg in the Boston marathon bombing, yet found the resilience and courage to not just walk but also run again! These are people of spirit and inspiration!

Sure, I've covered some things I wish I'd never encountered. Recently I was shaken up by my interview with a woman in prison who had tried to hire a contract killer to murder her boyfriend. And I still recall my rattled nerves while covering the Persian Gulf conflict, between the bomb sirens and walking through an active minefield. But just as my dad told me then, I always feel God beside me on this journey. I say a prayer when taking off for an assignment or before I go on the air for a live report, believing that God will guide me in all things. Thanks, Dad, for the reminder that I never walk alone. And, of course, if I get distracted or find myself momentarily harried, there's always a good cab therapy session, which sends me on my way with pep in my step, reminded that life is indeed good and I have much to be thankful for.

DEBORAH AND AL

Oh! Christmas Tree

AL

Each year around Christmas, we do our best to get into the holiday spirit. Deborah is especially fond of setting the tone by playing Nat King Cole albums—over and over. Many years ago, she got the wonderful idea that we should plan a family outing to cut down our own Christmas tree instead of buying one in the city like we usually did. I agreed it sounded like a great adventure.

DEBORAH

It was a classic December weekend, crisp and cold beneath a clear blue sky. That Saturday morning felt like the perfect day to get in the holiday mood and find just the right Christmas tree. I could already smell the fresh scent of pine as we headed out to our weekend home in upstate New York. We were all bundled up in our warm wool hats and scarves. Within an hour we had left our hurried and hectic world behind and were walking along the narrow paths of a huge Christmas tree farm.

Our first challenge was deciding what kind of tree we wanted.

A Fraser fir or a Virginia fir?

Long needles or short ones?

Tall and narrow or average and wide?

Who knew there was so much to think about in selecting a Christmas tree?

The choices were dizzying. As a result, Al and I had trouble agreeing on the perfect tree.

You see, we had never discussed our personal preferences, which meant a certain, um, escalating difficulty coming to a final decision.

Like a lot of couples before us, we'd soon learn a valuable lesson in the art of communication.

'Tis the season!

I tried to explain that when I was growing up, we usually had a small Virginia fir. That's before my parents gave in to the idea of saving money with an artificial tree (including a glittery silver tree we had for a few years back in the seventies).

Each year, as I run my fingers through those prickly, compact needles, I drift back to a time of wonder in my small Georgia home. That dazzling scent of fir was usually complemented by the fragrance of Mom's cakes and pies baking in the oven and the sound of laughter that always filled our small kitchen. That's how I knew Christmas was officially under way!

So as Al, Leila and I wandered the tree farm that day, I was partial to the Virginia fir for sentimental reasons. Once I shared my childhood memories with Al, of course, he finally gave in.

When we found a row of trees we liked, the man at the farm handed us a saw and said, "Here you go." Somehow I thought he was going to help us, but he quickly disappeared into the sea of green branches. I looked at Al, and he at me.

"Okay!" I said, holding the trunk while Al sawed.

Leila, who had just turned three years old, was running around in circles, singing and laughing, playing hide-and-seek behind the rows of trees, having a wonderful time.

"Fa la la la la, la la, la la," I caught myself singing.

AL

The temperature had dipped quite a bit while we looked for the perfect tree. And though we had hats and scarves, for whatever reason, we didn't bring gloves. That was our first huge mistake when it came time to saw down our tree. Soon my frozen hands were killing me from the back-and-forth motion of cutting through the thick base of the tree. When it finally fell over, some of the needles clipped me across the face, and in the commotion, we lost Leila somewhere among the thick brush. Luckily, she wasn't far, but for a moment I was panicked. I grabbed her in one arm and our tree in the other and began dragging it over to our car, wishing we had a minivan.

"Where is that tree man?" I thought to myself.

Actually, I was thinking something far worse, but this is a PG-rated book.

Deborah and I struggled and tugged until we finally reached the car with our prize. What had started out as a fun family outing had quickly become an arduous excursion that had put me in a pretty rotten mood.

DEBORAH

The tree was unwieldy and I couldn't feel my hands anymore in the biting cold. I jumped in the car, started up the engine and blasted the heat to warm up. Al, with his sore hands, was doing his best to hoist our large tree over the top of the car and tie it up. At this point, we all just wanted to get home. Al was crabby, and Leila was now cold and crying. I wasn't sure who was being a bigger baby! It wasn't the joyful experience I had envisioned when we left the city that morning.

Once we were all settled back into the vehicle, we drove in silence most of the way home. Surprisingly, the tree stayed on top of the car—which is where it stayed for the rest of the day, even after we parked, until Al could bring himself to cut it down and set it up in our house. Not exactly a Bing Crosby moment.

We vowed to never cut down our own Christmas tree again!

And that was fine by me.

All was not lost, though; there was still plenty of holiday spirit left in our home. Our new family Christmas activity going forward would become decorating the tree!

Not so fast.

Yes, when our kids were younger, decorating the tree together was a fun and festive activity we all looked forward to doing. However, the older they've gotten, the harder it has been to keep that Christmas cheer going. These days, Leila will grudgingly participate while blasting Beyoncé and Drake through her earbuds instead of "White Christmas" or "Jingle Bells." She's far more focused on texting her friends than on placing ornaments. And Nicky is definitely more interested in playing video games than he is in handling tinsel. But whether they want to or not, I like to get the Christmas carols going on the speakers, light a roaring fire and try to create another holiday memory around the tree.

Oh well. At least I get to hold on to those moments with the hope and wish that someday they might look back on these days and nights with the same fondness that I have.

Being from large families, Al and I both have a deep love for the Christmas season. Trimming the tree and, especially, having our children near us still create feelings of wonder around the holidays. In my heart, Santa is as real as ever and the spirit of fun and laughter is everlasting.

AL

I harken back to the days when Leila was barely two years old and for the first time was helping us hang ornaments on our Christmas tree. Everything for her was low-hanging fruit because she couldn't reach any higher! Chipper and excited, she'd do her best to place an ornament on a branch and we would hear, *crash!* One by one, the glass ornaments were shattered in tiny pieces on the ground. But it was so sweet because it was Leila's first time decorating the tree and she loved it and therefore we loved it. Unfortunately, Deborah hates my taste in Christmas ornaments. In fact, she once told me that she was embarrassed by the carton of plain brown balls I scored from the drugstore. She was convinced that if we had people over, my balls "would ruin the look of the tree."

DEBORAH

It's true. I can't stand Al's balls!

You see, while Al would be content with buying boxes of plastic ornaments and throwing them up on the tree, I love the special home-made kind and the ornate, specially crafted keepsakes we've collected over the years. I have ornaments from my days in Georgia, Florida and Tennessee, all places I lived before moving to New York. Every single one has significance and meaning. They spark memories and warm my heart. I don't know why this is important to me, but it is, and I wish Al felt the same way.

AL

You would think that I would have learned my lesson from chopping down that tree so many years ago, that I would never return to the scene of the crime unless I was absolutely forced to under duress or by threat of something worse—no Christmas tree at all. And that is exactly what nearly happened in December of 2013.

It was the weekend before Christmas and Nicky and I were heading to our home in upstate New York ahead of Deborah and Leila, with the idea of giving the ladies a few days in the city together and us guys a few days in the country to hang out. Our only mission was to get the Christmas tree for the house. Again, we didn't discuss this idea very much beforehand, which would lead to trouble later on.

The next morning Nicky and I got up with one thing on our minds. The tree.

The only question?

Fraser fir or a balsam?

Perhaps a Norway spruce?

Oh, right.

I've seen this movie.

We went to our local nursery, where we usually have great luck. When I pulled into the parking lot, I stopped short and stared with my mouth open, aghast. The lot, usually lined with trees of all different types and heights, was empty. Not a tree. Not a wreath. No roping. Nothing! For half a second I thought, "Are we in a time warp? Did we miss Christmas?"

I went into the shop and must've looked like a crazy man. "Where are all your trees? What happened?"

The nice lady inside explained they'd ordered fewer trees this year since they got stuck with a lot of leftovers last year. They had sold out of everything a week ago.

"No problem," I thought.

There was another nursery across the street. So off we went.

Uh-oh.

They were also completely sold out.

It's beginning not to feel a lot like Christmas.

That's when I knew I had to call Deborah with the news.

A lot of times when I call home, one of the kids will pick up the phone. When I ask to speak to Deborah, I usually hear my wife in the background saying, "Just find out what he wants." If I wanted to convey a message without speaking to her, I would have just sent an e-mail! Things get lost in the translation when I speak through one of the kids. And this time was no exception.

What I said to Courtney was, "Bad news. I've been to the usual places and so far everyone is sold out. I am about to go to one more store. If they don't have one, I am going to go cut down my own. Tell Deborah what's happening and that I'll check in as soon as I can with an update."

DEBORAH

Al generally calls me several times a day. Usually, he's just checking in to say, "Hi, how's it going?" So when I am busy chopping vegetables or about to take Pepper for a walk, I will ask the kids to take a message so I can finish up what I'm doing. If it's important, naturally I'll pick up. But I guess important is in the eye of the beholder, right? This time I should've picked up the phone. Instead I relied on Courtney's relayed version of events.

"Dad's got a problem," she said. "He sounds stressed because he can't find a tree." So, of course, I got upset. I had no idea he didn't have things under control.

Earlier in the week I had suggested that we ask a friend of ours to locate a tree for us or that Al should call the nursery that sells trees and reserve one. Despite my pleas, he insisted it wouldn't be a problem.

"No trees? What do you mean there are no trees?" I said when Courtney delivered the news.

Christmas was only a few days away. Given our disastrous tree hunt years ago, it didn't occur to me that Al was going to head back to the cut-your-own-tree place!

AL

———

I hadn't forgotten about the last time we had gone to cut our own Christmas tree. But now that we were in this bind, I looked at this as an opportunity for a do-over. I was actually looking forward to it, an adventure with my son. The first time, we weren't properly prepared. We weren't wearing boots or gloves, there was snow on the ground, Deborah and I were sniping at each other and we briefly lost Leila! That was the antithesis of the wonderful cut-your-own-tree experience Nicky and I were about to have. I would make sure of it!

Given the elevation of our upstate home and the usually frigid temperatures, we almost always end up with a white Christmas. There's normally at least three to six inches on the ground by the time we arrive for the holidays.

That was not the case in 2013. It was a record-setting brutal winter, but there was a three-week period of pretty mild weather leading up to Christmas. So it was an incredible *sixty-five* degrees when Nicky and I headed out in search of the perfect tree. I was in my best *Everybody Loves Raymond* look: jeans, a checkered shirt over a short-sleeve T-shirt. And this time I had all of the proper gear. It was fantastic! Best of all, it was dirt cheap! Cheaper than any tree I'd ever bought. I wanted to buy two.

Nicky and I each had a bow saw and walked leisurely around, debating the pros and cons of the different trees we saw. Eventually, we agreed on a terrific eight-footer. Unlike the last time, my hands weren't freezing, my feet weren't blocks of ice in the snow and I was enjoying this special time with my son. We were laughing and pretending to be lumberjacks in a great Canadian forest.

"Timber!" Nicky called out as the tree tumbled to the ground.

Our tree was a beauty!

And the best part was that we'd cut it down ourselves.

"I'm doing this every year!" I said to Nicky, as we both stood there for a moment, taking great pride in what we had just accomplished together. We even taped a selfie video of the entire experience and texted it to Deborah.

All in all, it was a really good day!

DEBORAH

I'll admit, I should've called Al back right away. But I assumed that I knew exactly what was going on: Al was miserable and panicked, we had no tree, and I needed to do what I usually do—jump into action. I am nothing if not a problem solver! I was going to have to save the day and rescue Christmas! Of course, not only was I stressed out over the lack of tree, but I was even more annoyed at Al! Hadn't I asked him to take care of the tree earlier in the week? Leila and Courtney rolled their eyes along with me as we all agreed that Dad had really messed this one up.

I began calling shopkeepers and neighbors near our place upstate to see if someone had a line on a Christmas tree for us. Finally I found Peter, the cheerful owner of an outdoor retail store not far from where we live. I pleaded with him to help me find a nursery or a group of Cub

Scouts who had Christmas trees for sale. He promised to call me back shortly. Two minutes later, bingo! Not only had he located a tree, but he offered to deliver it to our garage to save Al and me the trouble. What a great guy. Christmas was saved!

Relieved, I called Al right away with the good news, privately gloating how it took a woman to turn a near catastrophe around. Once again, it was Mommy to the rescue. So I was flabbergasted by his chipper tone.

"We don't need a tree. We got one! Look at your e-mail," Al offered in a matter-of-fact tone.

I had been so busy tracking down a tree I hadn't checked my messages for an hour. When I looked at my phone and saw Al's e-mail, I was stunned. There was a photo of him and Nicky grinning and high-fiving as they showed off a beautiful Virginia fir. They were having a great time and even sent a little video of the two of them growling in excitement like two mountain men. I didn't know if I should laugh or cry.

"It's the holidays! Chill out! It's all fine. I'm a lumberjack, and guess what? I'm okay!" Al said, quoting Monty Python.

AL

Deborah was seriously annoyed until she realized what a great time Nicky and I had had. The holidays can be a hectic time and can bring out the anxious side in all of us. I have found the secret to getting through the harried and trying moments is to remember that things have a way of working out. Even when someone has a full head of steam and the temper train has left the station, just take some deep breaths and let them vent until the moment passes.

Sometimes the most unexpected moments produce the very best memories, even—or should I say, especially—during the holidays. When things don't go the way you planned, be open and be flexible. They might turn out even better!

I hadn't planned on cutting down my own tree, but there we were, smelling the fresh pine, with sap all over my hands and pants and loving every minute of it. It doesn't get more authentic than that. Nicky had a great story to tell his friends, and we had an amazing father-son experience doing something neither of us will ever forget.

The best part of all?

This time I had a minivan and didn't have to strap that damn tree to the roof!

DEBORAH

Al and I learned a lesson about the importance of communication. Or I certainly did, anyway. If I had simply taken Al's call or if we had thoroughly discussed our feelings about either buying a tree or getting it ourselves, we could've avoided a stressful afternoon. I also learned that the two words "communication" and "information" are often used interchangeably but they really aren't the same. "Information" is about giving out and "communication" is about getting through. In the end, family harmony is all about talking to each other even when you don't think it's important. After twenty years of marriage, one thing I have learned is that communication is always key. Clarifying what you want and taking the time to listen can solve a multitude of problems and misunderstandings. It takes only a few minutes to talk things through. But it can take hours to smooth out a problem.

Family moments are not always going to be tied up with a beautiful, shiny bow. But cherish every one just the same. They become lovely memories even if they didn't unfold exactly as you thought they would. In the moment they may be exasperating and chaotic, but appreciate that you are together. For most of my life I was the type of person who wanted everything to be perfect, beautiful and seamless, like the advertisements for Hallmark cards I grew up with. That was my picture of a happy life. But the truth is that happy is sometimes messy and disorganized and definitely imperfect. Moments that are disappointing at first can turn into the funniest and fondest memories.

DEBORAH

What's the Hurry?

I am a very high-energy person, maybe even a bit manic at times! After a jolt of coffee, I generally hit the ground running first thing in the morning and just go, go, go. When it comes to getting things done, I'm a lot like that famous athletic swish—I JUST DO IT! I have a daily regimen mapped out that I follow on a regular basis. Sometimes the details change, but the routine primarily stays the same.

I am one of those people who rarely use an alarm clock. I have a middle schooler who gets up at about five forty-five or six a.m. So the minute I hear those footsteps upstairs . . . BAM! It's go time. The Energizer Bunny's got nothing on me! I get out of bed and within minutes my mind is racing with ideas and questions about the day ahead.

What blouse should I wear to interview a police detective?

Did I remember to move the parent-teacher conference since I'm shooting today?

What about the expired car registration? Is Al handling that or should I?

Remind Leila—again—to turn in the note for her excused absence.

And did we get a gluten-free cupcake for Nicky's classroom celebration? Oh boy. So much to sort out!

But after a cup of coffee—half caffeine only (doctor's orders)—I'm good to go.

After making breakfast for the kids and sending them to school with our sitter or dropping them off myself, I have forty-five minutes of "me time" for a workout.

No matter how chaotic it all is, exercise will be squeezed in somewhere. It is my secret weapon. Since college, I have been an avid runner. When I worked at a local station in Orlando, I ran 5 and 10Ks on weekends. Running is my sanity. Twice a week I wedge in a forty-minute trek through Central Park. No earbuds, just the gentle sounds of birds and ducks, punctuated by an occasional screeching cab in the background. There's nothing like that burst of adrenaline I get while pounding the crunchy dirt along the bridle path or around the reservoir. Some days it's a tough slog. My stomach feels tight and I can barely get my achy knees to move forward, but somehow I do. And as I round the corner toward my turnoff, that dopamine, the happy brain chemical, kicks in. I am overcome with an exhilarating feeling of victory. My mind and spirit take charge. Now I can face other obstacles!

Running is like brain medicine for me, but these days my body doesn't take the pounding as well as it used to. I've had shoulder and knee pulls. So I've been spending more time on strength training and floor work. I'm fortunate to be able to splurge on a personal trainer at least twice a week to punish me with twenty-pound weights, boxing gloves and killer plank exercises. By eight a.m., I'm usually asking myself, "Why would any sane person invite someone to inflict early-morning physical torture!" But within fifteen minutes, my brain fog clears and I have found a happy place.

By nine a.m. I am physically pumped, clearheaded and energized for my day. Within minutes I am showered and out the door to ABC, where that strength training really pays off.

Don't ask me where this blast of energy comes from. I call it mania. Maybe it is a chemical imbalance. But I have been driven for most of my life, which helps, given my unpredictable schedule. Recently I left the house at five thirty a.m. for a flight to Columbus, Ohio, to interview a man suffering a rare illness. Five hours later I was back on a plane, flying home so I could be there to see the kids off to school the next day. As hectic and tiring as it was, it was worth it! My producer and camera crews don't always see it that way when I ask to keep rolling, but when I offer to spring for dinner, all is usually forgiven.

I'm just as aggressive outside of work as I am at the office. If a cabdriver is taking Sixth Avenue instead of Madison Avenue to get uptown, it drives me nuts. The green lights are so much longer on Madison. I thought everyone knew that?

But this same trait that helps me manage my busy life has a negative side. For example, Leila routinely calls me out for finishing her sentences. "Mom, let me finish, PLEASE!" she begs.

My teenage daughter is also quick to point out how annoying it is when I talk over people—even if it's out of enthusiasm. I try to catch myself, but I have to admit, she is right.

I am learning to slow down and reel it in a little, but it's an effort. I try to listen patiently, but sometimes I want the short version. Let's cover this subject and move on to another.

I often complain to Al that we don't spend enough time sharing the details of our day. In an effort to share with me one night, he began to tell a story about a shoot he had that day with the cast of *Ghostbusters* for the thirtieth anniversary of the movie's debut.

"Bill Murray was running late," he told me, and then rattled off lots of details about what he, Sigourney Weaver and the others had chatted about before the cameras rolled.

As Al went on and on with his story, my eyes began to drift and my mind wandered. I really was interested in his day, but I was also waiting for an opening to say Pepper still had to go for a walk before we got into bed.

Yikes!

I was doing it again. I was allowing my thoughts to race ahead and not really listening. This is such a negative habit—one I'd like to break. My son can attest to this for sure.

Since Nicky struggles with learning and processing delays, he takes in information at a slower pace than many of us. It also makes it harder for him to express his ideas, and he'll stammer through an explanation or a story. But I've come to realize that I can be part of the problem! Maybe it's doubly hard to process language when the other person is speaking a mile a minute. A few weeks ago, he was telling me about a book report he was doing on Jackie Robinson. After a few *um*s and *uh*s, I started jumping in to fill the gaps. "So you need pictures? Will you talk about his wife, Rachel?"

"NO!" he finally said. "I already have a plan."

"Oops." Suddenly, embarrassingly, I realized that if I just slowed down, maybe he'd feel more comfortable explaining it. I took a breath and *slowly* asked him to tell me all about it, hanging on to his every word. And sure enough, he articulately detailed his plan for the essay. I was so proud of him. I was also proud of me. My son had taught Mom a serious lesson. If I can just slow down, I can enjoy my kids and maybe even the world a bit more.

I actually love getting critical feedback from my kids, and I take it to heart. As the old expression goes, "Out of the mouths of babes . . . wisdom comes." Both of my children can be so wise in their observations and interpretations of life. They are in tune with their feelings and are brave enough to share them (when they can get a word in edgewise). Sure, there are times I walk away feeling bad, hoping my children won't grow up with memories of a hard-charging mom who was more of a talker than a listener. But I think lately I'm showing them that I'm willing to try harder and to change.

Last summer I made great progress. One Saturday Leila and I were home alone. Al had taken Nicky with him on a trip to Washington, DC. After a rare day of sleeping in and a run through the park, I came home to find Leila still in her pajamas and making a smoothie.

"So what shall we do today?" I asked.

"I don't know," she replied. "Maybe just sit around and chill."

Hmm.

Later, I joined her on the couch for an episode of *The Real House-wives of New York City*. As Ramona began lighting into someone, I couldn't take it anymore. I suggested we go for manicures or to the Jeff Koons art exhibit. Then Leila offered a firm dose of wisdom.

"Mom, why can't you just *be*?" she pointedly asked. "You know you don't always have to have a plan . . . or something to do. Sometimes life is calmer if you can just do nothing."

Her words hit me like a ton of bricks. My sweet daughter was absolutely right. There is no reason that every single moment of every single day must be filled with something. When it's time to work and do . . . boy, do I work and do. She has seen me in action many times and even told me how much she admires my work ethic. But it's just as important that my children know that I value calm and peace.

For the rest of the day, Leila and I did nothing. We made tea, watched *Breakfast at Tiffany's* and chilled.

It was wonderful.

My friend Brenda, who has two grown children, recently told me that your family feeds on your energy. How right she is! My goal is to make sure that my energy is positive and calm. I know that there will be days when we are running late for the dentist or tae kwon do. But it's up to me to help make those frenetic moments less stressful and even meaningful.

I think I am on my way.

Nicky started a new school in the fall of 2014. On his first day, the bus was very late and he was anxious, so I calmly offered to get the car and we drove. As he fretted, I relaxed, telling him that finally I would see what it's like to get to another part of the city in the morning traffic. We laughed and he relaxed. When we finally pulled up in front of the school, we gave each other high fives. I offered him a drink from my water bottle and he sprinted up the stairs.

"You okay?" I called.

"Yup!" he shouted with confidence.

Maybe I'm getting the hang of it.

11

The Importance of Friendships

DEBORAH

Your Husband Can't Be Your End-All

Michelle Obama is an impressive, powerful woman, but she also comes off as the kind of woman you'd like to have as one of your girlfriends. Maybe that explains her widespread popularity. I first interviewed her a few months before the 2008 election, and I admired her intelligence and candor. A few years later, I was deeply inspired by something she said in another interview: "Your husband cannot be your be-all and end-all." Early in his career, Mrs. Obama was frustrated by her husband's frequent absences as he worked tirelessly as a community organizer. Often she found herself at home with the kids, feeling resentful and angry. It's a common scenario many women can relate to these days. But Michelle Obama didn't remain angry and upset; she discovered something that I now understand too: the value and the rescuing power of friendships with her girlfriends. Every word Michelle Obama spoke about the importance of female friendships resonated deep within me, as I knew what she said was true.

In the beginning of a romantic relationship, it can feel like this other person is the sun, the moon and the stars and that you'll never again need anyone else. Like most couples, Al and I were best friends bonded by that powerful biological attraction that early love brings. But, of course, after years of marriage and the draining power of that other biological wonder called children, the single-minded intensity of our relationship waned. He doesn't understand why I keep droning on and on about someone who annoyed me or why I sometimes feel irritable instead of sexy after the kids finally go to bed and I discovered one of them jammed a DVD into my computer and deleted all of my phone contacts "by accident." At those moments all I want to do is pass out . . . or simply vent. The last thing I want is sex. That's a situation where those estrogen alliances come in real handy! There are feelings women share that men simply don't have the capacity or the interest to understand.

As much as we love each other, Al and I are indeed from Mars and Venus. He can't understand why I like to talk late into the evening or maybe into the next day about someone who insulted me or grated on my nerves.

"Either tell them about themselves or move on," he says.

After we've watched a particularly disturbing or provocative movie, I want to discuss it more before bed. Was the ballerina imagining all those crazy acts in *Black Swan* or did they really happen? Why did the *The Help* strike such a chord and make its way to the Oscars?

Al is happy to discuss these things for a bit, but then he wants to move on to other things.

"Why beat a dead horse?" he wants to know.

For me, that's where close girlfriends come in.

Like me, most of my female friends want to talk about who and what is bothering us. Yes, we want to resolve a situation and trade advice on how to handle it, but we also want to lay out our feelings about whatever it is and then discuss the implications.

My friend Agenia and I can talk for an hour about a fight we had with our husbands and why they are wrong, or how a colleague just drives us crazy. When we hang up the phone, both of us feel heard and validated in ways that our men simply can't seem to understand or have the patience for. Rather than get annoyed by Al's lack of understanding for these types of things, I've learned to save certain topics for a female friend, to be shared over a cup of coffee—or better yet, a glass of wine.

I am fortunate to have an amazing "sisterhood" of women in my life, Robin Roberts among them. Robin and I not only have a last name in common, but we also share a deep commitment to family and spirituality. Over the years she has been a treasured friend I can always depend on for kinship and great career advice in our famously high-pressured, competitive work environment. Every few months Robin and I get together with our friends Gayle, Tonya and Theresa for a soul-nurturing lunch to talk about our joys and struggles and anything else that may pop up! We all agree that we walk around beaming for days after our afternoon get-togethers. We're always the first to offer shout-outs when one of us has received an award or support when someone has an ailing family member. Second to my sisters, these friends are among the most important women in my life. Whether face-to-face or courtesy of Verizon, a girlfriend pow-wow can be as restorative as a therapy appointment. One of my oldest and dearest friends lives in South Carolina, but we have wonderful phone dates. With glasses of chardonnay in hand, we laugh or cry for an hour or so until we both feel we can face another day with our sanity fully intact.

Simply being heard by a woman who knows exactly what it's like to have a husband forget to pick up the laundry or leave a smelly banana peel next to the computer overnight is like balm for an aching soul. Every other morning I find myself on the phone with Agenia, my dearest friend of thirty years. Usually, sometime around eight a.m. (seven a.m. her time), we begin the conversation with a hearty "Are you ready for this?" Within ten minutes we are cracking each other up over the ridiculousness we both deal with on a regular basis. A mom and a CEO of a national organization, she understands my stresses, and she knows how to tell me what's worth sweating over and what's not. And most important, she knows when to just listen.

Most men simply don't get the point of long, emotional exchanges, and trying to engage them just ends up in frustration. Though we've been together for twenty years, Al simply doesn't understand why I obsessively talk about something that is bothering me. If we have had a fight and made up, he feels like it's settled and done, and I feel like I still want to explain how I felt. I mean, why *not* clear the air over and over . . . and over? That's why talking with my female friends often feels lifesaving.

What works great one-on-one can also work wonders in a group. Besides my lunch gal pals, I have a core group of close women friends in New York—Marva, Judy, Jonelle, Angela, Dale, Yolanda and Tawana—and we loosely call ourselves a "book club" because we initially bonded at a dinner discussing the bestselling book *The Help.* I loved the book, but there was so much I wanted to talk about with others who had read it. The story of oppression and dashed dreams resonated with me because my grandmother and mother had both worked as maids at one point in their lives.

When I was done reading the book, I was grateful to have a place to process my roller-coaster emotions and the many questions I had about the author. Did a white author have the right to tell this story? Did she capture their struggles? Did she stereotype? As a journalist, I was fascinated by the story, but as a Southern black woman, I was intrigued by other people's take on it. Everywhere I went, from cocktail parties to the set of *Good Morning America,* people had been talking about this book. (In fact, it was Charlie Gibson who recommended that I read it.)

The night our "book club" was born, we opened a bottle of wine and talked about *The Help,* but we also delved into one another's stories. I talked about growing up in the South. One friend spoke of losing a child to SIDS, sudden infant death syndrome. Another talked about growing up black and middle-class in Oklahoma in the 1960s after unexpectedly losing her father, and her mother bravely going forward as a single mom. Everyone willingly peeled away the layers we all hide behind in our otherwise busy daily lives and made ourselves bare. We shared tears and laughter, and it was a rare moment for each of us. We felt safe enough to be vulnerable. With no particular expectations going into the evening, we discovered a sense of connectedness in a way that only girlfriends can truly understand. It was almost like a religious experience of sisterhood.

We whooped it up and hollered until midnight, when our host's husband came out and gave everyone that certain "look" that meant it was time for us to go home. I hadn't felt that way since my sleepover days in high school, when my best friend's father used to tell us to hush up and go to bed!

That night I realized once again the power of female friendships. I came away thinking about my childhood and examining feelings that I had once thought belonged only to me.

Sisterhood has always been healing to me. Talking to my friends helped me to realize that I'm not alone in the pain I've carried over the years due to colorism in the black community. When I disclosed my insecurity about growing up as a dark-skinned girl and feeling unattractive, it was my female friends who understood and made me feel beautiful. It has been liberating to share experiences with other women because it has helped free me from burdens I've long carried. I am a better partner, mom and friend because of my deep female friendships.

I really want to share with my daughter, Leila, this lesson about the importance of girlfriends. I want her to see that gift at work in my life.

When she sees me with a few female friends in the kitchen or hears my loud, syrupy *"Gurlll* . . . let me tell you!" on the phone, she may roll her eyes, but then she smiles, knowing I'm connecting with someone I feel close to. She's happily come along to a musical revue featuring my friend Pauletta, an actress and singer who's reclaiming her career after stepping back for years to raise her children.

Leila's even becoming "one of the girls," once coming to lunch with Robin and me. She's always adored Robin, and Robin, like so many of my "sisters," embraces Leila, encouraging her endeavors and interests. I hope Leila learns that as much as we love our guys, there's something special about women in her life. Isadora James said, "A sister is a gift to the heart, a friend to the spirit, a golden thread to the meaning of life." There's nothing quite like the wisdom and power of the lifelong friendship of women. Amen to that.

The Value of Friendship

I've always been the kind of husband who encourages my wife to take time with her girlfriends. I appreciate it and I understand it's what she needs. Even though I am around a lot of people on a daily basis, the truth is, I'm not terribly social. I prefer being with my family and a small handful of people I enjoy spending time with over groups of people I barely know and have no interest in getting to know better. I have a couple of close buddies, but for the most part, I'd much rather be with my wife and kids or alone.

It's one of the reasons I resent Facebook. All these contacts are called your "friends"? Um, no. Some may happen to be friends, but for the most part they are total strangers and will most likely remain that way.

Though I don't need people around me all the time, I have a great appreciation for someone who knows you and just lets you say your crazy stuff without judging. I confide in my wife, and a sibling or two, although even then, I'm guilty of not always sharing with them. I can't tell you the number of times I've picked up the phone to hear a complaint from a not-so-happy wife, offspring or sibling who read about an interview or something else I'm doing in the paper or online. Mea culpa. I know I need to share more.

But even I have times I need to unload to someone who isn't going to take it personally or be offended by what I say or how I feel—someone outside the family, like a close buddy. When you have that kind of friend, you almost instantly feel better once you get things off your chest, and if you don't, that good friend, with a clear head and a terrific sense of humor, can usually talk you off the ledge. I consider that an invaluable friend to have—someone who can cut through the clutter and help you find your way.

My buddy Jon Harris has been one of those guys for me.

Jon is the type of person you feel like you've known your whole life a few minutes after meeting him. He has the gift of gab and an insatiable thirst for knowing people. He's a combination good-time Charlie and the Wedding Singer. He's half Jewish and half Irish. I call him the world's tallest Yiddish leprechaun!

I've known Jon for at least twenty years. He is the king of global communications. When we first met back in the early nineties, he was working for Pepsi. Then he went to an Internet start-up, fitness powerhouse Bally's, and finally Hillshire Brands, the international food company, where he was responsible for touting (and tasting) everything from Sara Lee pound cake to Jimmy Dean sausage, which proved problematic, given his family history and his love of food.

His dad died very young from a heart attack; Jon, the father of three young kids, knew he needed to make some changes in his life so he didn't end up the same way. I never really thought of him as heavy, but he lost forty pounds and got into terrific shape. After that he turned me on to his nutritionist, Melissa Bowman Li, who helped me lose weight after my gastric bypass surgery. Ever since, Jon and I have shared both our love of food and our struggle to stay fit. We have a great camaraderie, and Jon has been a constant reminder of the power of a positive attitude. He has moments of doubt, as we all do, but he has such a deep-seated optimism that won't allow him to feel defeated, no matter how hard life gets sometimes. He genuinely lets stuff roll off his back, which I admire because I have a tendency to absorb my feelings, whether I show my emotions or not. It may be effective in the short term, but boy, does it catch up to me. The pressure builds up, and eventually, the tiniest thing will push me over the edge. And when that happens, believe me, it isn't pretty. Just ask Deborah and the kids. Jon's example is really helping me in my efforts to change that.

One of the ways I think I help Jon is being his "No" coach. Jon is a people pleaser; whether it's family, friends or colleagues, if it's humanly possible, Jon wants to say yes to the many requests that come over his transom and land on his desk. The problem is, he can't possibly do all the things people want him to do, so he's stressed and exhausted by the end of the day.

That's where I come in! I've learned the cathartic and transformative power of those two letters N-O. Unless it's a "must do" for work or a "need to" for your kids, most of the things we get asked to do can be dealt with by saying no. Nicely but firmly. Doesn't need an explanation or an apology. Just a simple no. You will be amazed at how much clearer and focused life is when you use that word. Forget about "please" being the magic word. It's "no."

And so when Jon and I talk, he will often run through his calendar and we prune away the requests so that he can focus, laserlike, on the things that really mean something to him and to the people he loves.

One evening we talked forty minutes, taking a Weedwacker to all the requests Jon had by saying no. It was thrilling to look at Jon's iPhone calendar and see days upon days with almost no blocks of color clogging up the screen.

Jon and I may not speak every day, but I know he is there for me and he knows I am always there for him. When it comes to real friendship, that's the bottom line—and I believe that meaningful solidarity among his peers is what my father cherished the most.

In my professional life, there have been a few men I've met along the way who have reminded me of my dad. It's pretty well-known that NBC's Willard Scott has long been a mentor and second dad to me. In the last few years, another father figure has come into my professional and personal life, Vice President Joseph Biden. To me, he is a politician in the very best sense of the word, meaning someone who isn't afraid to mingle with the people; someone who values loyalty, commitment and your word being your bond. Values too often forgotten today.

The first time I met him, at the second inaugural parade, I was immediately taken by his warmth and generosity. He said hello, treating me like an old friend, not a lowly weatherman standing on the sidelines, aggressively waving him down for a network scoop. He's the kind of guy who, if he were your local councilman, would get that pesky pothole fixed!

Vice President Biden and I have had the opportunity to get to know each other a bit since the parade. I've attended his annual Christmas party a few times, and he took part in an extended interview with Willie Geist, Tamron Hall, Natalie Morales and me. We've gotten friendly—as friendly as one can be with the Vice President of the United States!—and I truly admire the guy.

When I was covering the floods last year in Boulder, Colorado, I was so impressed by the way the vice president talked to people, from the locals who were displaced to the state and city politicians, Democrats and Republicans, who had to deal with the damage. I could see he was genuinely worried about what these people were going through and how they were being affected. He shook hands, reached out and hugged those who needed it and was there to offer whatever support he could. That means a lot, especially when you have just lost your home. He was more like an uncle than a polarizing politician. You can just tell that he cares about the American people, loves what he is doing and believes he can make a difference. That is such a rare gift these days, especially in our "what-are-the-polls-saying" and "friend-me" society. At least it feels that way to me.

The vice president graciously granted me an interview in Boulder, and at the end of our walk and talk, we wound up in front of Air Force Two. He turned to me and said, "I don't know which way you're going, but I'd be happy to give you a lift as far as Andrews Air Force Base."

I thought he was joking.

My producer looked at me and said, "You are going, aren't you?"

"But what about my things back at the hotel?" I wondered.

"Forget your stuff! I'll take care of it!" my producer said. "The vice president just invited you to fly back on Air Force Two with him! You've got to say yes, Al!"

Of course, I knew he was right, so I turned and made my way up the steps of the vice president's plane.

It was one of the most surreal experiences of my life.

As a weatherman, I don't get a lot of opportunities to travel with politicians like some journalists, so I didn't know what to expect. I found myself with a couple of other members of the press, the vice president's staff, Secret Service agents, a full complement of medical professionals, and navy stewards, who were on board to prepare and serve meals.

As we took off, it sank in that I was on board the second-most powerful plane in the world—as a guest of the Vice President of the United States.

Yeah, I felt pretty cool.

Shortly after takeoff, I was summoned to the vice president's office on board the plane.

"How ya doin', Al?" he said.

We sat in his office and chatted about family, kids, weight and life.

It was all so . . . normal. As if I were with an old friend.

When we were done, I went back to my seat.

About twenty minutes before we landed, the copilot asked me if I would like to sit in the cockpit for the approach into Andrews Air Force Base.

Just as I was heading forward, the vice president stuck his head out his office door and said, "If I knew this guy was going to be so much trouble, I would never have invited him on board! Way to go, pal. You're a good man!" He laughed and slapped me on the shoulder.

When we landed, the vice president and I shook hands and did that "guy hug" before he deplaned, got into his waiting car and drove off.

I'm not sure why he invited me on the plane that day, but it was the beginning of a deeper friendship that I didn't expect or see coming. Sometimes in life, the unexpected twists are the best and most precious.

A few months later I had rotator cuff surgery I'd been putting off. A day after I got home, my phone rang. I really wasn't feeling well enough to speak to anyone, but the odd caller ID made me curious enough to pick up.

"Hey, Al. Vice President Biden calling. How ya doing?"

"Vice President Biden!" I said. I will freely admit I was stunned. "I'm fine."

"Listen, Mrs. Biden had something like that, and you have to do what the doctors tell you to do, okay?"

"I always do what the doctors say. I'm a good patient," I assured him.

"Listen, pal, anything you need, you just give me a call . . ."

That phone call, and the ones since, such as for my sixtieth birthday, have meant the world to me.

Are we best buds?

No!

But it's sure nice to know there is someone who values our relationship. I know I do. And I know my dad must be smiling.

I think about Dad every single day, wondering what he would do or say about something. I think about how proud he would be of Leila, Nicky and Courtney, and I smile because I know deep in my heart that he has to be looking down on our family with a great sense of joy.

And now, more than ever, I appreciate what he got from his friends.

Losing My Best Friend

The end of life is not easy to contemplate. But, at the risk of sounding maudlin, I do consider it from time to time. I've lost so many relatives and friends in recent years. Some, like my grade-school friend Mattie, died too soon of illness, and others, like my aunt Annie, lived a long and incredible life. Big Annie, as she was known, was my daddy's older sister and the matriarch of his family and died at the age of 103. What a blessed life. After hearing of someone's death, Big Annie often asked, "Why her and not me?" It may sound strange to some, but we all laughed. A sweet woman with a warm smile, Big Annie was secure in her Christian faith and ready to go home to God. Death was a welcome passage for her when it finally came.

Big Annie's death was filled with the grace of God's love, and her funeral was a celebration of a life well lived. And we were prepared for it. I *wasn't* prepared to lose my oldest friend.

Denise Ingram was my best friend in the world. We met in the first grade at the segregated Houston County Training School and became inseparable. Both of us were dark-skinned and wore our hair in pigtails with colorful bows, and of course, both of our names started with the letter *D*. People often confused us because we looked so much alike. Only when I got glasses in the third grade did teachers seem to know who was who, and eventually I went out for cheerleading while Denise excelled in chorus.

I called Denise so often that I can still recite her phone number to this very day. Remember, this was long before cell phones and texting; we actually talked to each other on the phone, sometimes late into the night, gabbing about which boy we liked or didn't like, whether the Three Degrees would appear on Friday night's *Wolfman Jack Show* or whether arm-toning exercises really help make your breasts perky. We traded beauty tips—it was Denise who advised me to use my ring finger to apply eye cream because it's a weaker finger and easier on the delicate skin. Denise and I talked about everything and sometimes nothing at all.

Her parents were younger than mine and college-educated. Mr. Ingram was a teacher at Perry High School, and Mrs. Ingram was a school secretary, which meant that Denise grew up solidly middle-class, unlike my working-class family. Denise lived in the Creekwood subdivision, a new development across town, where higher-earning black families in Perry built two-story homes and had a neighborhood swimming pool. In my neighborhood, Old Field, the homes were smaller and rather simple. Most of my neighbors worked as cooks or construction laborers or in nearby factories. From the outside looking in, Denise was more likely destined for success. Her relatives, parents and neighbors were primarily professionals and most of mine were not. But our lives took different turns after high school.

By senior year I had developed a strong sense of my ambitions. I had big dreams to go to the University of Georgia, to work in television and maybe one day move to a major city like Chicago or New York. Some of my classmates thought I was pretty cocky. Denise was shyer than I was and, although smart and talented, was less certain about her plans. She chose a slightly smaller college with a little less prestige just south of Perry.

Once we went our separate ways, Denise and I didn't talk as much. For the first time in years, hers wasn't the first number I called when I had a problem. I suppose it happens to so many of us after high school, as we venture out into the wider world. But we stayed in touch and saw each other during holidays and summers. Eventually I moved out of Georgia, and after getting her degree in marketing, Denise worked in Washington for a congressman. Later, she landed a staff position at the Social Security Administration and a few other government agencies but never seemed to have a fire in her belly about her work.

Whenever an assignment brought me to Washington, we'd get together, but we definitely weren't as close as we had once been. Still, I always felt like we remained best friends forever.

Then one fall, when we would both celebrate our thirty-third birthdays, Denise gave me some disconcerting news. She had always been a gifted singer, but she was no longer able to sing at weddings or in the church choir because she had sarcoidosis, an autoimmune disease. In Denise's case it was attacking her lungs and causing emphysema-like symptoms.

Eventually she decided to follow her doctor's advice to seek a warmer climate, which might make her feel better. But her condition worsened, and a few years later she moved back to Perry, into her old bedroom at her parents' house—something no adult child wants to do unless they have to.

By this time Denise and I were in our forties. She had once been filled with such joy and love for music. She even sang "The Lord's Prayer" at our wedding, bringing Al and me to tears. But a debilitating disease was robbing my childhood pal of her passion and most everything else she loved too. Whenever I came home to see Mom and Dad, I made it a point to call and invite myself over. Sometimes Denise would wave me off, saying she hadn't gotten dressed or was too tired for a visitor. She had become more and more reclusive because her illness was tough to bear. Mrs. Ingram loved it when I persisted and pushed my way in for a visit anyway. She would give me a secret wink whenever I sat next to Denise on the sofa, watching TV or regaling her with stories about my travels.

I loved Denise so much, and I encouraged her to seek out the best medical care, possibly a lung transplant. But she was reluctant on all fronts. She felt uncomfortable about taking risks, even if it might possibly save her life. She prayed for healing but was at peace with whatever the future would bring. But I was frustrated because I was convinced that Denise felt defeated by her disease. Much to the dismay of her parents and brother and sister, she wasn't interested in a long, brave fight.

Each time I came home to Perry, I would call and try to see Denise for a cheer-up visit. She became very thin, and her breathing was labored. It pained me to see her so weak and diminished. The sicker Denise got, the less she wanted people to see her in such a fragile state. By now Denise rarely went out in public, fearing germs and looks of pity over her frail condition. I pleaded with her to go to a movie with me or, even better, to visit me in New York. I assured her that I had seen people all over New York City eating in the finest restaurants carrying a little oxygen tank and bag. "It's the must-have fashion accessory of the season!" I'd say, trying to bring a little levity to the situation, with the hope of lifting her spirits. It didn't work. Even so, I insisted on seeing her whenever I was in Perry, if only to sit with her and reminisce, tell stories and be together for a few hours.

"You really think you can avoid me?" I'd ask. "Well, it's not going to work! I am going to be right here for you, because I am your friend and I am going to be here and help you get through this," I'd say.

If she wasn't going to fight for herself, I'd fight for her. I'd be her cheerleader. That's what best friends are for!

Then one day I got that call.

That same dreaded one I got when my dad was dying.

This time, however, I would catch the next plane. Denise was in intensive care at a Florida hospital that specializes in autoimmune diseases.

Something inside told me that I needed to be there. Denise needed another voice there to tell her not to give up.

At first I convinced myself that this would be like any other visit, that I would see Denise and cheer her up. When I got to the hospital, her brother, Hervia, quickly shattered that fantasy. With a stricken face, he pulled me aside in the lobby and cautioned me that I needed to be strong. He warned me that his sister was unconscious and that I should prepare myself before going into the room.

I wasn't sure what to expect, so I took a deep breath and walked through the door. Denise was lying in bed, as if she were asleep. She had a slack mouth and a frozen, almost scared expression on her face. There were tubes running down her throat and wires connecting her to an oxygen machine and a heart-rate monitor. It took my breath away to see my friend like this—so frail and fragile.

Mrs. Ingram was asleep on the sofa, and I didn't want to wake her.

I took Denise's hand and held it tight. And I could've sworn she squeezed my hand back.

When her mother awoke, she explained that the doctors had induced a light comatose state so Denise could get some respite from the constant coughing. Her body needed a rest. Mrs. Ingram spoke quietly and confidently about her daughter coming home. I wanted to share her hopes, but I feared that Denise was in a fight for her life. Even so, I had no idea this would be our last visit.

With the beeps of the heart monitor and other machines purring in the background, I talked to Denise, rubbed her head, and smoothed back her hair with my brush. My mind was flooded with memories of our blissful childhood and happy times together. I struggled to hold back my tears, keeping things light, hoping that somewhere deep inside, Denise sensed my presence. With the ventilator pumping oxygen into her, she lay still and peaceful, a knitted blanket draped over her thin legs. My heart was cracking. I stayed for a couple of hours, until the nurses said visiting hours were over.

I had taken a hotel room on the grounds of the hospital so I would be close just in case anything happened. Emotionally drained and physically exhausted, I walked through the darkness and into my hotel feeling anxious and eager for a hot shower and a bed. I was slipping into my nightgown when the phone suddenly rang. Hervia was on the line and said I should come over—right away.

"It's not good," he said.

I threw on my sweats and a T-shirt and dashed back to the hospital and straight up to Denise's room. Mr. and Mrs. Ingram looked stricken as the doctor told them gently that they should consider disconnecting the life support to see if Denise could breathe on her own. Denise had asked long ago not to be left on life support. The Ingrams tried to remain hopeful, but somehow I knew what the outcome would be.

My heart was in my throat.

I couldn't speak—and worse, I felt out of place, like an intruder in a private family meeting. But at the same time I also felt privileged to be part of the family during this critical moment.

I will never forget that night for as long as I live.

Holding my breath, I stepped back from Denise's bed and watched the doctor disconnect the breathing tube.

We all held hands and took a deep, nervous breath. Mrs. Ingram, a deeply religious woman, began to pray for her daughter in a tiny voice, pleading, "Dear God, lift her up and give her strength." We watched the monitor as her heart rate slowed. Mrs. Ingram gently reached for the heirloom blanket at the foot of her bed and placed it across her body.

Seconds later, the machine went flatline.

My friend was gone.

Mrs. Ingram softly wept and gently kissed her daughter. She stared at her for a long time, then finally stepped into the hallway, where she let out a plaintive howl, the kind of heart-stopping cry a mother makes after losing a child. She had held it together for so long, but now that her first baby was gone, she had to let it out.

I just stood frozen in disbelief, tears running down my cheeks, feeling almost out of body. I grabbed Denise's still warm hands and bent over to kiss her. "Good-bye, my precious friend," I whispered. I turned to her brother and hugged him tightly.

"Thank you for being here," he said as he placed his arms around my shoulders. "It meant a lot to us, and I know it meant a lot to Denise."

Denise will always hold the place as my best friend in life. Although she pushed me away toward the end, I know she held on to our bond as tightly as I did. I understand that it must've been painful to face her loved ones when she was losing her grip. She no doubt wanted to make the difficult decision to move on without causing me pain. But I also believe that she wanted me with her once she was on her way. I often think how strange it was that Denise held on until I arrived, then passed away just hours later. In my heart I truly believe that she waited for me, just as we had waited for each other at school or on the phone so many times when we were growing up. My childhood twin allowed me to be at her side as she made her final journey from this life.

As tragic as it was to lose Denise, to watch her die so young, I'm thankful she was surrounded by the people she loved and that I was able to see her out of the world. God had cradled her and taken her away. Although it was heartbreaking, I cherish my memory of being at Denise's bedside as a reminder of the power of friendship. Whether old, battered or strained, true friendship never dies.

My best friend—my childhood double—was gone. I never expected to say good-bye to her so soon, and I certainly never thought I'd witness her walk into the arms of God.

Though I wanted her to fight, Denise clearly knew how much she could bear. A strong-willed woman of deep, unshakable faith, she had grown weary in her struggle to live. I think she knew it was time to surrender and find her final peace.

A few days later, when I spoke at Denise's funeral, I realized that it was her birthday. "How ironic to say good-bye to my friend on the same day she was brought into this world," I thought. I guess that is the true circle of life.

I always imagined that we would grow old together, calling each other up, laughing and gossiping about our lives. But God had another plan.

A year after Denise passed, her mother reached out to me during one of my visits back home. She said, "Deborah, if you could come by the house, I have something I'd like to give you."

Truth be told, it had been hard for me to stay in touch with her since Denise's death. It was just so painful, and I missed my friend very much. But when I got her message, of course I stopped in for a visit.

Mrs. Ingram had finally gone through Denise's things and had come across some wrapped presents. One had my name on it.

It took me a minute to open it. My hands trembled as I bore the paper away.

I opened a small box to find a white ceramic cross decorated with magnolias and dogwoods. The card read, simply, *To my friend Deborah.*

As I held the cross in my hands, tears fell from my eyes. It was as if Denise and I were together again. In this bittersweet moment I felt the meaning of true friendship. No matter how near or far, we will always be connected in each other's hearts. When I tell this story to my children, I want them to understand the meaning of the expression "friends to the end."

AL

The World's Greatest Puppy!

I am going on record that I did not want a dog. Not that I am antidog. I had a dog from the time I was ten years old until well into my thirties. But a couple of things happened.

1. I moved to Manhattan. The thought of following behind an animal, bending down and picking up its poop was not the way I wanted to spend my evenings.
2. With children who were past the point of poopy diapers, who could dress and feed themselves, why would I bring what amounts to a perennial two-year-old into my home?
3. I developed an allergy to dog hair late in life. And Nicky and Leila are allergic as well.

Of course, as the kids got older, they saw the cute little Yorkies, pugs and Labs walking around Manhattan, and I knew it was only a matter of time before I would hear, "Daaaaad! Can we have a dog? Pleeeeeaase?" accompanied by a look not unlike the kids in those paintings with the huge eyes and the little pouty lower lip.

When that day finally came, they trotted out all the reasons why they should have a dog: companionship, responsibility, an antidote for loneliness; all their friends have a dog—why not us? We're old enough. We'll take it out, we'll walk it, clean up after it. Pleeeeasseee? This despite the fact that Nicky was actually afraid of dogs! He was following his sister's lead.

These children think their mother and I were dropped on this planet, fully formed, without having run the same scams, arguments and promises on our parents.

Who are you kidding?

My brothers and sisters and I had used the exact same arguments. And this was at a time when your dog didn't live in your house. In my neighborhood, unless there was bad weather, your dog stayed outside. It didn't eat gourmet dog food; it had table scraps. And sadly, if your pooch got sick, the vet told you when it was time to say good-bye. There were no diagnoses of cancer, kidney disease or arthritis. No vet in my time or neighborhood would think to suggest chemo, dialysis or hip replacement.

When you took your dog for a walk, it pooped and you left it there as long as it wasn't on someone's lawn.

I steadfastly refused to even think about getting a dog until Nicky and Leila were old enough to take said dog outside *by themselves* and walk same said dog and pick up its poop and deposit said poop in the corner trash receptacle.

End of story.

By early 2012, though, the cacophony had grown to an incessant drone. Deborah and I talked about it and decided they were old enough to help take care of a dog. Friends suggested we have the kids sign a contract accepting their responsibility.

Are you kidding?

Major League Baseball players break multimillion-dollar contracts more often than you and I change underwear. Do you really think some unenforceable pact is going to keep the kids walking the dog or cleaning up after it?

And what if they don't?

Are we really giving the dog back?

Not likely, so scratch the contract idea.

But we hatched a plan.

Leila was already researching the breed of dog she thought might be perfect for our family. I told them I would talk to Jill Rappaport, our *Today* show animal advocate. We insisted on a rescue or shelter dog, and Jill is the best at hooking people up with the right rescue/shelter folks. When I called Jill, she was ecstatic. She said to give her some time, but she would find the right dog for our family.

We all had our wish list. The kids wanted a puppy, they wanted it to be a girl, and they wanted something small and hypoallergenic, obviously, and it had to be *the world's greatest puppy*! Okay, I added that part, but I figure, since we're putting in our order . . .

Week after week, the kids were on me. "When is the puppy coming?"

About six weeks went by and then came the call we'd all been waiting for. Jill wanted to know if we would be available to meet with Bill Smith, director of a well-known animal-rescue shelter, at the end of the week. He had a puppy he'd like us to meet.

I must admit, I was suddenly nervous. This was a big, honkin' deal. Once this happened, there was no going back.

Plus, I started doing the math.

Both Leila and Nicky would be out of the house at college in eight years. Deborah would be stuck with an incontinent, irascible poop machine that would most likely be a flatulence factory. And then there would be the dog.

Under a cone of silence, Deborah and I planned the meeting for the early afternoon *before* the kids got home from school. This way, if things didn't go well, no harm, no foul. They'd be none the wiser. (I always feel that when you say that, you have to twiddle your tie and look into the camera like Oliver Hardy.)

Jill and Bill showed up to our home and brought in not one but two crates. As soon as we met I could see that Bill was a man of incredible dedication to rescuing dogs and finding good homes for them. He has a kind demeanor and gentle manner, but I could see him as a staunch defender of these animals.

"GAME ON!" I thought.

We decided to meet a future member of our family in the backyard. Bill left the crates inside the door, reaching into one and walking out back with us. There in his hand was a beautiful light brown ball of fluff. We all sat down on the stone patio, and he let this little guy down on the ground. The puppy looked around curiously, and he was so very cute that I could see falling in love with him. He seemed easygoing and chill; this guy would clearly fit into our home, I thought.

Then Bill brought out the inhabitant of the other crate. He set this one down, and suddenly a black bundle of energy started sniffing and licking and kissing me and Deb. A Havanese mix, she was peppered with white around her chest and her feet and had a wonderful personality. She had been rescued from a Pennsylvania puppy mill, where she would have spent four or five years breeding before meeting a grisly death. You could tell right away this puppy had charisma and a tremendous intelligence that radiated from her core. Can you tell I was smitten from the start?

Just at that moment, Nicky came home from school. He walked into the backyard and came to a halt, his eyes wide and his mouth open.

Among some of Nicky's issues, he had a fear of dogs. It didn't matter the size, the temperament or the gender. If we were walking on the street and he saw a dog, he would place me between himself and the offending dog.

This was going to be interesting.

The first pup had snuggled into Deborah's lap and fallen asleep.

The second puppy trotted right over to Nicky, who amazingly and fearlessly dropped down onto the patio, where this newcomer climbed right into his lap and started licking him!

And he let her!

Then he started kissing her.

Deborah and I looked at each other.

And . . . we had a winner!

Any pup that conquered Nicky's fear was destined to be our dog.

This little girl chose us.

We felt bad that the other pup would go home without being adopted, but Bill assured us that this little guy would have no problem finding a home. He said that although the light brown lad with the sleepy eyes was originally his first choice, he felt in his gut that this black-and-white beauty belonged with us.

With Bill's help, we concocted a cover story about "watching" the puppy while she got ready to be on the *Today* show, in case it didn't go well with the puppy, but that immediately went out the window as this little one was quickly burrowing into the fabric of our lives. Leila, too, had fallen under the new pup's spell.

Some things are just meant to be.

Of course, the next question became, "What do we call her?"

Deborah wanted to call her Sugar, as an homage to her Southern roots—"sugar" being a term of endearment.

Leila came up with Pepper, since she was mostly black with a little white thrown in—Salt-'n'-Pepper.

And it stuck.

Over the weeks and months that followed, Pepper quickly became house-trained. She also quickly became Deborah's third child. Wherever Mommy goes, Pepper is sure to follow. And true to form, while the kids help, the bulk of her care and dog walking fell to her adopted mommy and daddy. And we are happy to do it.

I promised myself that whatever dog we got would *not* be sleeping on the bed or on the couch. So guess where you can find Pepper just before bedtime every evening?

On the comforter at the foot of our bed. And she looks truly offended when I tell her it's time to head downstairs. I am almost booed by my wife and children. That said, Pepper has developed a habit of growling and barking if she hears a perceived threat from some inter-loper passing our threshold. At one a.m., that is no fun. Does she have any idea what time I get up?

She should ask the kids. They'll tell her.

Many families struggle over whether or not to get a pet. Sometimes it's an issue of dog versus cat. (I contend dog people are dog people and they simply can't coexist with cat people.) And as I've just said, even the subject of whether or not the dog can sleep on the bed can divide the happiest of couples. But the one thing Deborah and I never expected when we fulfilled the promise of bringing home a puppy was the incred-ibly positive impact Pepper would end up having on our son. Of course, how could we, since he was afraid of dogs?

I would have bet my last dollar Leila would be the more conscien-tious about walking and caring for Pepper, but it turned out that Nicky is the one who volunteers his time more often and is far more diligent about keeping the poop, pee and food diary up-to-date than the rest of us. He would even leave the house early in the morning to walk Pepper without telling us where he was going, which scared us! But now we're thrilled that he's taken on the biggest responsibility of his young life. He stepped up and took ownership in a way that none of us did, and we were all happy to allow Nicky to do it. It has been endearing and heart-ening to see him grow and mature from his love and care for the dog.

And there's another thing. Through this connection, Nicky has dis-covered the power of unconditional love. Pepper doesn't care what he got on a test or whether he has learning disabilities. She cares that he pets her belly and gives her treats. She likes when he speaks to her in a funny voice and plays ball. It's a simple, loving relationship, and though we couldn't have imagined it at the time, Pepper was the greatest gift we could have given him.

In a sense, to us Nicky is a lot like Pepper. Everything *we* have learned through him has been a gift. He is an inspiration with a bright outlook and a good heart. He continually amazes me as well as the people he comes into contact with every single day. He is indeed a gift—one that keeps on giving.

It's now been four years since we brought Pepper home and I can't even imagine life without her. In fact, I wrote the bulk of this book with her right by my side. She is an integral part of our family and of all our lives. I am so glad I convinced Deborah and the kids to drop their opposition and allow Pepper into our home. After all, she *is*, in fact, the WORLD'S GREATEST PUPPY!

12

People Are Not Labels

AL AND DEBORAH

Don't Label Your Kids

The *smart* one.

The *pretty* one.

The *sporty* one.

The *wild* one.

The *ambitious* one.

The *dark* one.

We've all heard it said that children are like little sponges: They absorb everything we adults say and do. Our words and actions imprint to their memories and may very well influence their reactions, responses and behavior throughout life. It's the classic nurture theory. Experts say who we are is largely defined by our experiences and how we learned to define ourselves early on. This is why as parents, we try to be hyper-aware of those moments when we characterize any of our children. Let's face it—we all fall prey to it, and though it's not our intention, labeling a child can inflict lifelong damage.

DEBORAH

While parents don't consciously mean to label their child, it can happen in the subtlest of ways. One of my sisters vividly recalls a childhood incident. One afternoon she and an older sister got into trouble for climbing up on a stool with the intention of sneaking out through the kitchen window. Before they succeeded—or possibly broke their legs—my mom spotted them. Her scolding is one that my sister still can't shake. Mom declared that this prank had to be the older sister's plan, since the younger one couldn't possibly have been "clever enough to devise such a strategy."

Ouch!

Even at the age of six, those words stung and lingered.

My sister has *never* forgotten them.

Throughout childhood she carried feelings that she wasn't very smart.

Because these two girls were close in age, they were often lumped together and compared. The older one was usually praised for being the smart one and the younger for being pretty or quiet. Of course, my mom meant no harm, but with those simple words, the labeling was done.

Fifty years later, my sister still wrestles with insecurities about her intellect even though she is a very bright woman.

Psychologists and child development experts have long cautioned that if children hear a negative label attached to them, they will eventually believe that label to be true and will fall into line with the behaviors associated with that label. Many of us label our kids in the same way we were labeled as kids. It can start with seemingly harmless phrases like "She's shy" or "He's a real go-getter." But those comments can set the tone for things to come, and sometimes it isn't good. If you grow up hearing that you are "bad," that description becomes as toxic as any chemical seeping into a home. Soon the child will unconsciously display more behaviors associated with their understanding of what a "bad child" is.

With this in mind, Al and I are conscious of all the adults in our kids' lives, from teachers to babysitters, and whether they are sensitive and aware of how they speak with kids. Specific labels can create problems where no problems may have been. They can negatively impact a child's self-esteem and create situations that will lead them on a downward-spiraling path, predisposing them to a life that may have been different had the labeling never occurred.

AL

My dad was a really athletic guy. When I was a kid, we used to go watch him play softball with his bus depot team every Friday night. Mom would pack a cold dinner of fried chicken and potato salad and a thermos of lemonade, and we would cheer Dad on against the other teams. I think my dad realized early on that I wasn't destined to be the next Jackie Robinson or Willie Mays. I wasn't athletic and had no interest in sports. I'm so appreciative that he never pushed me to be athletic; sometimes we would throw the ball around, but if he was ever disappointed that I didn't do more, he never let me know that. Instead, he nurtured the things I seemed to gravitate toward, such as television, movies, comics and cartoons. Unfortunately, all of these things also produced a sedentary lifestyle. By the time I was in seventh grade, I had a real weight problem, although no one in my immediate family ever talked about it—at least, not that I ever heard. I knew I was heavy, but my parents never gave me a hard time about it and they never pushed me to get out of the house and do something active, either. I was one of those kids who liked drawing comic books and making my own movies. As I chronicled in my book *Never Goin' Back: Winning the Weight-loss Battle for Good*, I'll never forget the night I watched the prime-time NBC animated special *Fat Albert*. I loved animation, and one of my dreams was to become an animator for Walt Disney or Hanna-Barbera. But now a horrible reality fell over me. The medium that had spirited me away to solve mysteries with

Scooby-Doo and fight Bluto for the unnaturally skinny Olive Oyl's hand was about to deal me a crushing blow. In a split second, I realized that I was that animated blob on the screen. I was Fat Albert. I was black, fat and named . . . wait for it . . . Albert! I thought my life was over. This was the worst thing that could have happened to me. My head was spinning from the thought of having to go to school the next day. I knew every one of my schoolmates was home watching this show like I was.

The next day I went to school terrified, but much to my surprise, no one said a word.

"Well, maybe nobody saw the show," I thought.

But within five seconds of that hopeful thinking, sure enough, I heard eight or ten guys shout out, "Hey, hey, hey!"

I spent the rest of that week enduring everyone's imitations of Fat Albert. I laughed along with everybody else even though on the inside I was dying. I know many people with similar stories; we make self-deprecating jokes or embrace the label others put on us as a way to hide the hurt. At the height of my weight issues, I used to joke that some people want to see Europe, and I wanted to look down and see my johnson. I used humor as often as I could to deflect how I was really feeling about myself. I had become a self-fulfilling label. I was the fat, jolly guy.

DEBORAH

When I was in the sixth grade, I had an English teacher who made an enduring impact on my life. I still picture Mrs. Hardy with that shock of white hair, bright red lipstick and shiny crimson nail polish on her fingers. She was prim and proper, always dressed in a cardigan sweater, pearls and glasses, which often dangled around her neck. She introduced our class to the classics in literature and assigned poetry presentations. Works by Kipling, Dickinson and Frost are etched in my memory to this day, thanks to Mrs. Hardy. Her class was my first exposure to the beauty of the spoken and written word.

Mrs. Hardy, a true Southern belle, demanded a lot from her students, and you can bet there was no gum chewing and no speaking out of turn. She also insisted that all of her students—black and white—practice proper grammar and speak clearly and concisely. Even today I cringe when someone says "you and me" instead of "you and I" or when I get an e-mail with "your" when it should be "you're."

Thank you, Mrs. Hardy!

There are some teachers who are simply frightening and off-putting to their students . . . but others have an intrigue to their edge. You are drawn to them like a moth to a flame. To me, Mrs. Hardy was indeed an inviting flame—a beacon of light. It was as if she was saying, "I challenge you to win," and I thought, "Game on!" I found myself inspired to work hard and to excel. Whenever Mrs. Hardy praised me for a job well-done, I knew I had truly earned it—and the words somehow carried more weight coming from a white teacher. This was just two years post-segregation, and I was a dark-skinned black girl being told I could be *somebody*.

I didn't mind being labeled as someone who wanted to achieve. I loved it. But because of my drive, ambition and tenacity, some kids in school weren't so kind, calling me an "Oreo," a black girl who acted white. Because I went out of my way to drop my Southern drawl in favor of proper grammar, I was accused of trying to act white. I also made friends with a number of white students . . . something new in my world.

For some kids in my school, my ambitions were at adds with the black experience. In their eyes, I wasn't representing. My desire to reach beyond the boundaries of my small Southern town challenged a lot of my peers in a way I didn't expect. I still recall the taunting and teasing. Likewise, I've never forgotten the important influence Mrs. Hardy's belief in me had on my belief in myself. My English teacher had lit a fire in me that would burn for a long time. From then on, I thought, "She's right! I really can be somebody!" The power of a few words gave me the strength to reject negative labels.

AL

I think I have a pretty good sense of my kids' strengths and weaknesses. Nicky has some learning and development delays, so each day is busy, filled with school and appointments to help him grow and overcome his challenges. There is occupational therapy once a week to help him get better at fine-motor skills like using a screwdriver or scissors. There's physical therapy twice a week to help him to become more coordinated while running or playing catch. And then there is tae kwon do, swimming and chess club.

Nicky is a very outgoing kid, but he is different. And even though I know in my heart he is going to do just fine in life, there are days when it's difficult. Although I do my best to stay focused on the positive, sometimes that's easier said than done. If we're honest, parents of children with special needs will admit to occasionally thinking, "I can't wait to get back to work," after a ten-day vacation with the family.

Come on, I know if you're a parent, you get what I'm saying. You've thought it yourself, even if you won't say it out loud. And God bless all of you stay-at-home moms and dads who choose to be with your kids full-time. I've been working full-time since I was a junior in college. I sometimes fantasize about stepping off the train, at least for a while, to spend more time at home with my children and watch them grow, but I'm not sure I'm cut from that cloth. Besides, I haven't come to a stop long enough to really think about it.

When we first learned of Nicky's learning disabilities, many of the doctors we saw wanted to label him with a specific diagnosis. In fact, Deborah and I also wanted a name we could use for his condition! Naming the problem seemed like a prerequisite for solving the problem. However, after years of neurological testing, he still falls under the vague heading of "otherwise health impaired" or "processing delays." The upside is he doesn't have a label. And the downside is he doesn't have a label. We just don't know the exact cause of his disabilities. We know he exhibits some quirky behaviors close to the autism spectrum, but he is not officially autistic; he's too verbal, social and self-sufficient to fit the label. He has a keen wit, dresses himself, makes his bed, walks the dog on his own; he also reads and writes below grade level and sometimes asks you to repeat what you just said so he can process it. He is who he is.

In many ways, our son is an enigma, but he is also a very loving kid who looks you in the eye, wants to please and make everyone happy, and who knows when he has done something wrong and immediately feels sorry.

While I got good grades in school, I had to work at it. A few years ago, after neuropsychological testing, we learned Nicky was a couple of years behind where he should be for his age, but wow, I admire the fact that he works harder than I ever did. He is the first one to open his homework folder and wants to get it done right. He loves math challenges and is proud to solve a problem. I believe this kid's sheer will and determination will get him wherever he wants to go. We spend lots of time organizing tutoring and experiences to help Nicky reach his goals, and we feel blessed to do it. Nicky is now on the lower end of his grade level, and I know he's going to just keep growing and learning.

I remember the day I heard that Nicky got his Top Gun badge for attending four hundred tae kwon do classes. Very few kids achieve this level. I was as proud as if he'd just gotten his black belt—and he's on track to earn *that* in the coming year! That's the kind of commitment and determination our son has and that's what makes me so proud of him every single day.

Leila, on the other hand, is a girl who has an embarrassment of riches. She is smart, funny, sassy, quick-witted, extremely talented and beautiful to boot. I think she defies labeling.

She is growing up on New York's Upper East Side, but she rejects a lot of what that entails. She has said she is not a "skinny minnie" and never will be. She has lamented the unfairness of her baby brother inheriting Deborah's lean physique while she was saddled with mine.

And yet she refuses to be defined by the fate nature dealt her. Unlike her old man, who didn't get "religion" about exercise and proper eating until later in life, Leila is on a regimen of exercise and mostly sensible eating that will hold her in good stead down the road.

For high school, she chose to leave her predominately white private school for a public school filled with economic, racial, geographical, religious and ethnic diversity. Some kids at her new school have tried to pigeonhole her because of where she lives and who her parents are. Her response? "You don't know me just because you know where I live. Don't try it!"

My older daughter, Courtney, has also worked very hard to avoid labels. When she was in middle school, her mother, Alice, and I were concerned because her grades were slipping. We hired tutors and got her extra help, but Courtney still struggled. After having her tested, we discovered she had an auditory processing problem. Courtney needed to break up information into smaller, digestible chunks.

As time went on, we moved her from public school to a smaller private school and then another. After a while, she began to act out. Her label was "troubled student with learning issues." The story could've played out in predictable ways, and for a while, it did. Difficulties at home, failing grades, a couple of episodes of running away. It was one of the most painful times of my life. I felt guilty for not being there for her because of the divorce, and that led to much soul-searching about what I could've done differently.

Was Courtney's label going to doom her to a life of educational and emotional failure? Her mom and I, and ultimately Courtney, refused to accept that label.

After extensive research, therapy and discussion, Alice, Deborah and

I all agreed that an Outward Bound–like experience in Maine followed by a therapeutic boarding high school was what Courtney needed. It was a gut-wrenching choice. For eight weeks, Courtney would be living in a tent with other girls, doing heavy-duty therapy, team-building exercises and soul-searching.

I picked her up from her mother's house on a Friday and told her on the drive back to my house about the plan and the timeline and that we needed to do something drastic if we were going to alter the path she was on. I was braced for an explosion, an eruption of denial and anger. Instead, she started to cry and said, "Okay, I want to do it."

The two of us flew from New York to Boston and then on to Bangor, Maine.

While we were waiting for our connection, I had to use the bathroom. I was so worried Courtney might bolt. She seemed calm and accepting of the plan but given half a chance, might she try to put some distance between herself and the person taking her to an unknown fate?

I asked a nice lady at a concession stand to keep an eye on her while I popped into the bathroom. That felt like the longest whiz I've ever taken. When I came back out, Courtney was gone. My heart sank. Where could she have gone?

"Don't worry. She's in the bathroom," said the concession lady.

Sure enough, out came Courtney right on cue. I started breathing again.

Forty-five minutes later, we were on our way to Bangor.

When we landed, I rented a car and drove twenty minutes to the program's headquarters, where I handed my daughter over to strangers to begin a journey with an unknown destination and outcome.

After filling out forms and doing her intake interview, Courtney was relieved of all of her personal belongings. All she would wear for the next eight weeks were sweatpants, sweatshirts, jeans and T-shirts. No makeup, no iPods or cell phones. We were leaving our daughter in the hands of strangers who would hopefully help Courtney change her label from "troubled dropout" to "high school student with a hopeful future."

On her program graduation day, after a tearful reunion, we watched her get a certificate, and I could see the pride on my daughter's face. She had set out to do something, albeit not of her choosing, and had accomplished her goal.

DEBORAH

The greatest lesson Nick (he's thirteen and now insists on Nick) has taught me as a parent is to understand, acknowledge and embrace who your kids are versus who you want them to be. I have to let go of the notion of what is ideal for me and accept what reality is. Yes, I'd love for him to be a calm, easygoing kid who makes friends easily, has no trouble completing his homework and follows directions without resistance or anxiety. (Does that child actually exist?) But he is the beautiful child who was gifted to us, and I glow each time I see him. Sometimes when Nicky's therapists talk to us about his capabilities, about how in some areas he is progressing and others not as much, it can be hard to accept. As parents, we all want our kids to soar. No one wants to hear their kid is below his age level or challenged in any aspect. But over the years, we have learned to meet Nicky where he is . . . and to accept him for who he is. And who he is is great! Right now he is obsessed with tae kwon do, movies and travel. He loves watching baseball and doing all kinds of physical activity. He is the first one to join me for a run through the park on a Saturday morning. We are learning how to nurture Nicky's many interests with the hope that they lead to other exciting accomplishments for him.

The same philosophy holds true for Leila even though she's a completely different kid. She has a keen intellect and excels academically. She is *not* excited join me for a run in the park, or for any grueling physical activity for that matter. But she is passionate about theater and the arts. This is important to her, and therefore it must be just as important to us as her parents to help Leila become the best she can be too.

I plead guilty to occasionally pressuring our kids . . . and then worrying about it. I want to push them to be their very best but of course without stressing them out. Like every other mom, I fret over whether I am raising our children well and the thought of adding to their concerns or insecurities breaks my heart. I wonder especially if I am too critical of those crop tops Leila likes to wear, or whether I am cracking the whip too hard on homework. I know I'm the kind of mom who can convey approval or disapproval with a single glance—that "look." Am I too judgmental? Does she resent me for making her play volleyball last year? Will she always remember the time she burst into tears as I corrected her math homework?

On the other hand, I think it's good to set the bar high; I want both of my children to know that I expect them to have big goals. I want them to work hard and to aspire to great things because I know they have it in them. I have encouraged both kids to participate in sports, not because I expect them to be stars on the team but because I truly believe that team sports build character and discipline.

But I also want them to be happy. And finding that balance is one of the most difficult parts of parenting. Some days I think I've nailed it . . . and on others I feel like I've ruined their lives. So I remain a work in progress every day, as do they.

What I know for sure is that I have to listen to my kids. They don't want me to label them any more than I want someone else to. They know who they are and I need to trust in them.

It has not been easy . . . but I am trying to take cues and learn to button it up a little more—to keep my opinions to myself.

I am trying to learn it with my husband and my children so they can be who they need to be and who they feel like they are and not who I want them to be.

What a valuable lesson.

Sometimes we have to get out of the way and let our children become who they feel they are.

We don't always realize it, but in our quest to shape our children into competitive, high-achieving people, we are often labeling them . . . casting them in the light we want to shine. In this era of praise parenting, we also have a tendency to create "positive" labels as our way of socially stamping our children in a way we want others to see them.

But what I have discovered is that as hard as it may be to surrender our goals for our children, it represents the biggest vote of confidence in their abilities. I'm reminded of the movie *The Breakfast Club*, in which five students serve a Saturday detention together. They all come into it with preconceived ideas about one another because of the various cliques they come from; there's the jock, the brain, the bad boy, et cetera. After spending the day together, they learn that each of them is much more than a stereotype. And to me, that is the biggest lesson for not labeling our children. We may miss out on knowing their true potential.

DEBORAH

Jumping into the Lake of Life

Before his first birthday we knew that something was different about Nicky. On baby playdates, he mostly sat quietly, while the other babies scampered about. He cooed but he also drooled quite a bit more than other babies. We knew from our experience with Leila that by now he should be busier and pulling up.

"Don't worry. He's just taking his time," my mother-in-law, Isabel, consoled. "Albert was late to walk and talk," she offered, "and look at him now!"

We wanted to believe she was right. By eighteen months, Nicky was a cheerful, happy boy but still wasn't walking and was uttering only a few words. We decided to begin testing, to find out what was happening with our sweet little guy. The doctor ordered a battery of tests, including hearing and cognitive exams. He also prescribed therapy to help develop Nicky's low muscle tone in case he simply needed a physical jump-start. After several months, we were finally given a diagnosis of pervasive development disorder. In other words, Nicky was not autistic but was a slow developer with his motor, language and processing skills.

By Nicky's fourth birthday, when he entered preschool, he was walking and laughing and enjoying the company of his sister. But he still spoke very little and watched his classmates more than he interacted. It was wonderful to see him progress, but silently, we ached at his ongoing limitations. When other little boys rambunctiously jumped off the steps at school, or scaled the jungle gym, Nicky stepped back, frightened about navigating any uneven terrain. At a gym party, he ran and rolled around but never climbed the stairs to the slide or crawled through tunnels. Our boy would sometimes tremble at the top of a narrow staircase, frozen in midmotion.

Nicky's life now revolved around speech therapy, physical therapy and occupational therapy to help him button and open and twist with his chubby little fingers. We were blessed to find wonderful therapists, including a high-energy OT specialist named Lori Rothman. Lori, with her red hair, quick, toothy laugh and direct manner, was a godsend. Within months, she had coaxed Nicky to play on a tire swing in her gym and to try zipping up his coat. She was positive, encouraging and determined. In that New York way, Lori didn't mince words. She believed in gentle truth and honesty. So it meant the world to us when one day she declared, "Your son is so determined and driven. That will take him far." Then she said something that brought me to tears.

"Don't give up for a second!" she said. "He's going to college and he's going to do well in life! I just want you to know." Lori often ended her sentences with "I just want you to know."

Over the years, it has been difficult and often painful watching Nicky strive, stumble, get back up and then achieve. It was heartbreaking for me to admit that he would not follow his sister into a competitive New York elementary school but would need to be admitted to a school for special needs. On more than one occasion I broke down in tears, mourning the things that Nicky may not be destined for. Let's face it—we all have dreams for our kids tucked away in our minds. But Nicky has taught our family that dreams can morph into other magical and rewarding realities. Al was clear about that from the beginning. We simply have to have faith, and as Lori advised, not give up for a second.

By the time Nicky was ready for kindergarten, Al and I had wrapped our minds around the idea that we would always be his advocates but that Nicky would chart his own unique path. We found a wonderful school for him that would turn all of our lives around. The Parkside School serves kids with special needs from all over the city, regardless of need. In this warm, happy building filled with loving teachers and therapists, Nicky thrived, learning to read, write, deliver book reports and even steal the show while participating in his first school play. Each day Nicky happily bounded up the stairs to claim his place in the school line. Was this really the same kid who was afraid to jump down two small steps at preschool?

There were other successes over the years too—accomplishments that made Al and me incredibly proud. For example, Nicky became a skilled competitive swimmer. Then he discovered tae kwon do, which Leila had been taking. He wanted to do that too, and he has succeeded wildly. In fact, last summer he realized his longtime goal: he earned his black belt!

Of course, there have been bumps along the way. Sometimes Nicky grew frustrated when he couldn't write as quickly as he wanted or spit out his times tables, but he was making great progress, and most important, he was always determined. It didn't occur to him that he couldn't do what the others were doing. He always remained determined to keep trying.

Despite his challenges, Nicky has been blessed with steely determination. One thing we've noticed is that he suffers from bouts of vertigo.

When approaching a steep escalator or narrow staircase, he can become paralyzed. It once took him ten minutes to make that first step down, but once he did . . . he was filled with confidence and pride. "I conquered my fear," he said later. Nicky longs for success more than anyone I've ever seen.

I will never forget one particular Labor Day weekend at our country house. We had escaped the oppressive summer heat that had fallen over New York City most of the summer.

Leila and Nicky have always looked forward to the time we spend together at the upstate house. It's the only time all four of us are together with no outside distractions or obligations. It's also the place where so many of life's "firsts" have happened for our children: where Nicky first ran barefoot through the grass as a toddler on the front lawn and where Leila learned to ride a bike in the driveway and to swim in the pristine lake just down the hill.

Although our home isn't on the lake, our neighbors and friends Bill and Maggie do have a charming cottage that sits right next to the water. It's a sweet community that reminds me of small-town Georgia, where people leave their doors open, kids can skip down the gravel driveway and you can hear cackling laughter late into the evening. Across from Bill and Maggie's place is a beach club. Don't let the name fool you. It's basically a shack with a lifeguard stand and a sandy shoreline the home-owners' association brought in to make a beach.

(Side note: In the sixteen years we've owned that home, Al has never been in the lake. He thinks lakes are, and I quote, "squishy and icky!")

I mentioned that Nicky is a terrific swimmer. But that's in a pool, not in the lake.

It was no different on that warm Saturday afternoon in September. The hot summer days were giving way to cool, crisp mornings. Maggie and Bill had invited us all over for a last hurrah: a barbecue and a boat ride, the last of the summer. A final dip in the cool, fresh water sounded heavenly. Al had no interest in the boat or a dip, so he stayed behind to help guard the charcoal and the grill!

Although Nicky loved swimming in a pool, he's always been skittish of the vast depth of the lake. He had gotten in only once, lowering himself gingerly into the green water from the boat ladder as he clung tightly to a foam noodle.

But today was different.

Just as I was about to jump, he called to me to wait. After several starts and stops, my sweet, nervous guy had decided it was time to conquer a fear.

He would jump in.

He grabbed my hand, and together we plunged into the cold, refreshing water and bobbed up together, grinning and basking in the glow of success and cheers from everyone on deck.

We were all shocked and happy. Nicky had leaped confidently into the water! Then he insisted on doing it again—plunging unaided into the eighteen-foot-deep lake.

The more he jumped, the more he wanted to do it again.

When we got back to shore, we all felt triumphant. I also had a very special photo for Al that Leila had snapped, a shot that will remain dear for the rest of my days. Leila had caught the precious moment when Nicky and I jumped. It captured the essence of who Nicky truly is—a curious, brave young man jumping into the lake of life with abandon.

Of course we take great pride in all of our children. But there is something so inspiring about Nicky's sheer determination. Although he struggles in school, he is a hard worker who always does his best and never gives up. Even though reading came slowly for him, he's now reading books like *The Hunger Games* alongside many of his friends. We learned early on to never say never when it comes to our son. We're committed to nurturing him along his path and to doing our best not to get frustrated with his limitations.

But what brings him and us the most pride is his mastery of tae kwon do. Nicky has aspired to become a black belt ever since he started the program five years ago. The kicks and forms haven't always been easy. Nicky's muscular strength wasn't great when he began. But he was determined, always practicing his moves at home . . . often startling us with his loud "kiya!" He goes to class three or four days a week and has earned—*really* earned—belt after belt. He's now just months away from his prized black belt!

It can be hard as well as disappointing to watch your children struggle, because you want only the best for them.

But we have learned to nurture each stage of his development until the next success comes along. It hasn't been easy, but we've learned patience and acceptance. Our children can teach us many things, but the greatest lesson our son, Nicky, has taught us is to accept and embrace our kids for who they are instead of who we want them to be. It's a simple lesson but sometimes hard to do. So often we mistake our goals and expectations for those of our children, losing sight of who they are and who they were meant to be.

We are learning to give our children the freedom to grow and blossom and to discover their individual gifts. As parents, we want to give them everything—and protect them from making mistakes, from getting hurt, from falling into the wrong crowd. But both of those dreams are just that—fantasies. We can't give them everything; the most important things are the ones they discover themselves. And we can't protect them from pain, either; sometimes those experiences are the greatest teachers offering the deepest lessons. All we can truly hope is that by giving them the right tools and opportunities to make their own choices, our children will make good decisions. And if they don't, we'll both be there ready to guide them and love them. At the end of the day, we can't expect our kids to swim with the safety and security of a noodle forever. At some point we have to stand on the shore and allow them to take a running dive from the dock. We promise to watch them with great pride, even if we're holding our breath, as they jump into that great lake of life.

13

Life Is Full of Hard Choices

DEBORAH

Sacrifices We Make as Moms

Eight months after Leila was born and I was settling into a new routine at ABC, I received a call from Meredith White, an accomplished senior producer at 20/20, asking if I could hop on a plane to Ethiopia in two days to cover a story about an Ethiopian-American woman who was looking for her long-lost mother. Meredith had just worked out the details and I'd have to scramble to catch up to Lydia Dawson, who had left her Seattle home and was already in Addis Ababa. Meredith thought it would be the perfect story for me. Lydia, a social worker and mother of three, had not seen her mother since she was a baby. Lydia had been just five months old and cradled in her mother's arms while her mother was cooking the family meal at the outdoor fire of her African village. Suddenly, her mother, who was only thirteen at the time, suffered a seizure. She fell, accidentally dropping her baby into the open fire.

The nearest medical care was one hundred miles away. By the time her frightened and weary family reached the hospital some five days later, Lydia's legs were burned and infected so badly, they had to be amputated, one above and one just below the knee.

Lydia's parents, poor farmers who were too frightened to remain away from their home and their other children for very long, made an agonizing choice: to leave their injured baby daughter at the hospital to be cared for and raised by American missionaries. I can't imagine any greater sacrifice.

Lydia spent the next four years in the hospital, mostly because there was nowhere else for her to go. The staff cared for her and taught her English and Lydia learned how to crawl because walking wasn't an option. She managed so well, she barely noticed how different she was from everyone else around her.

One day a photographer from the *Saturday Evening Post* snapped some photos of Lydia, "the African girl with no legs." That picture would change Lydia's life forever. A group of strangers was moved so deeply by that single image that they banded together to give Lydia the promise for a better future. The first donation came from a Philadelphia maker of artificial limbs, who was so moved by Lydia's story that he offered to make her a set of prosthetic legs, which would give her the ability to walk on her own and the hope for independence.

Next, a group of women from a Presbyterian church in New Jersey decided to finance a first-class education for Lydia. With the help of Lydia's nurse, Mary Nell Harper, they sent her to an exclusive boarding school in Addis Ababa, the capital of Ethiopia, and later paid for college in the United States, where Lydia studied to become a social worker.

Admittedly, Meredith, a friend as well as my boss, was reluctant to ask me to go because Leila was just eight months old and she wasn't sure I'd want to leave her on such short notice. But I was blown away by the story and I wanted to be part of Lydia's remarkable journey. Suddenly, adrenaline was coursing through my body along with the dopamine a new mom feels. I was pumped to get back in the saddle, but first I had to figure out the logistics on the home front. Al was gung ho for me to grab such a big assignment, and our babysitter was on board. I was in agony over one other major decision. I would have to wean Leila cold turkey, because I had to get several immunizations for the trip. I had already been considering closing my "personal kitchen," so I decided it was fine.

Twenty-four hours later, I touched down in Addis Ababa, Ethiopia. By the time I got there, Lydia was waiting and anxious to begin her quest. Tall and strikingly beautiful, with her smooth raven hair and warm, happy smile, Lydia was perfect for television. She was also sweet and open, so we connected right away. Lydia knew a little bit about her background, and of course, the story of how she got to the hospital, but she knew very little about her family or the village where she was born. She had no idea if her mother was dead or alive. As we sat talking in the hotel restaurant, a lovely dark-skinned waitress brought us coffee. I scanned the charming breakfast room and took in the array of black faces at every table . . . a rarity even in New York City, which is considered the melting pot of America.

Being a dark-skinned girl from the South who has never felt totally comfortable about my blackness in America, where light skin is treasured, I soon noticed something. In Ethiopia, surrounded by beautiful, dark-skinned people, I felt like I was "home." I had been to Africa once before, for a story on the anniversary of the genocide in Rwanda. It was an excruciatingly painful trip with so many horrifying stories of murder and betrayal. But this trip was hopeful and uplifting to my spirit. I was much more able to take in my surroundings and enjoy the journey.

Using a ham radio to communicate with various villages, we received a lead on where Lydia's mother was living. We also found someone who had an old airplane he could use to fly us to where she was.

This was joyful news to everyone, especially Lydia, who now had confirmation, albeit secondhand, that her mother was, in fact, alive. But it wasn't a sure thing; the lead could turn out to be a bust, so I warned Lydia not to get her hopes up too high. I was so afraid she'd be in for a great disappointment if this turned out to be a dead end.

As we boarded the rickety single-engine plane, four thoughts popped into my mind.

1. I had no clear idea where we were headed.
2. Did this guy Solomon really know how to fly a plane?
3. How would anyone find us if something went wrong?
4. I was a new mom. . . . How would I get back to Leila if something happened?

It was exhilarating and frightening and the very reason I love my job as much as I do.

We landed on a dirt road on the edge of a tiny village. From the small window of the prop plane, I could see the villagers running toward us as we rolled to a stop. It was like a scene out of a movie. Children of every size and shade of brown gleefully swooped in and gazed in wonder at this flying machine, trying to figure out what it was and who these strange people getting out of it were.

Lydia hadn't been to this village since she was a baby, but she looked just like the people who now surrounded us.

I was filled with excitement and pride, especially because some of the people there thought I was African too. They spoke to me in Amharic, which filled my heart in a way that I can barely explain.

We met our contact, a man who was waiting to take us the rest of the way in his Jeep. We drove along rugged, narrow, dusty roads, nearly breaking down a couple of times as we made our way into the village. It had looked a lot closer from the air, but two hours later, we came to a clearing and had finally arrived.

The villagers had prepared a cinder-block house with slab floors as a guesthouse. They beamed with pride as they showed us to the finest accommodations they had to offer. Gracious and warm, they were thrilled that a village girl had come back home and explained their plans for an evening feast of goat, boiled eggs and injera.

Dusk began to settle in, and there was still no sign of Lydia's mother. Someone had radioed to say her Jeep had broken down, that she had been delayed.

Was it true, or was this some kind of ploy?

Were they stalling for some reason?

We had no idea.

As night fell, there was no sign of the mother and no chance we could fly out. The pilot explained it was too late—that we would have to spend the night.

We had no provisions, but what choice did we have?

As wild monkeys screeched in the background, freaking out my producer, the villagers brought us cots to sleep on and that dinner they had promised.

"I'm not eating this! We have no idea what it is!" my producer quietly said to me.

Given my own humble roots, I understood the depth of this moment. I didn't want us to offend our gracious hosts; this impoverished but proud community was graciously reaching out to foreign guests.

I told my producer to eat whatever she could swallow down.

There was something sweet and exciting about this adventure. I was in remote Ethiopia with a woman who was one of their native daughters. When would I ever have an opportunity to experience anything like this again? I wanted to soak in every last morsel of the moment, including the culture, so I happily ate whatever they put in front of me.

Well past midnight, just as many of us were beginning to doubt this story would happen, the wooden door to the cinder-block house swung open, and from the darkness of the African night, a shadowy figure emerged.

Our camera crew quickly shone their lights on the doorway. Then, in a moment of wonder and majesty, the figure of a petite woman, her head covered with a scarf, gently stepped across the threshold of the door.

It was Asha, Lydia's long-lost mother.

She glided into the room in silence, staring into the eyes of the daughter who stood before her trembling.

Time stood still.

No words needed to be spoken.

Lydia slowly stepped toward her and burst into tears. And so did I . . .

Passionate hugs and kisses and tears marked this unforgettable moment of a mother being reunited with her daughter.

I haven't experienced a more emotional moment before or since.

The two women stood for ten minutes, gazing and looking, kissing and hugging.

A tiny, beautiful woman, Asha was no more than fifty years old. Her drawn, thin face and sunken cheekbones made her appear older, but at this moment she was radiant, cloaked in a silken red scarf.

When they finally sat down to talk, one of the villagers translated for all of us. In Amharic, Asha told of her heartbreak when her daughter had been injured, a tragedy she remembered like it happened yesterday. Softly, she explained how not a day goes by that she doesn't think about her daughter and what happened to her. She wept as she told her daughter how her heart had ached to give her up . . . but that she could see her decision had given Lydia a better life.

As I sat on a wooden chair witnessing this dramatic moment, I knew I would never forget it nor the lesson I'd take with me from this small African village. Asha's decision was the ultimate sacrifice born of a parent's love for a child. She had taken a leap of faith that a heartbreaking choice would ultimately save her precious child. And it had.

This was a moment of warmth and humanity that transcended continents, culture, race and economics. It was this moment that would guide me as a new mom.

The next day, as we prepared to leave, we stepped into the African dawn to find another surprise. Dozens of people—men, women and children—were crowding the yard of the guesthouse. Asha's neighbors had walked for hours through the night to greet her long-lost American daughter—another powerful and unforgettable moment for all of us in this story of discovery. After hugging every single person, Lydia would now have to say good-bye to her mother . . . again . . . not knowing how long it would be before they would reunite once more. She promised to come back and bring her children to meet their courageous grandmother. As we boarded the plane, the villagers all gathered to say good-bye, and in the center of the crowd, I saw Asha, wrapped in her red silk head scarf, clutching photographs of the daughter she had finally reclaimed. She was hunched over in a squat with her head cradled in her hands, sobbing. She had endured the heartbreak of saying good-bye to her daughter once. Now she was doing it again. It felt cruel and unfair.

I flew back to New York with the image of Lydia's mother sobbing on the ground seared in my mind. It got me thinking about my mother and all of the sacrifices she'd made for her children throughout the years, and about me as a mom too—and the incredibly deep love I felt for my new baby. I no longer had to question how far I would go to make sure my child was always taken care of because I already knew and understood what it felt like to put my own desires aside to make sure I was there to give her what she needed.

I spent that long flight back from Africa to New York giving thanks for the experience I had shared with Lydia for many reasons, but most of all for the confirmation that every mother needs that sacrificing for your child is the greatest gift of unconditional love.

From time to time I still think about my decision to pass on the job offered to me before Leila was born. But I have made peace with it. Perhaps it was my first major sacrifice for my child. I knew that motherhood is about love, commitment and sacrifice—and now I understand just how deep that can run. Thankfully, both of my children are healthy and I have never had to make a life-or-death decision the way Asha had done. But I do make choices every day to put them first. I often tell Leila and Nicky that whatever the obligation or opportunity, they are my first consideration. Over the years I have turned down invitations, events and occasionally assignments to be there when they were sick, needy or celebrating a big moment. I will never regret a minute of the time I sacrificed to have with them. Nothing else in life can come close. Of this, I am certain. It's a lesson that was driven home for me in an African village and one that I will always share with my children.

DEBORAH

Struggling with My Decisions

It was just a few days before Christmas 2006. Though my father was declining at home in the final stages of colon cancer, I was struggling to get through the holidays with the family. I had been down to Perry to visit Daddy just a couple of weeks before and had decided to come back home. I had a pressing assignment at work and the kids were wrapping up school projects and presentations. And there was the Christmas celebration at church, a program that both Leila and Nicky excitedly looked forward to being a part of every year. Nicky was set to play a shepherd boy, and Leila was cast as one of Mary's companions.

New York was all aglow with Christmas decorations and excitement. There isn't a prettier time of year in the city. I've always loved the holiday season and I wanted to be in the spirit, but it wasn't easy, given my father's condition.

At the kids' urging, and as a way to attempt to cheer me up, Al got tickets to the Broadway production of *How the Grinch Stole Christmas*. My friend Karen joined us, along with her daughter Catherine. Al hoped it would bring a smile to my face to spend some quality family time together. Just as the curtain opened, my phone began to vibrate. It was that dreaded call we all fear. I quickly stepped out of the theater. When I answered, my sister Tina said shakily, "I think we're losing Daddy."

My voice echoing in the empty lobby, I said, "Can you please put the phone next to his ear?"

As Tina did, I could hear my sister Bennie crying in the background.

"Hi, Daddy. It's Deborah," I managed to choke out through muffled sobs. "I'm so very sorry I'm not there with you, but I want you to know that I love you very much." By now Al had joined me, his eyes brimming with tears too. What do you say in those final moments to a dying parent? Trembling now, I told Daddy I knew he was going home and how sorry I was for not being at his side. I tried to express how much I appreciated him as my father.

Dad held on overnight.

On Sunday morning, Al and I took the kids to church like always, and prayed for Daddy. This was also the day of the church Christmas pageant. Nicky and Leila were both excited about their roles. So was I, but my heart hurt and I was also deeply torn about where I should be.

Should I fly home right away to my dying father, uncertain if I would make it in time, or do I grab this precious life-affirming moment with my children and then scramble to go?

Al, who'd lost his dad a few years earlier and who understood the pain in my heart, asked if I wanted him to call the airline to make a last-minute reservation. I was seized with fear and sadness, somehow frozen in my tracks. Tough decisions can be difficult for me. Whether it's a work assignment or a personal choice, I often wrestle with the right answer. Why wasn't I in a cab at this moment, racing to LaGuardia Airport to catch the next flight to Atlanta? But how could I miss being with my family during a cherished moment? And would I make it before Dad passed?

Looking back I think I was terrified to come face-to-face with the loss of my dad. For years he was such a tower of strength, and now he was terribly weakened, his life almost over. I thought about my last visit with Dad as we sat in the small wood-paneled den back in my childhood home. He was alert and able to smile, but he was so frail he couldn't speak. It was excruciating to see him slipping away. For reasons I can't really explain, I felt paralyzed and decided that I would stay at home and hold on to my children, gathering strength from their free and happy spirits. Daddy was eighty-three. He'd lived a full life, made peace with his illness and turned everything over to God. I believe he was ready to go.

Through tears I told Al that while I was in knots about it all, I desperately needed to hold on to him and the kids at this moment . . . celebrating life instead of racing to witness the end of a life.

We gathered at church for the children's pageant. St. James' was resplendent in poinsettias, wreaths and hay bales for the manger scene. Kids were running everywhere, squealing with excitement. Vicki Hall, the children's ministry director, was showing her incredible and enviable level of patience and firm control. Vicki knew that my dad was terminally ill and understood the pain I was grappling with that afternoon. She gave me a knowing hug and said quietly, "You're in our prayers."

Although I ached all over, my heart felt a flutter of warmth when I saw Leila and Nicky parade down the church aisle with the other children. Leila flashed me a proud smile. At that moment I knew I was in exactly the right place and was where God wanted me to be.

Just after the pageant ended and the cast headed downstairs for a party of cupcakes and punch, my phone buzzed again.

I knew.

Al took the call as we stepped outside the church building into the December chill.

"Honey," he said in a choked whisper, "your dad is gone."

We both collapsed in tears on the sidewalk just outside the church.

Today I sometimes still wrestle with the hard choice I made on that winter afternoon. Would I feel any differently if I had rushed to Georgia that afternoon, even if I hadn't made it in time? Or was it better for me to be in the arms of my family as I processed the heartbreaking loss of my father? Who's to say what the right choice was?

I have come to realize that we all must follow our hearts and make the decisions we feel are best in the moment. Looking back doesn't change a thing. What matters is finding peace with your judgment. I am grateful that I had time with Dad before his passing and felt his love one last time. Some of my siblings didn't have that chance.

Over the next few days we all gathered at home in Perry to prepare for Daddy's funeral. There was a heavy sadness in the air, but in the spirit of the black Baptist church, there was also hope and happiness as we honored a life and a spirit now in heaven. The night before the service, we all sat around telling stories and reconnecting, then suddenly heard the sounds of a beautiful choir. We stepped onto the back porch and discovered church carolers singing Christmas songs for us. My sister Bonita and I smiled through our tears. "We know this is a tough time for you all and you're in our prayers," the choir leader shouted.

What a beautiful moment.

I was with my family, celebrating my dad's life.

He was at peace. And, somehow, I was too.

Making difficult decisions is a part of all of our daily lives, but it can be a tough skill to master. When it was time to choose a new school for Leila, I tossed and turned at night, agonizing over the decision long after Al had made up his mind and was able to settle into a deep, restful sleep. And I still recall my difficulty in coming to the conclusion that it was time to move my mom into a nursing home. After lots of family discussions, my siblings were all on board and yet I continued to worry over it for weeks.

Some things come quickly to me and from the gut, like moving to ABC to join *20/20*. However, when it comes to matters of the heart, I often struggle. But once I make a call, once I put my hand to the plow, I am learning not to second-guess. After all, I want my children to know that we all make difficult choices, and even then you may never know the absolute right answer. That's why it's best to accept it no matter what, especially if you cannot change it. In the words of Jon Kabat-Zinn, the father of mindfulness and an advocate for living in the moment, "You cannot change the tide, but you can learn to surf!"

Acknowledgments

As I reflect on the deeply personal moments shared in this book, I cannot do so without a debt of gratitude to the incredible sisterhood in my life. First, to my blood sisters, Annette, Bennie Ruth, Janet, Celestine, Bonita and Belinda . . . thank you for the love, hard times and happiness you shared with me over the years, along with my big brothers, Jackie and Ben.

Where would I be without the women friends who helped shape, nurture and encourage me through so many ups and downs? What would become of me without my book club girls (Marva, Judy, Tawana, Jonelle, Angela, Yolanda, Dale, KC, Pauletta, Gloria and Jerri), who keep it real and sane? Who cares if we don't always read a stimulating book? Or my lunch club, which makes life so much richer: Robin, Gayle, Theresa and Tonya are like a ray of sunshine.

I am stronger and wiser because of many mentors who brightened my life, like Dorothy Hardy, my unforgettable English teacher, who helped me truly believe in myself. Thanks to my confidante, honorary sister and cheerleader, Agenia Clark, who always gives me reason to smile even during the dark moments of parenting and living; I'm also so grateful for the friendship of Ruhanna Neal, my spiritual mentor. Thanks to the brilliant Laura Morton, who discovered that I had a story to share, and to Mel Berger and Tracy Bernstein, who nurtured it along for so very long. And most of all to my kind, passionate and extraordinary husband, Al, who makes me believe in the beauty and challenge of love!

—D.R.

I want to thank my brother, Chris, and sisters, Alisa, Desireé and Patricia, for being family.

Thanks to someone I talk about all the time, Dr. Louis B. O'Donnell, my professor at SUNY Oswego who was instrumental in setting me on my career.

I want to publicly thank the man who gave me that first job doing television weather, Andy Brigham, the news director at WHEN-TV in Syracuse. He gave me my first invaluable piece of advice. "Roker, remember. No matter how hard you try, you can't chrome-plate sh*t!"

Thanks to my second dad, Willard Scott. Your generosity and humor are still what help guide me today. And to my buddy Jon Harris, who was a great sounding board for thoughts, ideas and concepts.

Without the writing talents of Laura Morton, we would still be looking at a blank computer screen. To Tracy Bernstein, thanks for the guidance. And to Mel Berger, living proof that there's no school like old school. You are a gentleman and a lover of the written word who gets it done.

Finally, to Deborah, the woman who has been my rock for the past twenty years, thank you for being the yin to my yang, the balance in my life and the mother to two wonderful kids and a guiding force to Courtney. I am so grateful to have been there and done that with you.

—A.R.